A Celebration of Comic Art and Memorabilia

A Celebration of Comic Art and Memorabilia

ROBERT LESSER

Photographs by Stefan Congrat-Butlar

HAWTHORN BOOKS, INC.
PUBLISHERS / *New York*

"I am for an art that does something
other than sit on its ass in a museum."

—*Claes Oldenburg*

A CELEBRATION OF COMIC ART AND MEMORABILIA

Copyright © 1975 by Robert Lesser. Copyright under International and Pan-American Copyright Conventions. All rights reserved, including the right to reproduce this book or portions thereof in any form, except for the inclusion of brief quotations in a review. All inquiries should be addressed to Hawthorn Books, Inc., 260 Madison Avenue, New York, New York 10016. This book was manufactured in the United States of America and published simultaneously in Canada by Prentice-Hall of Canada, Limited, 1870 Birchmount Road, Scarborough, Ontario.

Library of Congress Catalog Card Number: 74-22928

ISBN: 0-8015-1456-8

1 2 3 4 5 6 7 8 9 10

Contents

ACKNOWLEDGMENTS   vii

INTRODUCTION   1

1   ORIGINAL ART AND THE SUNDAY PAGES   3

2   COMIC BOOKS   46

3   COMIC-CHARACTER TOYS   68

4   COMIC-CHARACTER TIMEPIECES   118

5   BUCK ROGERS IN THE 25th CENTURY—
THE FABULOUS FANTASY   168

6   COMIC INSERT CARDS   228

7   THE DECODERS AND THEIR MANUALS   260

INDEX   281

Acknowledgments

I wish to thank Henry Mazzeo, Jr., of New York, Bob Lyons of Ypsilanti, Michigan, and John Tornquist of Minneapolis, Minnesota, for their cooperation and the photographs they have provided for the book.

Special thanks to Cass Hough, president of Daisy Manufacturing Company for his memoirs of Buck Rogers.

I wish to express my gratitude to Stephan Congrat-Butlar for his wisdom, perseverence, and photography and to Michael Toomey for the handsome cover.

For the education they have given me over a period of the last eight years, my gratitude to: Howard Bayliss, Van Dexter, Joe Sarno, Murray Harris, Kenny Harmon, Carol Beltran, Paul and Bob Gallagher, Larry Dalton, Phil Hecht, Bob Sheperd, Bill Morse, Dale Manesis, Bruce Hertzberg, Frank Whitson, Edward Mosler, Russ Cochran, Marc Zakarin, Joe Lozano, Robert Weinberg, Cosmo Sorice, Larry Bigman, Dave Weiss, Dave Kaufman, Peter Maresca, David Bausch, Joe Parente, Terry Bienstock, Robert Overstreet, Charles Crane, Evelyn Hyman, Don Hillman, Alan Frumkin, Lloyd Ralston, Maurice Sendak, John Fawcett, David Smith, Ty Singer, Bob Kane, Howard Godel, Jack Melcher, George Ward, Larry Whiteley, Dave Boyle, Richard Merkin, Ralph Whitmer, Bill Thailing, Mat Masterson, Joel Kopp, Dr. Lawrence Kurzrok, Gray Morrow, Eugene Seger, Jack Promo, Philip Ellenbogen, Elaine Ellenbogen, Jim Archambault, Abe Peskow, Fred Loranger, Robert Dille, Claude Held, Donald Kaufman, Michael Malce, David Kogen, Bill Lafferty, Roger Nelson, Dean Newman, Don Maris, Ernest Trova, Kenny Kneitel, Ward Kimball, Don Vernon, Hal Cohen, Kathy Aaronson.

A Celebration of Comic Art and Memorabilia

Introduction

The years from 1896 to 1950 witnessed the growth and golden age of a new and native American art form. Its pervasive influence reached into millions of minds in every country on this planet and through all the media. Its popularity and enthusiastic acceptance was and is worldwide because it appealed to an inner need . . . a hunger . . . for pictures and stories in combination. Today American comic art is recognized as legitimate art, and as a legitimate art its individual artists and their individual works are entitled to be judged separately and to have subjective evaluations thrown at them—genius, lousy, great, awful, poor, fair, ugly, beautiful—terms to be used here as they are there in the world of accepted modern museum art.

Our Raymond, Foster, and Hogarth should be judged as separate artists within a single art form as are Picasso, Léger, and Klee. The dimensions that they reached in terms of originality, imagination, and comic invention vary from artist to artist, but all exist within the confines of this particular genre of neorepresentational art. Its use of words with pictures is its mark, its strength. Its basic universal appeal is that it is easily understood and has the clarity that the mass of the world's population demands when it is being told a story. Yet flowing outward and upward from its basic, solid foundation of realistic art is a high tolerance for the surreal, which the better comic artists blended into their art, making the total form unique.

Is art a necessity or a luxury? Can the human spirit prosper and grow in a life without art? Does not a certain deadness set into any life that is divorced from a recognition that appreciation of art, any art, even comic art, can delight and excite the soul? One basic difference between the American rich and the American poor is that the rich own all the important art and the poor own none. The rich visit the museums they own; the poor don't. The children of the rich learn very quickly in their private schools and expensive colleges what art is and the money value of a Rembrandt, a Goya, a Picasso, or a Jackson Pollack. But the poor are kept outside the world of art. They rarely visit museums, they have never learned what art is supposed to be, because the schools of the rich don't teach the poor.

But art is a human necessity; without it there is a vacuum, an empty space inside the soul that must be filled. Today, the lower-middle-class young of America are filling this emptiness of inner space. They are putting into effect a revolutionary, almost anarchic doctrine that might be called "Aesthetic Civil Rights":

Any American citizen has the inalienable right to collect, cherish, love, and hang on his wall any object that he truly believes has beauty. And furthermore it is so stated that his act of nailing the tack into the wall to hang up his Mickey

Mouse Watch, *Superman* comic book, or Captain Midnight Decoder does not require prior approval of the faculty of the Yale School of Fine Arts, the Museum of Modern Art, or a special decision from the Supreme Court.

Without "knowing" what art is, the hordes from the LMC are deciding for themselves, teaching each other what they don't know, setting art and money values, and just enjoying the hell out of themselves amassing art collections that relate to the ocean-deep, mountain-high mass of comic art produced in the last three-quarters of this century. They are collecting art but they don't know that they are! And they are collecting with the compulsiveness of a Joseph Hirshhorn, with the encyclopedic knowledge of a Nelson Rockefeller collecting primitive art, and with the gluttony of an Egypt's King Farouk.

For hundreds of years, the question "What is Art?" was answered by whatever art the nobility of Europe collected, since they comprised the single class that owned culture. We have inherited and we accept their values, but their heirs and their museums own their art. We never can. But the new revolution says that "art should do something other than sit on its ass in a museum," that the mass of the LMC should be guided and welcomed into participation, that they should own art. Why not American comic art as a candidate? They have been relating to it all of their lives. Perhaps the time has come to name the creation and collecting of all the various aspects of the comic genre Prol Art. It was the prols who created it and it is the prols who collect it.

Until recently all comic memorabilia was considered worthless; much was destroyed during the patriotic scrap metal and paper drives of World War II and much was simply garbage-canned from coast to coast. Collecting comic art is very new. The patterns began to form in the early nineteen sixties as values were being determined for comic books and comic-character toys. Only in the most recent years has the collecting of this art form exploded to worldwide proportions. Values are still in a state of flux, and reliable records and authentic information are difficult to find since most of the companies involved in production have long since departed from the commercial scene.

It is the hope of this book to help reverse the still existing negative view and prove with pictures and some words that there is serious merit in the art and sculpture of this particularly American form. It is also hoped that the suggested list of collectibles at the end of each chapter will be of aid to both the new and the advanced collector and will inform the general reader of the vast quantities and imaginative varieties that were produced. Many of the photographs depict character items that have never before been published. Each chapter illustrates one particular area of comic collecting because collectors tend to specialize. The chapters deal with the original art of the comics, comic books, comic-character toys, character timepieces, a complete history of one of the most famous comic characters of all—Buck Rogers in the 25th Century—comic bubble gum cards, and the fantastic decoders and their manuals. Much more material could be added but not much more is needed to demonstrate the beauty and originality of comic art and memorabilia.

1

Original Art
and the Sunday Pages

The dimensions of comic art are incredible: billions of pictures multiplied by three-quarters of a century of distribution, providing pure pleasure and excitement for a large percentage of the world's population. The names have become the best known, most known names on earth, each conjuring up an exact image: Mickey Mouse, Superman, Tarzan, Donald Duck, Buck Rogers in the 25th Century, Batman, Orphan Annie, Captain America, from The Yellow Kid to Pogo.

The golden age of American comic industrial art had many beginnings, but they were slight in comparison with the breakthrough of The Yellow Kid, created in February 1896 by Richard Outcault for the New York Sunday *World*. It was the first successful comic creation: a bald-headed boy with an Oriental face, flap ears, only two upper front teeth, and wearing a yellow nightgown. It was always a group scene on an entire page, not the later series of separate panels, but all of the different inhabitants of Hogan's Alley in pursuit of the dogcatcher or celebrating the Chinese New Year.

And it was art, original, beautifully drawn, with a comic surrealism that separates The Yellow Kid from Buster Brown and Max und Moritz and other realistically drawn naughty boys of the era.

Richard Outcault was more than just an artist. What is not too well known about him is that he was an equally shrewd businessman who, early in his career, sensed the possibilities of mass merchandising. Cast-iron toys of The Yellow Kid in his famous goat cart, cigar-box plugola, cigarette cards, tie pins, dolls, and games were licensed to manufacturers that resulted in instant commercial success, so successful that the competition to control The Yellow Kid became cutthroat.

The publisher of the New York *World*, Joseph Pulitzer, had hired Outcault to create the full Sunday pages of The Kid. But a circulation war was in progress, and William Randolph Hearst of the New York *Journal*, furious at this comic secret weapon, pirated Outcault away. In October the *Journal* announced its own new color comic section: ". . . eight pages of irridescent polychromous effulgence that makes the rainbow look like a piece of lead pipe." Its superstar: The Yellow Kid. Counterattacking, Pulitzer hired the talented George Luks to draw another Yellow Kid for the *World*, and the circulation war of the Yellow Kids followed, with both artists trying to outdo each other.

The beauty of these full pages is so evident that many collectors collect and frame these rare Sunday pages from the *World* and the *Herald*, hanging them on their walls as others might a Picasso print. Among Sunday-page newspaper collectors, a Yellow Kid page is the most desirable of all and always very expensive.

George Luks became a famous and accepted artist, but Richard Outcault stayed with the trade and sensed where the real money was to be made. He invented a new boy, Buster Brown, a nasty, naughty pest and bigot dressed like Little Lord Fauntleroy, and changed the comic-art format from a single group scene into individual panels—the comic strip. It was an instant success.

Outcault set up shop at the 1904 St. Louis World's Fair with the purpose of licensing Buster Brown to toy and clothing manufacturers. Clothing and shoes may appear prosaic, but from this simple beginning the Buster Brown Shoe Company and the Buster Brown Textile Company were born. Both are industrial giants today and the most successful of the licensees signed up by the artist. There are 2,500 Buster Brown shoe stores coast to coast, and the textile company is even larger. Both have their own private museums of Buster Brown memorabilia, including rare German hand-painted tin toys, banks, pocket watches, dolls, games, advertising art, comic buttons, original art, proof pages, and jewelry, all of which are almost impossible to find anymore. Although the Buster Brown comic page was never great art, the merchandise was superb and was hawked with much publicity and show-business techniques by traveling teams of midgets dressed just like Buster giving free vaudeville shows!

The originators of American comic art were four. In addition to Outcault, James Swinnerton in 1892 created "Little Bears and Tigers," which depicted a jolly assortment of animal characters; Rudolph Dirks created "The Katzenjammer Kids," based upon Max und Moritz; and F. B. Opper created the popular "Happy Hooligan." Outcault, Swinnerton, Dirks, and Opper gave comic art its basic directions: a sequence of individual panels, continuous use of the balloon to enclose the dialogue, action and story moving from panel to panel, and the use of bright colors and excellent draftsmanship. These early directions became conventions that have not changed in form to this day.

Using the forms invented by these four, a giant began to appear on the horizon—the finest comic artist of all times, an artist whose work dissolved the distinction between "low art" and "high art," an artist who said of his compulsion:

> The principal factor in my success has been an absolute desire to draw constantly. I never decided to be an artist. Simply, I couldn't stop myself from drawing. I drew for my own pleasure. I never wanted to know whether or not someone liked my drawings. I drew on walls, the school blackboards, old bits of paper, the walls of barns. Today I'm still as fond of drawing as when I was a kid . . . and that's a long time ago . . . but surprising as it may seem, I never thought about the money I would receive for my drawings. I simply drew and drew.

Winsor Zenic McCay was born in Spring Lake, Michigan, on September 26, 1869. At seventeen he went to Chicago with a circus and designed advertising posters for the company, then on to Cincinnati where he was employed by Morton's Dime Museum as a scenic artist to design posters for the sideshow attractions.

McCay arrived in New York in 1903 and worked for *The Evening Telegram*, and then the New York *Herald*. During this time he created many comic strips, including "Dull Care," "Poor Jake," "The Man from Montclair," "A Pilgrim's Progress," "It's Nice to Be Married," "Little Sammy Sneeze," and "Hungry Henrietta." In 1905 he created "Dreams of a Rarebit Fiend"—a full color page devoted to the pictorial view of our weird world of dreams.

Unlike the earlier strips, there was no fixed cast of characters, and each story was based on a different character who would fall into a nightmare sleep after eating too much Welsh rarebit. Each depicted a mad, violent world gone out of control: a farmer walking on Broadway having his arms, legs, and head quickly cut off by city traffic; a missionary being boiled alive by black cannibals while listening to them argue about who gets his gizzard; a love-sick girl receiving an alligator bag from her boy friend that grows into a real alligator, chases her, and swallows her whole . . . All of them climaxing in the victim awakening from the nightmare mumbling the same promise:

> Oh! Pshaw! What a fool. It's that
> Rarebit I ate last night. Well I'm
> glad it was a dream at that. Oh but
> that was fierce. Never again!

This was a comic for adults filled with violence, death, nudity, madness, sexual anxiety, and social criticism. Its popularity grew, and in 1906 Edwin Porter of the Edison Company created a live action film seven minutes in length, "The Dream of a Rarebit Fiend." The fiend in this early classic, played by John Brawn, was an overeater tormented in his bed by devils, holding on to his bed for dear life as it flies high over the city, eventually dropping onto a steeple. McCay had discovered the nightmare as an art form that would permit the full, imaginative use of his creative talent.

This talent, perhaps genius, found its complete dimensions in the superb creation of "Little Nemo in Slumberland." At once it transcended in beauty and form all that had preceded it and made all aware that newspaper comics could reach the level of high art. Technique; talent; imagination; and exquisite draftsmanship detailing realistically baroque palaces while surrealistically distorting mirrored rooms, staircases, people, and large cities of the future all combined with an Art Nouveau approach to create the finest in American comic art. From the beginning in October 1905 to the present day the Sunday pages of "Little Nemo in Slumberland" have been collected as avidly as fine prints and paintings. McCay reached deeply into the dream world where the real and the surreal, the sane and the insane could combine to permit the freest flow of his imagination and artistic talent.

Nemo's first dream appeared October 15, 1905, in the New York *Herald*. The format was similar to "The Dreams of a Rarebit Fiend," which had preceded it. Nemo dreams that King Morpheus of Slumberland has sent Oomp the messenger to give him a pony named Somnus to bring him to Slumberland. Accepting the invitation, he leaves his bed and rides the pony up into the night sky, being warned by Oomp not to ride too fast. But along the way he is challenged to a race by a green kangaroo, a white pig, a red dog being jockeyed by a frog, and other strange creatures. Somnus stumbles on a star, and Nemo tumbles down "through miles and miles of space," falls out of bed, and awakes to end the dream. All the strips that followed used the same format of wild dreams ending in the rude awakening to reality.

Nemo, King Morpheus, Flip, Princess, Impy, Granny, Hag, and others traveled from the Candy Islands to the Moon from 1905 to 1911 in the New York *Herald*. This was the great period; the revival from 1924 to 1927 produced a less colorful and imaginative Nemo.

Winsor McCay was the comics' first artist, and his work transcended the newspaper comic to reach the level of pure art. McCay also had a serious interest in the development of the animated film and in 1909 made a short film of Little Nemo that was handsomely composed and is in the archives of the Museum of Modern Art. Another interesting short feature was

"Gertie the Dinosaur," made in 1911, in which both McCay and George McManus ("Bringing up Father") appeared.

But McCay's magnificent talent began to fade after he completed the last beautifully drawn adventure, a trip to the moon aboard King Morpheus' steamboat-like dirigible. After 1911 he left the *Herald* to work for the Hearst organization, and the quality of the art and even the printing went downhill. Yet his influence, particularly on other artists, grew. Walt Disney knew him and his work, and sequences from *Snow White*, *Fantasia*, and the pink-elephant scenes in *Dumbo* are pure McCay. Maurice Sendak's handsome children's book illustrations also show a strong Little Nemo derivation.

McCay, Outcault, Opper, and Swinnerton were the pioneer creators and inventors of American comic art. There were others, but none so important. The popularity of their comic creations developed a paying public who would buy newspapers to follow their favorites, thereby increasing circulation. Their success established the financial fact that a profit could be made from the art and the artist could become self-supportive. A market was created that attracted other talented artists, and it expanded away from the printed newspaper into toys, dolls, games, comic books, clothing, jewelry, animated films, and advertising, all derived from the newspaper comic strips. From the first few seeds sprang a large tree and from that tree branches and from the branches many leaves. This was the beginning.

It's always been the same. The comic artist prepares the daily or Sunday page on white cardboard with pen and black ink. A proof page is prepared, then approved by the artist, and the newspaper presses roll. That black-and-white art is the original art of the comics. Although most of it was considered absolutely worthless after it had served the purpose of printing and was destroyed, that which survived the furnace and garbage cans comprises an almost silent, growing, and very high-priced market of new collectibles.

A few astute collectors, museums, and members of the investment-oriented New York City Art Establishment have been buying in silence for years at very low prices. The result is that the best of American original comic art is held in a few hands, and the few pieces that are released for sale or traded command the highest prices paid for any of the various comic collectibles. A conspiracy of silence surrounds it. The value of comic books and Mickey Mouse watches is known by the general public, but newspapers, magazines, and other media do not print or speak about the fantastic rise in prices and selective determinations of art value that have been and are right now taking place as astute accumulation continues.

Even the names of comic artists whose work has soared from zero worth to thousands of dollars within the last few years are completely unknown to the general public. McCay, Outcault, Raymond, Foster, Hogarth, Iwerks, Calkins, Kirby, Herriman are important and valuable unknowns.

Worse, comic-strip art is dying as the newspapers die nationwide. Television started to kill this art form in the 1950s, and its slow death is continuing. With the exception of a few very popular strips, the market for national syndication has shrunk and is shrinking. Much worse from the viewpoint of the collector is that the current comic artists are holding on to all their art and are themselves collecting the best of the old, thereby decreasing the supply.

Original comic art is basically black-and-white inked drawings done on Bristol board twice the size of the printed panels and signed by the artist. It is the preparatory art for the Sunday and daily newspaper comics. But it is also magnificent oil paintings produced by exceptionally fine artists during the depression era for pulp- and comic-magazine covers. It is also commercial art for the packaging of comic-character toys and games. And it is the penciled animation sketches and "cels" that were required for the Mickey Mouse and Betty Boop animated films.

Behind the comic artist who drew the strip was a vast army of commercial artists and illustrators, ranging from genius to hack, schooled and unschooled, who used comic-strip art to design the millions of comic-related items that were produced. For each and every piece of comic anything there was an artist who conceptualized, created, designed, and drew his art on paper, cardboard, or celluloid, with pencil, pen, or paintbrush. And his work, when and if found, can be categorized as original comic art.

These artists, many brilliant and talented, remain unrecorded, unknown, and without names. Even the Sunday-page art was considered so worthless that it is not unusual today to find an original with next week's Sunday comics drawn on the other side to save the cost of another piece of cardboard—which means that the monetary evaluation of the artist's work was lower than a cheap piece of depression-priced cardboard! That was the thinking then, and this is the reason now why it is so difficult to collect American comic-art originals. Even the artists who drew the comics often shared the prejudice. Example: All of the magnificent Sunday and daily original art for "Buck Rogers in the 25th Century" from the 1930s had gasoline poured over it and was turned into a backyard bonfire by one of the artists who drew it because it took up too much space! And this crime against art was committed just a few years ago!

This art is unlike any other medium in that it is both real and surreal at the same time. Although the story is always logical and simple and the art is representational, the leading character is absurd. A mouse in short pants with yellow shoes talking to a duck dressed in a sailor's suit? A Superman who can fly faster than a speeding bullet and changes into a long-underwear uniform in a telephone booth to fight gangsters? A Buck Rogers trapped in a mine waking five hundred years later undecomposed to war against the villains of outer space? Only a child's imagination could suspend disbelief and become entranced in these worlds of absurdity. But it was this essential element of absurdity that permitted the artist to create this particular kind of surreal art and free his imagination and pen from the boundaries of strict realism. This freedom attracted the type of talent that could flourish within this new art form. The vast audience and the newspaper deadlines required speed, therefore much of the art was awful, but a few artists excelled and created the finest works in American comic-art history.

Whereas comic books and comic toys were produced by the millions, original comic art was one of a kind and handmade, and most of it was destroyed after the Sunday or daily strip was printed. There is little art available from the early period of Outcault's "Yellow Kid" and McCay's "Little Nemo in Slumberland" and not too much from the golden age of the middle period, which can be approximately dated from 1929 to 1939. Some original comic art will never be available. All of the Sundays and dailies of "Orphan Annie" were donated to a university, all of the nineteen-thirties "Buck Rogers in the 25th Century" art was destroyed, and not a single nineteen-thirties "Dick Tracy" can be found.

The scarcity of these items plus the growing demand for original art creates a seller's market and very high prices. Equally high are the prices for the work of those few artists who are considered the best of the middle period.

In 1933 King Features Syndicate decided that they had to meet the competition and popularity of "Buck Rogers" and "Tarzan." Alex Raymond was employed, and his answers were "Flash Gordon" and "Jungle Jim." He was an accomplished artist and illustrator, and both strips achieved immediate popularity. He used research and had a large personal science library to make his machines and actions plausible and thus avoid criticism. He saw comic art as serious art and labored long hours. Even in those days he was considered good; among collectors today he is considered one of the greatest who ever took to black ink and pen. Russ Westover, who drew "Tillie the Toiler," was aware of his skill and suggested that he should be working as a comic artist. His passionate interest in Jules Verne led directly to his creation of "Flash Gordon." From the very beginning fan letters poured in, and its syndication grew nationwide and around the world. He was a master of fine-line art and had a crisp modern style that differentiated his work from all others. Interestingly, "Jungle Jim" was drawn in a different style from that of "Flash Gordon," though they appeared together on the Sunday page. His art progressed, the 1934–1940 period is considered the best, and the twenty full-length Sunday pages of "Flash Gordon" that he drew without "Jungle Jim" are top prizes. He also did "Rip Kirby" and a strip called "Secret Agent X-9," the story line for which was provided by Dashiell Hammett. In 1956 Raymond was killed in an automobile accident, and the strip was continued by another fine artist, John Prentice. In recent years the prices for "Raymond-Art" have soared and the supply has dwindled to zero, but because the quality of the art was so impressive, much was saved from the early years and is safely placed in many collections.

The appreciation of the art of Burne Hogarth has been growing straight up. He drew the "Tarzan" page from 1937 to 1950, and of all the artists, illustrators, the talented, and the hacks who have drawn Tarzan in comics, books, posters, and everything since 1912, Hogarth was absolutely the best. He was a born artist. He started sketching at the age of twelve and at fifteen became an assistant cartoonist at Associated Editors Syndicate. At sixteen he created his own feature, "Famous Churches of the World," for the syndicate, and at eighteen, in 1929, he created his first comic strip, "Ivy Hemmanshaw." Then from Chicago where he was born he moved on to New York City where he worked for King Features Syndicate. But the task never used the talent until 1936, when the great Hal Foster, who had been drawing "Tarzan" since 1929 for United Features Syndicate, decided to quit the strip. Many cartoonists applied for the job, but Hogarth won. At first the style was similar to Foster's, but

soon it began to change into a new and unique approach to comic art based upon his studies of the anatomy of the human form and his appreciation of the fine draftsmanship of Michelangelo and the artists of the baroque period. Although the stories were "Tarzan" stories, the art was more and became a serious means for measuring and developing this fine artist's talent to its furthest limits.

The style was like nothing that came before: the accent was on anatomy in motion, long muscles distorted, apes and men and tigers twisting beautifully through the sky as if suspended in air by their own sheer strength, set against the background of a surreal jungle of razor-sharp trees, mountains, birds, and beasts with dangerous cutting beaks and claws and teeth all merging into a continuous illusion of motion.

He tried other strips, "Drago" and "Miracle Jones"; he was one of the founders of the School of Visual Arts in New York City, which trained many famous comic artists of today, and he wrote books on anatomy, drawing the human head, and figure drawing; but nothing before or after ever equaled Hogarth's art of "Tarzan."

Recognition came, not from his own country but from France. In 1966 Hogarth's works were shown by Socerlid (Sociètè d'Études de Recherches de Littératures Dessinees). The French critics were ecstatic in their praise, and the French museums bought. The brilliant French critic Francis Lacassin wrote in his "Hogarth Between Wonder and Madness," Paris, *Giff-Wiff*, No. 13, 1965:

> The twists of the plot are arranged to serve a set purpose: the dynamic depiction of Tarzan's anatomy. Pitted against him are opponents—men or beasts—well suited to free his kinetic energy. It is clear that Hogarth does not strive so much to develop the point of the narrative as to express the inner drama of the action: the furor of the bodies often reflects the torment of the souls. Rather than tell the story word for word, he elects to represent some of its significant moments. Nearly always these correspond to phases of acute dramatic tension . . . .
>
> In turn, the atmosphere yields to the frenzy which consumes the living. Nature seems in a feverish trance: the grass and the trees bow under the threat of an ever raging storm and the fire stirs up the bowels of the earth and illuminates, in some apocalyptic explosion, the peaks of the volcanoes. Still waters try to conceal quicksands.

Moving waters rolling into foamy swells, meditate some frightful tidal wave. . . . A high wall is destined to bring into display the hero's muscles while he climbs over it; a branch stands out so he might crouch down in a simian position in order to jump on his enemies; a sugarloaf-shaped rock allows Tarzan to hug it with nonchalance and contemplate the horizon.

Right now a controversy is raging among the astute collectors of original art. Which is more valuable, a "Tarzan" Sunday page by Hal Foster or one by Burne Hogarth? As the smoke of this battle clears, it appears that Hogarth is winning as the price for his originals soars. As recently as a few years ago a Hogarth was bought for a mere fifty dollars; now it can command hundreds. Francis Lacassin on this controversy:

> Foster's brush gave Tarzan a simplicity of purpose. Hogarth's invisible camera makes him into an actor whose behavior is shaped by the needs of the mise-en-scène. Theatrical convention succeeds realistic simplicity. The secondary characters in their death throes, the monarchs in the affirmation of their tyranny, and Tarzan in his most familiar gestures strike up stage postures charged and speeded up by the artist's obsession with dynamic action. The well-known pose of a figure standing with his arms folded against the chest meant only undisturbed power to Foster. As seen by Hogarth, the pose breathes defiance. The gesture of the arm with pointed finger has now become both sententious and imperious. The somewhat quaint majesty with which Foster sometimes froze Tarzan's silhouette is eclipsed by Hogarth's feverish contortions, signs of impatience, surprised starts, and interrupted motions of the figure.

But the issue is more complex. Hal Foster quit the "Tarzan" page in 1936 because it limited the full reach of his talents. He was a great comic-strip artist who needed a new vehicle to develop and who needed to measure for himself his ultimate creative dimensions. He had outgrown "Tarzan" and had become bored with the repetitive format. In 1937 he began one of the most beautiful and imaginative epics ever drawn, "Prince Valiant." Here he achieved the full limits of his capacity as a fine artist, which was precisely what he wanted to do in leaving "Tarzan" to Hogarth. To a large extent it was based upon knighthood and King Arthur's Court and was filled with perilous voyages,

violent fights with monsters and dragons, beautiful maidens to be rescued, and shining knights on strong steeds, all drawn across his Sunday pages in a panorama of pageantry. Medieval battlefields, huge sea-castles were drawn in splendid detail. In "Prince Valiant" he eliminated the old-fashioned balloons and instead printed the narrative below the drawing.

His art created another time and place and transcended the flat, childish scrawl of the comic strips. The incredibly detailed backgrounds and figures resembled illustrations for expensive editions of historical novels. Foster spent about fifty hours a week on each Sunday page, which can be seen in the amount of accurate detail drawn into the background of every fraction of an inch. From the beginning the art of "Prince Valiant" was recognized, and awards included the National Cartoonists' Society's Reuben and the Banshees' Silver Lady. Foster was elected into membership of Great Britain's prestigious Royal Society of Arts; popularity and acceptance were worldwide. His pages are avidly sought by comic collectors and noncollectors who admire his art, and they command extremely high prices.

So it's Raymond, Hogarth, and Foster who are the most desired in this middle period of American comic art, and their originals have become very difficult for collectors to obtain as the demand increases and prices fly upward to the sky.

There were others whose originals are in near equal demand, and one of the most interesting is an obsessed artist who gets up every morning at precisely 4:30 A.M., probably with pen in hand, and has drawn at dawn for forty-three years. He is today, at the age of seventy-three, a fine artist and imaginative story teller still: Chester Gould. His "Dick Tracy" first appeared in the New York *Daily News* in 1931 and continues in that same newspaper to this day. His was the first strip to show real violence in terms of blood and murder. It was a no-nonsense era, in which gangsters crawled the streets, headlined the newspapers, and were in the movies as both the heroes and the hated, and law and order and crime in the streets were the issues of the day.

Popularity was almost instantaneous: from a slight appearance on October 4, 1931, in the Detroit *Mirror* to an October 12, 1931, debut of the daily strip in the New York *Daily News* to its appearance in "The World's Greatest Newspaper" the Chicago *Tribune* in 1932 to today's 375 newspapers with 38 million readers around the world. According to recent surveys "Dick Tracy" ranks number one in readership among adventure comic strips, even though the serial strip has been badly hurt by television.

"Dick Tracy" was and is a modernized Sherlock Holmes using a sharp intelligence and the latest crime-detection devices. He was the first and most important of the detective comic strips that originated in the crime stories of books and pulps. But as a comic strip he could be seen in action. And what could be seen is seldom discussed: the art of Chester Gould. Flat, two-dimensional graphics predominate, using extremely bright colors. Our hero wore a bright yellow overcoat, a green snap-brim hat, loud stripes on the tie, and natty double-breasted suits that made him the best- or worst-dressed detective on the force. From panel to panel, action dominated that created the illusion of a Hollywood gangster movie.

But if the basis of all art is originality, then the surreal near-humans Gould created are testimony to his art: Sam Catchem, Flattop, Tinky, The Button, The Brow, Pruneface, B. B. Eyes, Moon Maid, Breathless Mahoney, Pouch, Groovy Grove, Ugly Christine, Scorpio, Mr. Snelt, Shaky, Gravel Gertie, Mole, Shoulders, Bribery, Piggy, B. O. Plenty, Steve The Tramp—all of the criminals were created ugly and deformed and dirty to prove visually Gould's point of view that crime is ugly, deformed, and dirty.

True, the stories are interesting, true he was the first to introduce the two-way wrist radio and the first to use television for crime detection and he culled the files of police departments for accurate research, but it is the ignored and undiscussed art of Chester Gould that demands attention. Look at the profile of Dick Tracy. His nose is that of a determined, hungry hawk, and the jaw looks as if it was carved from cast iron, the eyes coming directly from a killer cobra. All together it is the portrait of a hunter and killer of criminals. criminals.

The art was representational, but the characters were pure surreal. No way, nowhere on any street will you ever see characters like these. It is Gould's combination of both forms of art that makes his creations examples of the unlimited freedom available to the comic artist. And these departures from reality will be accepted by its vast unschooled public who is otherwise hostile to all abstract art. Again, unfortunately for the original-art collector, the excellent, early nineteen-thirties dailies and Sundays are impossible to find, but the newspaper pages, which are the end product, in full color, are easier and cheaper to collect and make superb framed prints.

Take comic art one step further: create both char-

acters and stories that are equally surreal, that do not relate in any way to any real world. George Herriman did just that with his "Krazy Kat." It was understood and accepted enthusiastically by the intelligentsia of the nineteen twenties and thirties. The poet E. E. Cummings wrote the forward to the first book on "Krazy Kat," and to this day many consider it the best comic strip ever drawn.

George Herriman was born in New Orleans in 1878 and never went to an art school. His career began as an office boy on the old Los Angeles *Herald* plus some political cartooning. Then on to the New York *World* and the New York *Evening Journal*, trying several strips: "The Dingbat Family," "Professor Otto and His Auto," and "Doc Archie and Bean," and finally his masterpiece, "Krazy Kat."

The setting is his Coconino County of open land and blank sky, a vastness of the "Enchanted Mesa," buttes, adobe houses, and Pueblo architecture. Indian designs appear on the clouds, trees, pots, and other objects on his stage. The characters never look and seldom speak like real humans, and the backgrounds are in continuous change as if in a dream. Sophistication and naïveté combine in this simple and complex world. A cat is in love with a mouse. Krazy Kat, the victim of Ignatz Mouse, is protected by Offisa Pup. Ignatz throws bricks at Krazy Kat, who continues to love his "liddle dahlink" anyway.

Each page was a complete story, and there was no continuity from episode to episode. They were filled with puns and jokes and odd characters, such as Bum Bill Bee, who was a bee named Bill and a bum; Mrs. Quack Wack, a Peking duck; Willi Mendoza, the Mexican jumping-bean bandit, and Old Joe Stork, who brought babies from the Enchanted Mesa. Herriman's art was unconventional and departed from the usual square panels; borders were eliminated, and large splash panels were drawn to any size, some of the best resembling film strips with no words to describe what was going on.

Luckily, he valued his work, and much of the original art has been saved, but even though a supply exists, the demand has made the original art of George Herriman extremely expensive.

Quite similar is the comic art of E. C. Segar, the creator of the first super hero, Popeye. From 1907 to 1917 he drew the daily and Sunday newspaper comic strip "The Adventures of Charlie Chaplin," then on to "Thimble Theatre" in 1919, and in 1929 Popeye made his debut. Popeye is the second most popular worldwide comic creation; only Mickey Mouse beats the spinach eater. The name Wimpy means hamburger to the world, and the intriguing characters of Olive Oyl, Ham Gravy, and Sea Hag and Eugene the Jeep, Sweetpea, and Bluto have held reader interest fast for decades.

There are others, many, many others, who were fine artists and made major contributions to American comic art during the golden age, and all of them together created this uniquely American heritage.

By logical and economic extension newspaper comic art led directly to the art of the comic book. Many comic books are merely reprints of the newspaper comics, but the bulk was original creations, and its art began a different look. Here, there was even more freedom; they did not have to pass the strict editorial censorship of newspaper comics, and most of the artists and writers were very young, writing and drawing for the very young.

The front covers are the real art of the comic books, every fraction of an inch used, filled with bright colors, violence, and action. They had to be because it was and is the cover art that attracts the eyes of the young to the newsstand and sells the comic book. And it is the original black-and-white art of the comic-book covers that is so avidly sought by collectors. Unfortunately, most of it has disappeared with the passage of time and the years of neglect and indifference to its true value as an indigenous American art form.

Even the names of the finest artists remain relatively unknown—Lou Fine, Jack Kirby, Will Eisner, C. C. Beck, Reed Crandall, Neil Adams—and forever nameless and unknown will be the army of their helpers who inked and lettered and also drew. During the golden age of American comics an explosion of inspiration was set off by the freedom to create in a new form, to innovate and experiment and yet be paid for doing your own wild thing.

Most of the art that was saved was requested art: A young fan would write to a cartoonist requesting a sample of his art; the cartoonist would then select a piece, sign it, and send it on to the kid. These are the ones that have survived from the early days and are extremely valuable now because they are signed by the artist. It is an exciting hunt to find black-and-white cover art, then seek the comic book itself and frame both of them together, the preparatory art and the end product.

Beneath this mountain the rumbles of a new volcano can be heard; it's a sleeper, it's "next," it's still a few years away, and only a few astute collectors are currently involved. It doesn't even have a name yet. It could be called Commercial Preparatory Art. All of that huge mountain of comic merchandise with its required packaging design and the advertising art necessary to sell it also required art and artists. Where is it all? The answer to this question is being sought by a new group of comic-art collectors who haunt the files of advertising agencies and hunt in the dead files of toy manufacturers' art departments.

One example that has been found and is shown is the giant "Gulliver Buck Rogers," a charcoal and watercolor sketch depicting our first space hero standing with one foot in New York and the other in Los Angeles, rocket pistol in hand guarding the U.S.A. against the Red Mongol Hordes who will of course attempt to conquer America in the twenty-fifth century, if not sooner. It was drawn by Dick Calkins, the strip's artist in 1935, for the advertising brochure and box design for the National Fireworks Company's Buck Rogers Kits. It was the best Buck Rogers art Calkins ever drew, and he knew it and kept it on the wall over his drafting board for years.

Like the Rogers piece, much of this art was drawn quite large, four or eight times printed size, and then reduced, which makes it extremely impressive when displayed. Not only was commercial preparatory art large, but it was also painted in oils or watercolors if it was to be printed in color. Giant sized, beautifully composed and colored, C.P.A.'s of Little Orphan Annie, Buck Rogers, Popeye, Dick Tracy, and, of course, Mickey Mouse are being sought and found. An additional attraction is the pure depiction of the subject only. There are no printed words! The mechanical type layouts that cited prices or names or advertising were done later and separately; it is free from interfering storyline or commercial messages that would detract from its visual impact.

The preparatory art for pulp-magazine covers were oils painted on canvas and were pure action art without the clutter of words. Typical is the September 1, 1933, cover for *The Shadow* pulp. As shown on page 40, it is pure Shadow, a portrait in bright colors brilliantly executed by the artist G. Rozen. The Shadow is caught in the net of criminals and is struggling to escape; his eyes are narrow slits of terror and his huge nose suggests heavy breathing. The black cape with red lining and the large floppy black hat combined with the yellow background results in a striking work of commercial preparatory art.

Similar oil paintings were prepared for *Doc Savage, Operator #5, G-8 and His Battle Aces, Spider, The*

Phantom Detective, Captain Satan, Weird Tales, Jungle Stories, Public Enemy, Black Mask, Argosy, Planet Stories, and a host of others, all with superb cover art.

The pulps were basically untrimmed magazines named for the cheap paper flecked with shreds of wood fibre used for printing. They measured nine and one-half by seven and one-half inches and were anywhere from 114 to 162 pages thick. They cost a dime and had to be printed cheaply, and were—in the millions. They were popular entertainment during the nineteen thirties, and at any one time there were at least 250 different titles on newsstand display—a measure of their popularity and devoted readership. Comic books were for boys and pulps were for men, and both thrilled, horrified, shocked, and satisfied their millions of lower-middle-class repeat customers. They were paperbacks before the publishing industry had invented the name. There is a vast number of pulp collectors who attempt in their lifetimes to complete an entire run of *Shadows*, *Spiders*, and *G-8s* and who patrol the bookstores that cater to their wants, quite like a policeman on his beat. But it is the original oil painting of the cover art of their favorite character that they consider the supreme collectible. Unfortunately, the large size of these paintings resulted in most being thrown away, and they are very difficult to find. It is tragic because these oil paintings were close to fine art, and in the opinions of many advanced collectors, some of them represent the most handsome and original art ever created for American popular culture.

In the vast world of the animated cartoon film, from the very beginning of the silents to the present day, thousands of artists were employed, and what original art still remains is known among collectors as Studio Art. The technical process must be understood, and perhaps the simplest explanation is from "The Story of Betty Boop," written by its creator Max Fleischer, in *Radio Guide*, March 26, 1932:

Betty Boop's talents are unlimited, or should I say limited only by the human imagination. She can sprout wings and fly like an angel or she can lift an elephant with her little finger. Betty Boop has no limitations.

True, she is a cartoon, but like any other star she is surrounded by over one hundred and fifty specially trained servants . . . a staff of scenic artists continuously engaged in designing her backgrounds; a staff of musicians who prepare special music for her; a crew of cameramen, sound men and studio technicians.

Do you wonder that her movements are so fascinating when I tell you that each step that she makes is carefully analyzed by a staff of twenty artists? Before Betty Boop can entertain you for seven minutes, over 14,000 drawings must be made.

Fourteen thousand drawings represent a lot of work to be sure, but what do you suppose happens when these drawings are completed? It will probably be a shock to you to learn that they are actually thrown away and never used. The reason for this is that the original drawings are made in pencil on sheets of paper and merely represent a guide for the crew of artists who ink in the drawings on celluloid. That is, a sheet of celluloid is laid over the drawing and upon this celluloid the artists apply the ink lines. The paper drawings are then discarded. Having completed the second set of 14,000 drawings on celluloid we still find that not a single drawing is complete for they must now be colored with paint and brush so that again each of the vast number of drawings is sent to the coloring department where the various shades of blacks, whites and grays are carefully applied and the little figures of Betty Boop take on a finished appearance.

Is the job finished now? No such luck. The colored celluloids are now sent to the music department and each one of them is carefully checked by men who are expert in the timing and synchronization of music with the action of the cartoons. . . . We now find the stacks of drawings in the photographic department where five specially constructed motor-driven cameras are ready. The photographers lay these drawings down one by one, press on a pedal, and the images of Betty Boop and her friends are in this way permanently recorded on the long celluloid film which becomes the negative of the picture being produced. From this negative a print is made. . . . Then the picture is carefully edited. And for the first time we can actually say "finished."

The mountains of studio art required can be visualized by the statistics from the first feature-length animated film, *Snow White and the Seven Dwarfs*. Twenty-five artists painted the pastel backgrounds. Then 300 animators drew the characters in motion on sheets of celluloid. Two million "cels" were painted before 250,000 were finally chosen to be successively photographed against the backgrounds. But the tragedy for original-art collectors, as Fleischer states, is that the strict policy of the studios was to throw all of it away. They had to; the huge piles of sketches and cels would have required a warehouse the size of an airplane hangar.

Because of this policy during the early years of film animation, collecting original studio art is very difficult. Basically there are, first, the studio animation charts that served as an instruction guide to show the artist how the studio wanted the character drawn. This ensured conformity. Secondly, there were the pencil sketches of the characters in action on thin tracing paper, and thirdly, the cels that were traced from these sketches and hand colored. These were the finished product that was sent to the photographic department. Much of the small amount of studio art that is available to the collector today is available because the artists simply stole the best and put it into their portfolios to help them obtain better jobs elsewhere. Some has been preserved as requested art, and the Disney Studios sold and gave away many of their best and earliest cels. There is a current and viable market for cels, and the handsome cels for the Beatles' *Yellow Submarine* and Disney's recent *Robin Hood* were sold at very high prices by studio-authorized New York art galleries.

An advanced collector can look at a Mickey Mouse pencil sketch from the studio, recognize the art as "early Mickey," identify the artist as Ub Iwerks, determine the date it was drawn and the film it was used for, and check the specially shaped and punched holes at the top to authenticate it. Original studio art is difficult to find and expensive to collect—but then there is always luck.

A word of caution: As the era of the syndicated newspaper daily and Sunday comic strip declines and eventually dies, the price value of the original black-and-white art is increasing to the point where reproductions are worth making. They are simply black ink on white cardboard and can be easily duplicated by merely tracing the newspaper page. One protection is that almost always a small printed newspaper strip stating the date of copyright and the particular syndicate's name was glued to the lower right-hand corner of the original. Since this is almost impossible to duplicate, its presence is evidence of authenticity. Studio sketches, cels, and oil paintings of

pulp-magazine covers often had the studio stamp or printed labels on the back that cannot be duplicated without severe legal penalties and much expense. Look for the newspaper strips, studio stamps, and labels on the back to be sure.

As this era in American comic art began to decline, a completely new group of legitimate artists became interested in its form and content and are currently engaged in its adaptation and adoption: Andy Warhol, Roy Lichtenstein, Edward Ruscha, Claes Oldenburg, Mel Ramos, and other pop artists. Their obvious talents are providing a new direction through superb insights into the basic elements of each comic character as well as the particular aspects of the flat, colorful graphics of comic art. Lichtenstein does not use known comic characters but rather uses and abstracts the form, the style. It is as if there is a center from which all explodes outward. The bright colors, the larger-than-life-size close-ups, and the outline techniques plus the halftone printing suggest a blowup of an actual newspaper comic-strip panel. It is the style of the genre, not the character, that is instantly recognizable. Claes Oldenburg's long love affair with Mickey Mouse has finally taken the magnificent form of a huge welded steel-plate sculpture of his favorite rodent, with a square, brutal face and near-representational round ears, all painted an orange red. It is successful because it displays the ratlike malice of Mickey's early character through abstract art, while other elements of the design, mainly the ears, are so realistic that the subject of the sculpture becomes instantly recognizable. It is an excellent example of the easy and imaginative mix in styles that comic art permits an accomplished modern sculptor or artist.

Andy Warhol's *Popeye* is perhaps the best of the Pop Art–Comic Art combinations. It is an acrylic on canvas painted in 1961, long before other artists joined the movement. A blank-faced Popeye has swung a haymaker and has knocked his opponent out of the picture. Only a star-shaped empty space surrounded by knock-out stars remains to suggest his presence. Above is the wide-stroke letters of Popeye's name, as if scrawled by a six-year-old fan. It is the essence of Popeye, the first of the American super heroes, capable of solving any problem with the simple and violent use of his fists.

There are other artists who have worked and are continuing to work in the comic-art style. They are attracted by the unique possibilities and far dimensions that permit a new and different freedom for the creative unorthodox. The point is this: Although newspaper comic strips and books may be declining, if not dying, the best in the comic-art style may be yet to come.

ORIGINAL ART AND THE SUNDAY PAGES
SUGGESTED LIST OF COLLECTIBLES

	Artist	Best Period
"Little Nemo in Slumberland"	Winsor McCay	1905–1912
"The Yellow Kid"	R. F. Outcault	1896
"Buster Brown"	R. F. Outcault	any
"Krazy Kat"	George Herriman	1916–1932
"Bringing up Father"	George McManus	any
"Popeye"	E. C. Segar	1929–1937
"Little Orphan Annie"	Harold Gray	any
"Buck Rogers" (Also any daily from this period is rare.)	Dick Calkins	1930–1939
"Terry and the Pirates"	Milton Caniff	previous 1940
"Dick Tracy"	Chester Gould	previous 1955
"Flash Gordon"	Alex Raymond	any
"Tarzan"	Burne Hogarth	any
"Tarzan"	Hal Foster	any
"Prince Valiant"	Hal Foster	1938–1950
"Skippy"	Percy Crosby	any
"Mickey Mouse"	Ub Iwerks	any
"Snow White"	Fred Gottfredson	any
"Donald Duck"	Carl Barks	any
"Alley Oop"	V. T. Hamlin	previous 1950
"Napoleon"	Clifford McBride	previous 1950
"Polly and Her Pals"	Cliff Sterrett	previous 1950
"Captain Easy"	Roy Crane	any
"Gasoline Alley"	Frank King	1921–1935

COMIC BOOKS

Any original cover or panel art from the comic books listed in the suggested list at the end of the chapter on comic books. Also any art by Reed Crandall, Carl Barks, Frank Frazetta, Harvey Kurtzman, Al Williamson, Wally Wood, Simon and Kirby, MacRaboy, Will Eisner, Lou Fine, Bernie Krigstein, and any E. C. Comics art.

	Studio	Best Period
Mickey Mouse	Walt Disney Enterprises	1928–1936
Minnie Mouse	Walt Disney Enterprises	previous 1938
Horace Horsecollar	Walt Disney Enterprises	previous 1938
Clarabelle Cow	Walt Disney Enterprises	previous 1938
Goofy	Walt Disney Enterprises	previous 1938
Morty and Ferdy	Walt Disney Enterprises	previous 1938
Pluto	Walt Disney Enterprises	previous 1938
Donald Duck	Walt Disney Enterprises or Walt Disney Productions*	any
Daisy Duck	Walt Disney Enterprises or Walt Disney Productions	any
Snow White	Walt Disney Enterprises	any
Popeye	Fleischer Studios	any
Olive Oyl	Fleischer Studios	any
Bluto	Fleischer Studios	any
Betty Boop	Fleischer Studios	any
Koko the Clown	Fleischer Studios	any
Bimbo	Fleischer Studios	any
Billy Boop	Fleischer Studios	any
Dora Duck	Fleischer Studios	any
Original Art from the Pornographic Films of Betty Boop and Popeye	Fleischer Studios	any
Felix the Cat	Pat Sullivan	any

* Walt Disney Enterprises was renamed Walt Disney Productions in 1939.

OIL PAINTINGS OF PULP COVERS

Adventure, The Shadow, G-8 and His Battle Aces, Spider, The Phantom Detective, Argosy, Operator #5, Captain Satan, Dime Mysteries, Black Book Detective, Secret Agent X-9, Wu Fang, Weird Tales, Jungle Stories, Dusty Ayres and His Battle Birds, Double Detective, Black Mask, Fantastic Adventures, Amazing Stories, Planet Stories, Top-Notch, Captain Future.

The Yellow Kid with a Chinese visitor to Hogan's Alley. The New York *World*, September 6, 1896.
Richard Outcault.

WHAT THEY DID TO THE DOG-CATCHER IN HOGAN'S ALLEY.

The Yellow Kid, with the help of a few friends, takes good care of the dogcatcher. The New York *World*, September 20, 1896. Richard Outcault.

Comic advertising art: The Yellow Kid Cigars. Richard Outcault, 1898.

Little Nemo in Slumberland lands on the moon to find giant Easter bunnies and lilies. The New York *Herald*, March 20, 1910. Winsor McKay.

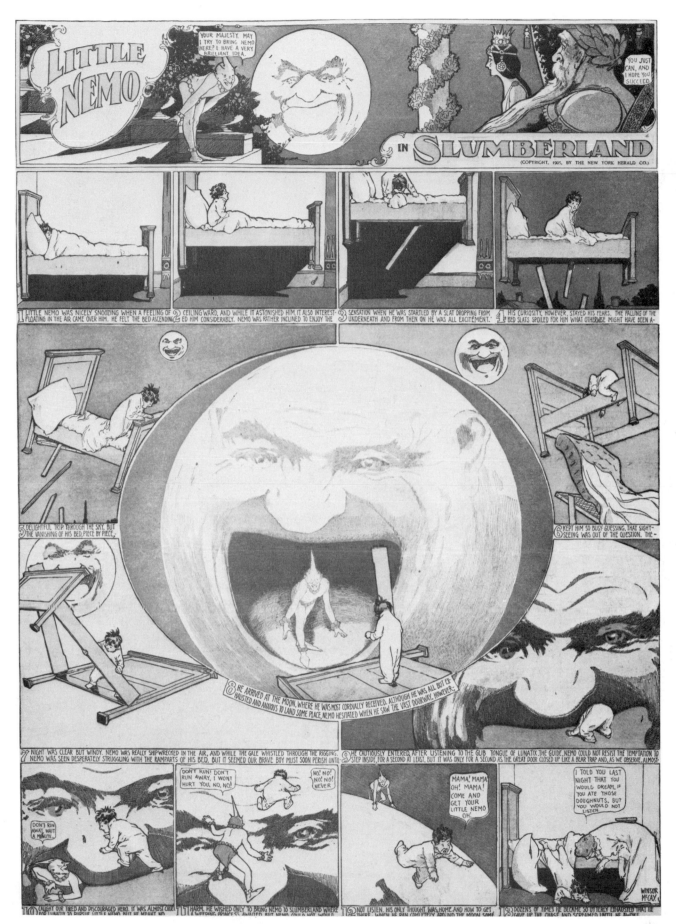

Little Nemo in Slumberland enters into the mouth of the moon. Handsome and imaginative nightmare art. The New York *Herald*, December 3, 1905.

A special "Toonerville" Sunday page drawn by Fontaine Fox for the fiftieth anniversary of the St. Louis *Post-Dispatch* in 1928.

The first pages of "Jungle Jim" and "Flash Gordon," introduced to compete with the popular "Tarzan" and "Buck Rogers." Drawn by Alex Raymond, one of the finest comic-strip artists, in 1933.

"Jungle Jim" and "Flash Gordon," May 22, 1938. The progressive development of Raymond's art is evident when compared with the first page.

"Little Nemo in Slumberland."
The New York *Herald*, February 2, 1908.

The Shadow. Preparatory oil painting by G. Rozen for the cover of "The Grove of Doom." *Shadow Magazine,* September 1, 1933.

Preparatory oil painting for the cover of *Dime Mysteries,* February 1943.

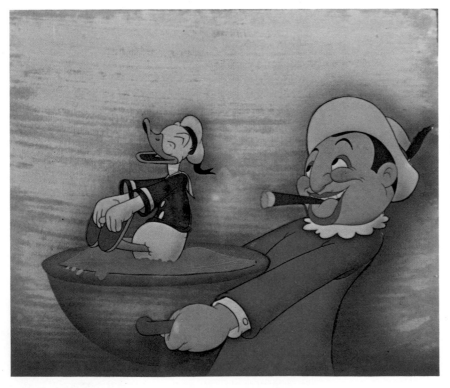

A Donald Duck and Joe Penner cel from the movie *Mother Goose Goes Hollywood.* Walt Disney Enterprises, 1937.

Superman, No. 1.

Captain America, No. 1.

Tarzan Single Series, No. 20. Hal Foster cover art.

Weird Science, No. 12.

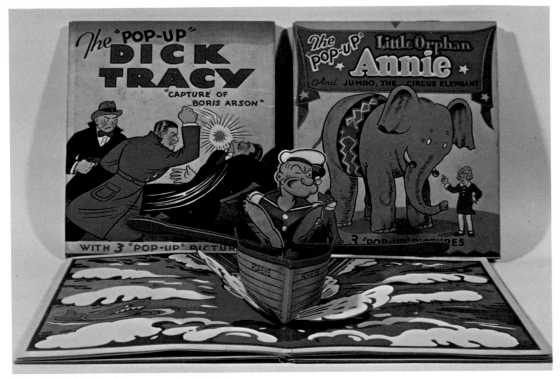

Pop-up books: Dick Tracy, Little Orphan
Annie, and Popeye.

Powerful Katrinka lifting Jimmy. (*Photo*
courtesy Bob Lyons)

Hi-Way Henry. (*Photo courtesy Bob Lyons*)

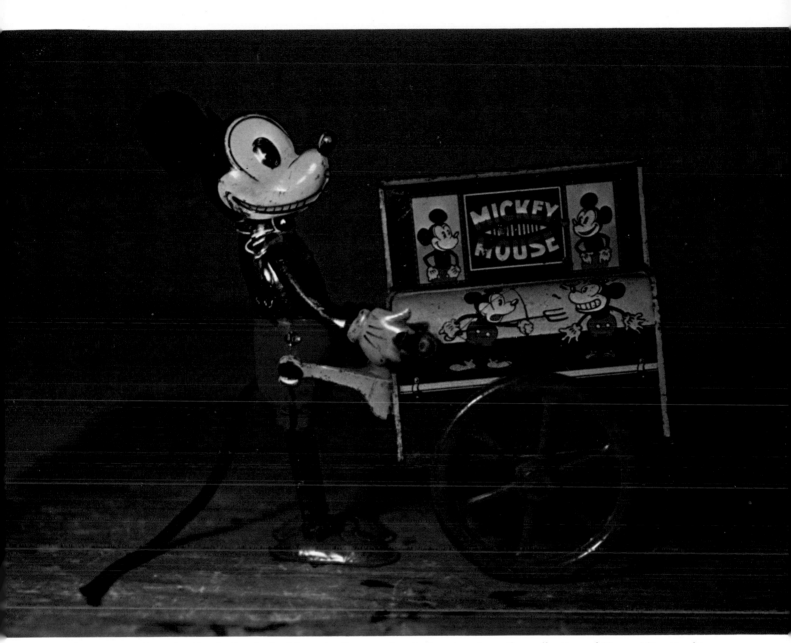

Mickey Mouse plays the Hurdy Gurdy in this early German tin wind-up toy from the collection of Henry Mazzeo, Jr. (*Photo courtesy of the collector*)

Mickey Mouse Lionel circus train. (*Photo courtesy Bob Lyons*)

The Amos 'n' Andy Fresh Air
Taxicab and walking figures.
Louis Marx, 1930.

Toonerville Trolley, Maggie and Jiggs,
and the Smitty Scooter.

Big Fight! Popeye the Champ. Watching the fight are Charlie Chaplin, Sandy, Little Orphan Annie, and Charlie McCarthy.

Superman group: Wood jointed doll by Ideal; Superman racing the airplane; dime bank; wrist watch; and *Superman*, No. 1.

Mickey and Minnie on the Piano, Mickey Torreador, Mickey Mouse Drummer, Spanish Mickey wire form, and the Schuco Donald Duck.

The Seven Dwarfs by Sieberling handsomely molded in solid rubber figures.

Mickey Mouse electric clock with pop-up box (Ingersoll, 1933) and the very rare Mickey Mouse desk clock.

Three Little Pigs animated alarm clock with pop-up box.

Pluto animated electric clock.

Popeye alarm clock, face view. 1930.

Popeye alarm clock, rear view. Handsome lithography.

Bugs Bunny, Charlie McCarthy, and Woody Woodpecker clocks.

Rare gold-plated Mickey Mouse Number One wrist watch with copper hands. American and English Ingersoll Mickey Mouse pocket watches, 1933.

Three Little Pigs pocket watch and wrist watch. Ingersoll, 1934.

Mickey Mouse lapel watch; perhaps the most beautiful of all.

Group: Buck Rogers, Popeye, Tom Mix, Betty Boop, and Donald Duck.

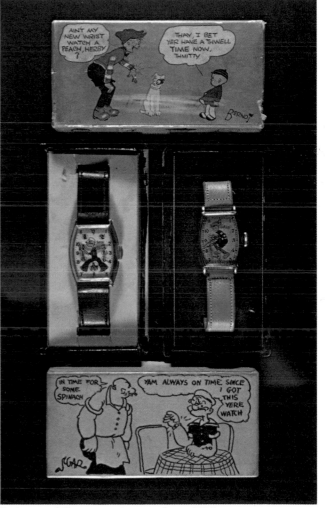

Smitty and Popeye wrist watches, 1935.

Orphan Annie wrist watch.

The beautiful masks of Buck Rogers and Wilma
Deering, 1933.

The Buck Rogers Solar Scout Map showing a 25th century
concept of the solar system. A very rare radio premium.

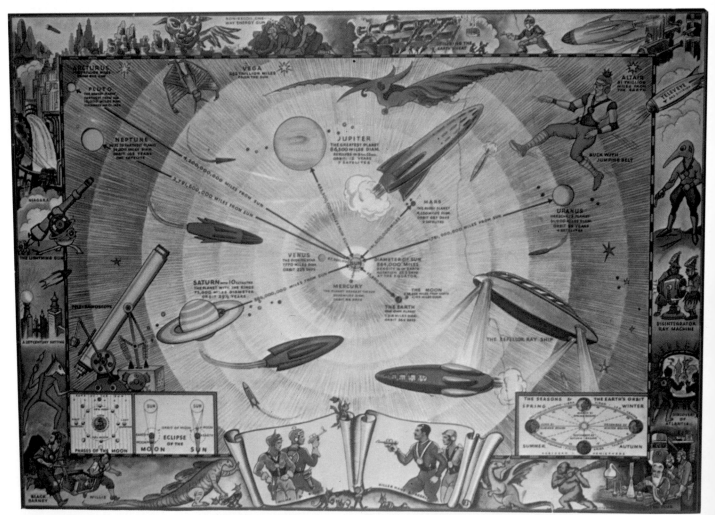

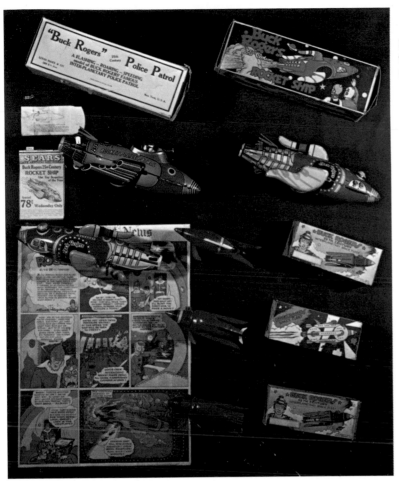

Display of metal wind-up rocket ships by Louis Marx and the Buck Rogers rocket ship construction kits with finished models.

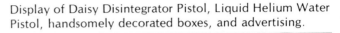

Display of Daisy Disintegrator Pistol, Liquid Helium Water Pistol, handsomely decorated boxes, and advertising.

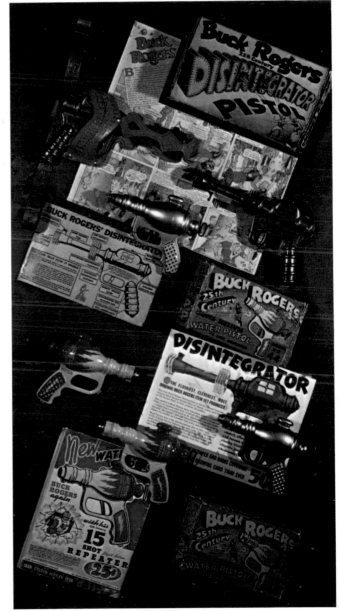

A display of the pop-up books: *Buck Rogers in a Dangerous Mission* and larger, *Buck Rogers Strange Adventures in the Spider Ship.*

Buck Rogers Helmet, box, and box for the model kit.

The *Buck Rogers Big Big Book* with complete set of Britains.

Complete set of the twelve *Buck Rogers Big Little Books*.

Mickey Mouse Bubble Gum cards. 1933–1935.

Group: Tarzan, Flash Gordon, Buck Rogers, Lone Ranger, Superman, Tom Mix, Dick Tracy, and Horrors of War cards.

Captain Midnight manual and decoders.

Dick Tracy and Justice Society of America decoders and badge.

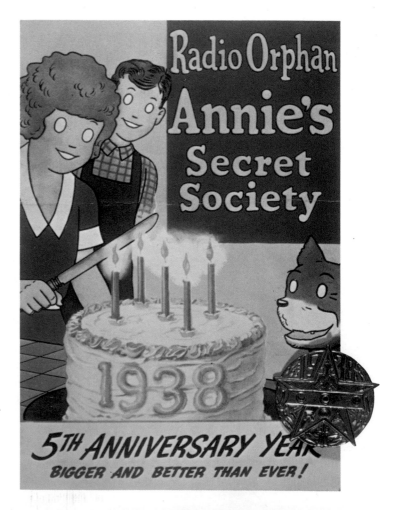

Orphan Annie manual and decoder.

A "Tarzan" Sunday page, drawn by the superb Burne Hogarth. This page is famous for its tiger scenes. March 6, 1949.

"Prince Valiant" art by Hal Foster, particularly his early period, is considered the finest of all comic art. August 28, 1938.

A handsome "Dick Tracy" Sunday page drawn by Chester Gould, February 13, 1938.

"Thimble Theatre," with Popeye as the leading man. Segar always drew a cigar butt in front of his name. December 9, 1933.

"Krazy Kat" was a creation that was an original world in its own place, outside of time, and with an unusual love triangle. George Herriman, December 25, 1932.

The handsome composition and comic draftsmanship of "Bringing up Father." George McManus, May 22, 1938.

"Tille the Toiler." Russ Westover, August 28, 1938.

"Napoleon," spoofing political advertising. Clifford McBride, 1929.

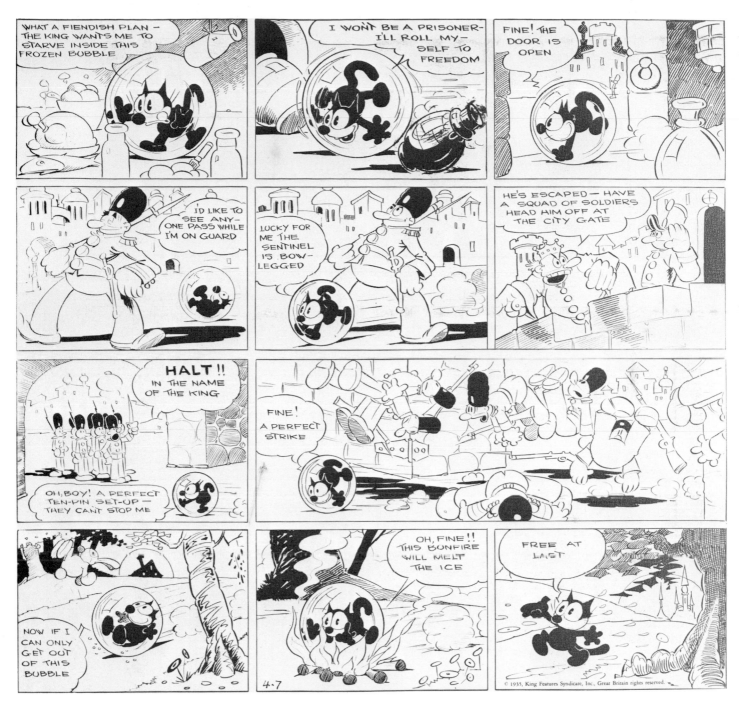

"Felix the Cat," always in and out of trouble. Pat Sullivan, 1932.

"Polly and Her Pals." Cliff Sterrett, 1947.

Snuffy Smith gets lynched by the Bulger Boys. Large "splash panels" are very rare, and it is usually a super effort by an artist turned ambitious. Billy De Beck, 1936.

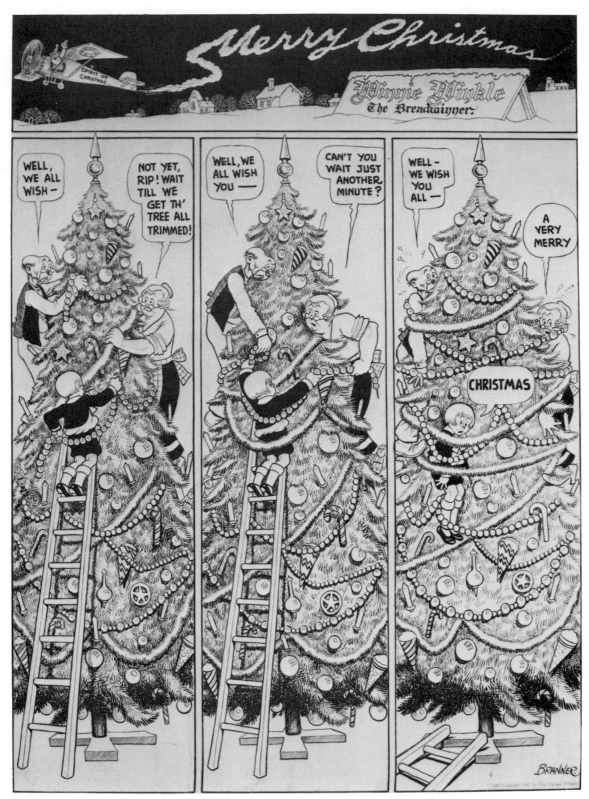

"Winnie Winkle the Breadwinner." Martin Branner wishes you a merry 1927 Christmas.

Moon Mullins has cigar trouble. Frank Willard, 1930.

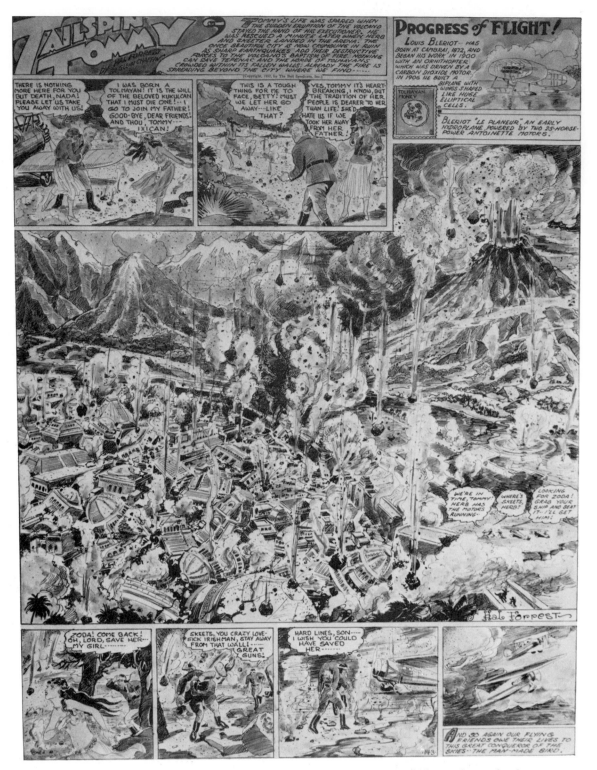

"Tailspin Tommy." An end-of-sequence super spectacular, with a huge splash panel completely hand colored by the artist to guide the printer. Hal Forrest, July 10, 1932.

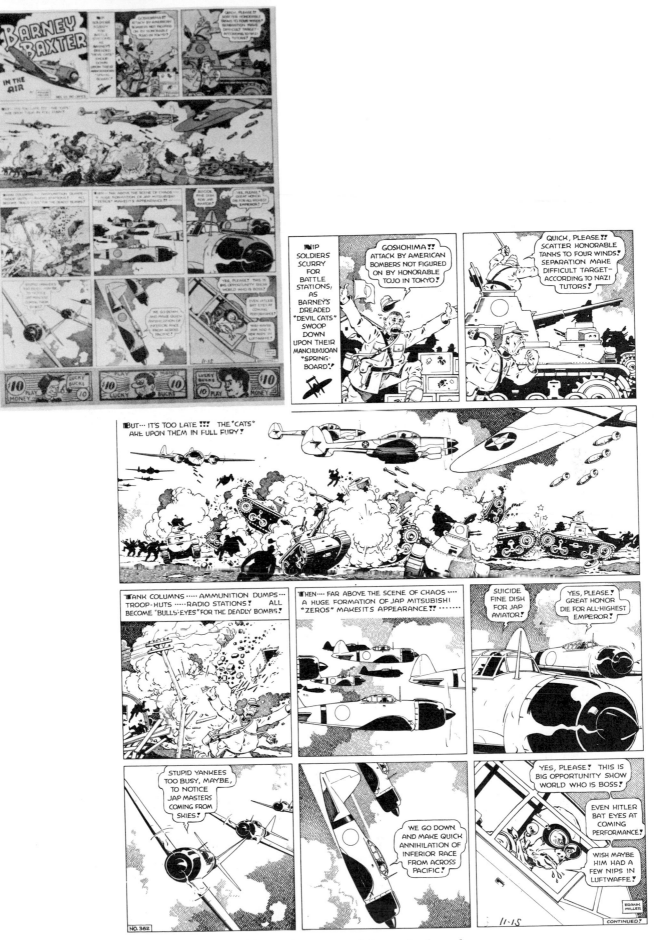

"Barney Baxter." World War II was on, and the comics showed
the Japanese as subhumans. Frank Miller, 1942.

A very rare "Buck Rogers" daily from the nineteen thirties. Dick Calkins, 1938.

"Buck Rogers" Sunday page. The style became quite different in the forties. Rick Yager, 1949.

38

"Buck Rogers in the 25th Century" commercial preparatory art. Drawn by Dick Calkins in 1935. Buck is a giant Gulliver with one foot in New York and the other in Los Angeles, protecting the United States from the "Yellow Peril."

"The Shadow." Preparatory oil painting, beautifully executed by G. Rozen for "The Grove of Doom," *Shadow Magazine*, September 1, 1933.

The production cover for the pulp.

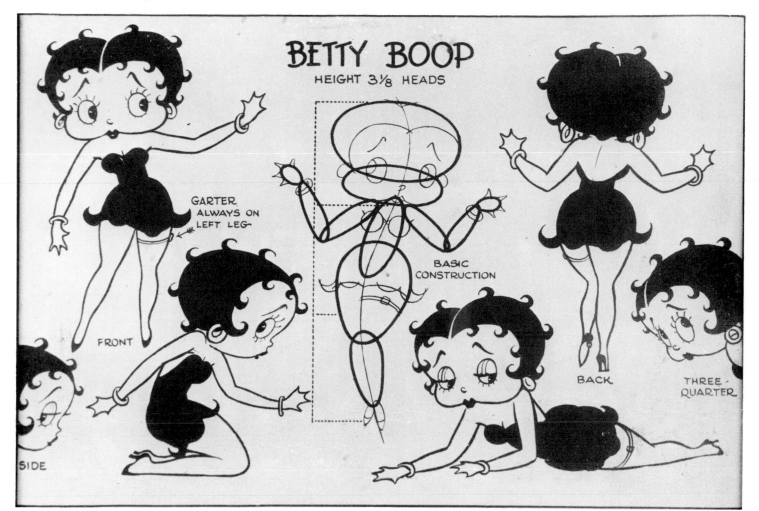

A Betty Boop animation instruction chart.
Fleischer Studios. Circa 1932.

A Betty Boop penciled animation sketch for
film. Fleischer Studios. Circa 1932.

A Popeye animation instruction chart. Fleischer Studios. Circa 1932.

A Bluto animation instruction chart. Fleischer Studios. Circa 1932.

"SNOW WHITE AND THE SEVEN DWARFS"
Disney animates a full-length film

At the Mickey Mouse studio in Hollywood, Walt Disney and his prodigious crew of artists have just finished the first feature-length animated film ever made. It is the story of *Snow White and the Seven Dwarfs*, which millions of children have read in *Grimm's Fairy Tales*.

Snow White cost $1,500,000 and took three years to make. Using human characters extensively for the first time, Disney began by making charts to show how each one should be drawn. The charts at left show (*top*) the seven dwarfs; (*centre*) their comparative heights; (*bottom*) specifications for Sleepy. Twenty-five artists painted the pastel backgrounds. Then 300 animators drew the characters in motion on sheets of celluloid. Two million "cels" were painted before 250,000 were finally chosen to be successively photographed against the backgrounds (*see below*). *Snow White* was aimed at the Christmas trade but was such a gigantic job that only Los Angeles will see it before mid-January. Meanwhile its advance publicity has reached such proportions that Mr. Disney may well worry lest his public expect too much.

A PAINTED BACKGROUND REMAINS THE SAME THROUGHOUT EACH OF THE SCENES

THE CHARACTERS ARE DRAWN ON CELLULOID, MOVE MINUTELY IN EACH DRAWING

CHARACTERS ARE SUPERIMPOSED ON BACKGROUND TO MAKE FINISHED SCENE

How *Snow White and the Seven Dwarfs* was drawn. *Life* magazine, 1937.

Mickey Mouse, a magnificent abstract steel sculpture of the famous rodent by Claes Oldenburg, 1974.

Popeye, an acrylic on canvas, by Andy Warhol, 1961.
Batmobile and the Joker, oils on canvas, by Mel Ramos, 1962.

2
Comic Books

Why are individual collectors paying as high as $4,000 for a mint copy of *Marvel Mystery Comics*, No. 1, or for *Action*, No. 1, when fourteen years ago these books sold for 10¢ each?

In order to provide an answer, perhaps it is important to look at the collector himself. The average comic-book collector is young and began collecting almost as soon as he could read. His search to complete a run or for a rare book is passionate, and a major portion of his waking hours is dominated by this interest. Usually his origins are lower middle class, and the surplus dollars available after the necessities of life are paid are few. Often he is forced to become a collector-dealer, selling comic books he doesn't want in order to buy and keep those he does. He hunts in his own neighborhood door to door, entangled in the passionate fantasy of finding hundreds of mint-condition Golden Age comics, including complete runs of *Superman*, *Batman*, *Captain America*, stored away in a dry attic by a nice old lady who wants them carted away because they are a fire hazard. More realistically, she is standing in the doorway with a copy of the latest comic-book price guide clutched in her sweaty hand, has watched the talk shows on television, and knows all about spine roll, browning of pages, tape on spine, and the differences between mint, very good, good, fair, and poor.

As knowledge about the value of the books becomes more and more universal, the possibility of his fantasy becoming a reality grows less and less, and he haunts the local store in his neighborhood that specializes in old comics, trades with other collectors, and attends the comic-book conventions that abound in almost every major city in the United States. But the fantasies persist, and the hunt never ends, because the comic-book collector is the most dedicated and passionate of all collectors in comic memorabilia. But he does pay a price in human terms. And the highest price paid can be witnessed at any comic-book convention: the teenage collector-dealer with his comics displayed on a card table covered with thick transparent plastic to prevent the younger kids from stealing his precious wares, shouting, screaming, hating, lying, bargaining shrewdly down to pennies like a Scrooge or an ancient Volpone. Often Mother and Father hover behind him, watching his books and counting the money, like vultures at famine time. He becomes an adult before his time, and the disease of greed, brutalization, and dehumanization sets in and eats away his childhood.

While growing into middle age, the disease eats deeper. Open the door to his apartment and look inside: It hasn't been cleaned in six months, the ashtrays haven't been emptied in a month and the unopened mail, mostly unpaid bills, has been gathering dust for weeks on the kitchen table next to the unwashed coffee cup and the greasy frying pan that he uses as a plate. The bed is unmade, the bathroom dirty, and there is only one chair because all available space is required for the thousands of comic books carefully stacked on wall shelves and in boxes, while the more expensive books he has acquired over the years are inside clear plastic bags for protection against dust, sunlight, water, and the corrosive sweat of human fingertips. Sooner or later, mostly sooner, his wife divorces him, and secretly he is glad to see her go so that he can devote all of his money to his passion. He hates his job but needs the money to buy comics and is always, but always, behind in paying the rent. Now open the closet door, but don't inhale, because the stench coming from that pile of dirty laundry smells like old cheese and might make you sick to the stomach. No hats, never an umbrella, or galoshes, only one wrinkled suit hanging from a hook, jeans, T-shirts, one necktie for parties, dates, weddings, and funerals, two pairs of sneakers, and one pair of extra shoes that need new heels and soles. Open the refrigerator door and it smells just like the closet. The ice is packed thick because it hasn't been defrosted since his wife left; inside is half of a pizza from last week with all of the cheese, tomato, and pepperoni scraped off the top, a six-pack of the lowest priced supermarket beer, and a ripped-open, near-emptied bag of potato chips.

As the gray hairs appear in his sideburns and creep upward, his comics become even more precious, and slowly but surely he stops selling. Even the coverless, torn, high-number comics are put into the plastic protectors and are stacked neatly on the shelves as if they were AAA Municipal bonds. The final acts of divorce from reality are his disconnecting the doorbell so that the special agents from the collection division of the Internal Revenue Service cannot intrude, the removal of his name from the mailbox downstairs, and the posting of a neatly typed notice scotch-taped to its front: "Return All Mail to Sender." Again, why?

It is art that these collectors can relate to because it is neorepresentational and understandable and yet it is at the same time surreal, because no superhuman beings like these could ever exist anywhere but in the imagination. Beauty is in the eye of the beholder, be he half blind, completely mad, or unexposed to the sight of orthodox art. Collectors at comic conventions talk about color harmony, fine linework, draftsmanship, composition, and action without ever having been taught them by a teacher or having learned them from a book.

A comic book consists of pictures and stories. If half of the explanation is the art, certainly the other half is the story. Simple, direct, easy to understand, often combining humor and terror in an original fashion. But the basic originality is not in the plots but in the superb, unreal characterizations of super heroes capable of superhuman feats; that is at least part of the fascination, and it provides a participatory attraction because the young reader can fantasize himself into the story. These are stories combined with pictures to tell a story, an even and integral balance that creates the uniqueness of this art form. And it works. These are not books that children are forced to read but rather want to read. Many ghetto children have learned to read only because they want to read comic books. These are books that they buy with their own money, not school books that are given to them free and that they are forced to study. To witness the powerful attraction of the comic stories, merely watch the kids run to the comic-book rack as soon as school closes in the afternoon and rip into them, trying to finish the story before the candy-store owner screams, curses, and throws them out.

Comic books since World War II have become a dominant force in the culture of American youngsters. Their circulation is wide, and several have achieved circulation in excess of a million copies per issue. And the truth is that they are read with an equal avidity by many adults. Even in Mao's China comic books are widely circulated and are popular though the stories are specifically slanted to indoctrinate the young. The appeal of pictures plus words is universal, and the castigation of the comics because of their excesses of blood-and-guts violence and sometimes inferior levels of writing and art have not reduced their magnetlike attraction. They are a uniquely American invention and they both reflect and form the imaginations of the young worldwide.

Although general appeal may be based upon art and story, value is not. The value of a comic book most often depends upon its condition, number, and if it is the origin story of its super hero. *Captain America*, No. 1, is appealing because of the Kirby art and the intriguing story, but its dollar value is based upon its being the origin story of Captain America and the first issue. General acceptance of this simple market evaluation by the entire community of comic-book collectors has skyrocketed the prices for *Action*, No. 1 (origin of Superman), *Detective*, No. 27 (origin of Batman), *Marvel Mystery*, No. 1 (origin of Human Torch and Sub-Mariner), and *Whiz*, No. 1 (origin of Captain Marvel, Spy Smasher, and Golden Arrow).

Not only is it difficult to find the scarce first and origin issues, but they were printed on cheap paper that becomes brittle with age and is easily torn. Yet price depends upon condition. The gradations range downward from Newsstand Mint, which means just that; absolute perfection—no printing or cutting errors, no color fade, white inside pages, and covers that have retained the same shiny gloss they had thirty-five years ago. Poor means brittle inside pages, spine roll, taped repairs, watermarks, tears in the covers, soiled condition, and damage from weather. In between are grades from Near-Mint, Fine, Very Good, and Good down to Fair. Comic books are delicate and easily damaged, and this is why collectors insert their best books into mylar—clear plastic bags—not in cardboard boxes that contain destructive acids, and store them in dark, cool, air-conditioned rooms to protect the low-quality paper from dampness, ultraviolet light that will fade the brightness of colors, and heat that will turn the inside pages brown and brittle.

Although many collectors are completists who try to achieve a complete run, the hottest demand, in reality, is for a very few books: the number-one issues, the origin issues, and issues drawn by special artists.

And it is precisely because comics were printed on the cheapest paper and considered worthless that they are so difficult to find today. Most of the comic books prior to 1944 were gathered by Boy Scouts during the patriotic paper drives of World War II and were destroyed by the millions. Hundreds of thousands were sent overseas to the soldiers to relieve the boredom of war and left there. And from the war years up to the early nineteen sixties they were burned and garbage-canned.

These criteria are not changing but are rather becoming more rigid and stronger. They apply particularly to the so-called Golden Age comics, from 1933 to 1955, and more particularly to the most sought-after super-hero books, such as *Superman, Batman, Captain Marvel, Detective Comics, Human Torch, Sub-Mariner, Green Lantern, Captain America, The Flash, The Spectre*, and others. These are the means comic collectors use for measuring value, to determine whether a comic book is worth $3,500 or just 35¢.

But the conflict remains. What is more important, the appeal of the art of the comics or the mere money value based upon external standards of rarity and origin? A forceful answer is coming, not from comic-book collectors but from famous modern artists, such as Roy Lichtenstein, Andy Warhol, Mel Ramos, and Claes Oldenburg, who have the eye to look at a comic book, whether old or right off the newsstand, and evaluate it on the basis of its art alone. These Pop artists have selected the best of Batman, Popeye, and Mickey Mouse and have restructured them into works of art that are sometimes far superior in both content and form to the best of the originals. If the appeal of comic art ever becomes of sufficient interest to wealthy museums and to the New York art-gallery establishment, then the opinions of artists, perhaps of these very artists working in this form, will provide final values based upon the quality and originality of the art alone.

Perhaps the first attempt at a comic book was *The Yellow Kid*, Vol. 1, No. 1, published at the turn of the century by the Howard Ainslee Company. The covers were beautifully drawn by R. F. Outcault, with a marvelous Yellow Kid, shown in the publisher's composing room surrounded by messy papers, a bad-luck black cat, a can of paste, a huge editor's scissors hanging from his neck, and a large pen dripping black ink on the papers scattered around the floor. Inside were the author's drawings and stories in a combined format.

By 1908 the idea occurred to the publishers that the newspaper comics could be reprinted in book form, and the Cupples and Leon Company reprinted Buster Brown in a soft-cover eleven-and-one-half-by-sixteen-inch book. The success enabled the publisher to proceed with similar books for other comic characters popular in those early years. But it was not until 1933 that the first true comic book appeared. It was *Funnies on Parade*, published by the Eastern Color Printing Company. It was standard magazine size, but it was an advertising premium.

In the same year *Famous Funnies* appeared. It was the first book to be sold to the general public through the chain stores and it was basically reprints of current newspaper comic strips. Since the resulting sales were excellent, Eastern Publishing decided to publish *Famous Funnies* on a regular basis, and the marketing plan changed to distribution through the nation's magazine outlets.

Even during the worst of the depression years the kids had money for comics, and supply and diversity increased. In 1936 Dell Publishing brought to the marketplace *Popular Comics*, and in the same year

King Comics was published by David McKay. These were still only reprints of newspaper comics, but sales climbed, permitting expense on original material. The first to make this departure was *New Fun Comics*. In 1937 *Detective Comics*, No. 1, appeared, with all of the strips relating in terms of a single theme.

A breakthrough came with the appearance of *Action Comics*, No. 1, in June 1938. This issue originated Superman, certainly the greatest and most popular of all of the super heroes in long underwear. It immediately captured the public's imagination, sales soared, and a new publishing industry was created almost overnight. Dozens of old and new publishers came in, hundreds of new titles appeared, and the golden age of comics came into being. Comic books became the largest selling magazines all over the world, and new millionaires were created.

The fantasy and the participation of the reader that it involved is made clear in *Superman*, No. 1:

Scientific Explanation of Superman's Amazing Strength—!

Superman came to earth from the planet Krypton whose inhabitants had evolved, after millions of years to physical perfection.

The smaller size of our planet, with its slighter gravity pull, assists SUPERMAN'S tremendous muscles in the performance of miraculous feats of strength.

Even upon our world today exist creatures possessing SUPER-STRENGTH! The lowly ant can support weights hundreds of times its own. The grasshopper leaps what to man would be the space of several city blocks!

Is it not too far fetched to predict that some day our very own planet may be peopled entirely by SUPERMEN!!!

Joe Shuster drew it and Jerry Siegel wrote it. They also created Slam Bradley and Spy, who appeared in *Detective Comics;* Radio Squad for *More Fun Comics,* and Federal Men, who appeared monthly in *Adventure Comics.* But none of these equaled the popularity of Superman.

The first four Superman stories went into *Action Comics* and were later reprinted in *Superman,* No. 1. The stories were plain and the art plainer, but it was the originality of the character of Superman that appealed universally and created the financial success. And it was the explanation of his strength, so bizarre

as to make the unbelievable believable, that fired the imagination. Because he could burst past the borders of reality, fly faster than a speeding bullet, run faster than a streamline train, hurdle the highest skyscraper, stop bullets with his chest, and because he championed the oppressed, Superman excited the fantasies of the young. As Clark Kent he was an ordinary nothing; as Superman everything you wished you could become.

After the first year of publication Superman was selling well over a million copies of the books he appeared in. And because of the large printing and his popularity it is not too difficult for collectors to gather a complete run. Imitations abounded, and since National Periodical Publications could not stop them, they joined in the race. *Superboy* was the first venture. It concentrated on the adventures of Superman when he was a boy and depicted him shooting marbles and winning the soapbox derby. *Supergirl* was followed by *Superdog* and *Supercat,* and the successful format continues into the present.

The originators, Siegel and Shuster, have long since departed, and Shuster stopped drawing our hero as early as 1940. Wayne Boring was the artist who drew most of the stories, and certainly many staff people made their contributions.

One of the most rare, high-priced, and sought-after comic books is *Detective,* No. 27. It is the origin of Batman, and the first story was entitled "The Batman . . . The Case of the Chemical Syndicate." The artist was Bob Kane and the writing of the scripts was done by Bill Finger, and, like *Superman,* its popularity was instantaneous. The introduction to the origin story spells out the reasons for his appeal:

The *BAT-MAN,* a mysterious and adventurous figure, fighting for righteousness and apprehending the wrong doer, in his lone battle against the evil forces of society.

His identity remains unknown!

Unlike Superman, this character created fright. His black mask, with Oriental slanted-eye slits and sharp twin horns, his huge cape that became two giant bat wings, his black boots and skin-tight costume revealing bulging muscles made many young readers tremble with terror.

Like Superman he was two men. He had had normal Earth humans for parents. Returning home on a dark night the Waynes were shot and killed by a crook named Joey Chill; their young son Bruce swore vengeance on the Underworld of crime and devoted himself to the study of law and criminology and to developing muscular strength. One night a bat flew in the open window, and the idea struck him that he could become a batman! He assumed the costume, thinking that it would strike terror and panic in the evil denizens of crime. And it did, because the crooks were so panic-stricken by his appearance that they froze and allowed him to punch them in the face, toss them into the air and off of roofs, and even shoot them dead without any resistance!

Both the stories and the art were excellent. The appeal of the stories was the suspense of detective-story fiction. Batman had brains and used them like a detective to find the plot of the crime and the identity of the criminal. The reader simply had to finish the story to relieve the suspense.

But the major, original accomplishment in terms of art is the magnificent figure of Batman, which has become instantly recognizable to millions around the world. Superman, and certainly Mickey Mouse, belong in this category of immediate recognition also. Batman has entered the consciousness of millions; show his picture and in two seconds they'll say his name; say his name and his picture is instantly conjured. Perhaps no other art form can make this claim, and in this claim is one very important element of comic art.

Other characters were equally original and well drawn. Robin, The Boy Wonder, was one of the first sidekicks accompanying the hero on his adventures. Dick Grayson could do what his boss could do, because he was a superb, circus-trained boy aerialist, and since he was lucky enough to be an orphan he didn't have to worry about worrying his mother or coming home on time for supper.

But it was Batman's enemies who were fascinating —original in art and characterization, they delighted the imaginations of the young. The Joker was introduced in 1940, and his face resembled an insane harlequin clown, rouged and chalk white, straight from a better deck of playing cards. He was a menacing hired killer and he fought Batman with brains and skill. The Penguin was another original; fat but very dangerous, hung up on birds and umbrellas, his anti-Batman schemes were brilliant, but in the true tradition he always lost. The Catwoman was Batman's most fierce enemy and she and her gang fought him hard, as did the Fiddler and a host of other opponents.

The best of Batman can be isolated into the 1940–1946 era, but the television series contributed excellent stories and marvelous acting, such as that of Burgess Meredith as the Joker, and it sparked a merchandising revival that included everything from kids' wallets to Batmobile toys.

Both *Batman* and *Superman* of the nineteen forties offered original, superb comic art and well-written stories, far superior to the bland fare of their current comics. But what they also proved was that comic books could be commercially successful, creating a vast market of kids with nickels and dimes ready to buy. They made the breakthrough and built the foundation and made an audience that wasn't there before. Because of this, during the next thirty years zillions of comics were printed and bought and perhaps saved for the future.

The first issue of *Whiz Comics* is another super collectible because it is the origin of another great comic-book long-underwear-clad super hero: Captain Marvel, affectionately known to collector friends as The Big Red Cheese. Charles Clarence Beck, a staff illustrator in 1939 for Fawcett Publications, was assigned to do the artwork for the new *Whiz Comics*. He was an educated and trained artist and had provided illustrations for the famous *Captain Billy's Whiz Bang*, which was one of the first magazines published by Fawcett, hence the title *Whiz Comics*. C. C. Beck was a movie buff and based the face and figure of Captain Marvel on the actor Fred MacMurray, and the early art shows our hero easily recognizable as MacMurray.

Certainly the reason for the excellent comic art and the tremendous commercial success was simply that a competent and talented artist was the boss. Beck did it all, penciling, inking, and lettering, even editing and rewriting to maintain consistency from story to story. Bill Parker wrote the first stories, and as sales soared, other artists became involved. Since Beck's style was simple, the new artists could draw the characters in the same style.

But *Whiz* was a variety book that had different stories with different heroes. It became obvious to Fawcett that, due to his growing popularity, The Big Red Cheese demanded an exclusive book. *Captain Marvel Adventures* appeared and was so successful that it was followed by an entire family of Marvels. The demand had the printer working round the clock: They had to publish *Captain Marvel Adventures* every three weeks; then, at the peak of the demand, every two weeks! Circulation soared to the amazing figure of 2 million comic books per issue, never exceeded by any other comic book before or after. On delivery day lines of kids appeared at newsstands and candy stores, and in minutes the books disappeared. More than one thousand stories featuring Captain Marvel or members of the Marvel family were published.

Although *Superman* set the format, *Captain Marvel* was raking in the cash. The two were almost identical, so National started a lawsuit against Fawcett, charging that *Captain Marvel* was in violation of the copyright of *Superman*. They definitely looked alike: strong tall men with muscles and tight, bright-colored costumes, with similar emblems on the chest. Superman's other self worked as a news reporter for the *Daily Planet* and Captain Marvel's Billy Batson was a radio newscaster for station WHIZ. On and on it went, and finally in 1972 National bought the rights to *Captain Marvel*, and an attempt was made to rehire C. C. Beck for a revival, but it fizzled out.

Captain Marvel, Mary Marvel, and Captain Marvel, Jr., remain as the great family in American comics and certainly the most successful.

When *Captain Marvel Adventures* was given the green light by Fawcett, a new artist did the art for the first issue under Beck's direction. His talent, originality, and fine draftsmanship were immediately obvious, and in the following years of the great comic boom, his work and reputation spread. Today the comic books and original art that he created are eagerly hunted by collectors, and there are many who collect Jack Kirby art exclusively (sometimes called Simon and Kirby). Their *Captain America*, No. 1, is one of the most sought-after comic books today, and the selling price has soared toward the stars in the last few years.

Captain America was issued in 1941 and ignited the World War II comic-book explosion. Our super heroes went out to fight the war. They now had a purpose; real live villains to fight, like Hitler Nazis and yellow-faced, rat-toothed Japs, sock 'em, kill 'em, beat 'em up! This is what the kids wanted and this is what they got. Nazis and Japs were savages, degenerates, mean bastards, and anything our hero did to foil their plans, defend America, and humiliate them was O.K. The writers and artists of this period were very young and enthusiastic about this opportunity for publishing new material. It was the only way that the kids could get into and relate to the war. They desperately wanted to understand, and comic books spoke their language—with pictures. The comics had found a reason for being.

On the cover of *Captain America*, No. 1, is our red-white-and-blue-garbed hero delivering a smashing right hook into Adolf Hitler's jaw, while evil-looking fat Nazis are shooting at him to no avail. Maps and sabotage plans are on the floor, and a large wall-mounted television set (yes, this is 1941) shows a spy blowing up the U.S. Munitions Works. "Smashing thru, CAPTAIN AMERICA comes face to face with Hitler!" Typical of Kirby art, every fraction of an inch of cover is used. The art and action is so full it almost has to be read.

It is interesting to notice the monetary relationship between wars and comic books. The first big boom occurred during World War II, and comic-book publishers still speak of that era with fond financial remembrances. After the war, sales dropped, only to soar again during the Korean War, then drop again. The third boom period occurred during the Vietnam War, and as soon as American involvement stopped, sales went straight down. Perhaps the attraction for kids is the excitement of war and of simple good guys versus simple bad guys; nevertheless, the relationship is measurable.

The top comic book, even more rare and expensive than *Action*, No. 1, is *Marvel Mystery Comics*, No. 1, put on the newsstands of America in November 1939. The art is bad and the stories are very poor, but the high price is based upon the presence of the origin stories for two very popular super heroes: the Sub-Mariner and the Human Torch. The first cover depicted a man on fire who looked like he was made of fire. He was created from the test tubes of a near-mad scientist, Dr. Horton, who sought to make the first artificial man, but something went wrong and his humanoid burst into flames on contact with the air. All the reporters and scientists present for the unveiling urged Horton to destroy this monster; instead he sealed him in a glass container, put that in a steel tube then embedded the whole thing in a large block of cement. One night air seeped through, the tomb burst open, and the Human Torch was free and ran wild, starting fires everywhere. But Human Torch was a good guy, a flaming Boy-Scout type, and resisted being used by Sardo the gangster and Horton the scientist to make money in evil ways.

His young sidekick was called Toro, and they both had the power to burst into flames with the cry: "Flame on!" During the war his enemies were the Japanese, who all had awful yellow faces with buck fang teeth and wore thick glasses. In one scene the Human

Torch is happily burning off the arm of a Jap who is screaming in pain while a pretty young patriotic American girl cheers him on in the torture! A Nazi spy and a gestapo agent were called Rabbit and Python, and they looked like a rabbit and a snake.

The Human Torch was created by Carl Burgos, who worked with a group of artists and writers, and all during the war Human Torch and Toro fought and humiliated Hitler, Goebbels, and Goering.

Prince Namor, better known as the Sub-Mariner, was introduced in the same issue of *Marvel Mystery Comics*, No. 1. He was the strange son of Princess Fen of Atlantis and Commander McKenzie of the U.S. Navy. Here's how it happened: McKenzie was sent to Antarctica to blast the giant ice formations. The beautiful and near-human-looking princess was sent to vamp the commander and stall for time while they got an army together. But they fell madly in love with each other: Then man married mermaid!

One big blast destroyed the entire army of Atlantis. Angry Fen jumped ship and returned to what was left of her people beneath the sea. Soon after Namor was born, Mom poisoned his mind against surface people and persuaded him to destroy them. He was, of course, muscular, with big shoulders, but had thin arms and small wrists and pointed ears, like Mr. Spock in television's *Star Trek*. Small wings on his heels gave him the power to fly.

Bill Everett was the creator of Sub-Mariner, and both the art and stories improved as time progressed. Torture, brutality, gore, violence, mass murder aimed at the Jap rats of World War II were to his taste and that of his young readers. And there is some proof that many of these stories were written by the famous guts, blood, and more guts author Mickey Spillane.

Sub-Mariner was mean, had a raging temper, was sometimes stupid, treated all girls like you know what, and hated the Human Torch. It was fire versus water, and Sub-Mariner wanted to destroy the human race while Human Torch wanted to save it, so Sub-Mariner became the super villain. During the war they each had their own armies, which were often completely wiped out and instantly replenished as if by the stroke of a pen! And one book showed Franklin Delano Roosevelt reading a copy of *Marvel Mysteries*, smiling at the exploits of our super heroes!

What about girls, that other half of the human race? The publishers discovered that young girls were also buying and reading comic super heroes, so in January 1942 *Sensation*, No. 1, featured something for the girls: Wonder Woman! It was the brainchild of Dr. William Marston, a psychologist and one of the inventors of the lie detector. Harry Peter was the artist and a very good one. Popularity was immediate, and by the summer of the same year *Wonder Woman*, No. 1, appeared. Long before Women's Liberation became a worldwide movement, Wonder Woman was fighting for female-human rights! It was controversial even then; perhaps that's why Dr. Marston adopted the pen name Charles Moulton. The introduction sets the tone:

WONDER WOMAN!
Like the crash of thunder from the sky comes the WONDER WOMAN, to save the world from the hatreds and wars of MEN in a MAN-made world! And what a woman! A woman with the eternal beauty of Aphrodite and the wisdom of Athena—yet whose lovely form hides the agility of Mercury and the steel sinews of a Hercules! Who is Wonder Woman? Why does she fight for America?

She was born Princess Diana on Amazon Island amongst a tribe of white Amazons who hadn't seen any men for years. Steve Trevor, a wounded airman, was forced down on her island, and she fell in love with him and returned to the outside world in her transparent, invisible airplane to save his life. She switched her name from Princess Diana to Diana Prince and slipped into the uniform of a nurse to be near his bedside in the hospital. Her magic bracelets turned back the bullets of ugly, fat gangsters and Nazi spies; in fact, all men were shown as fat, incredibly ugly, hairy, malformed, and treacherous. Also, the overtones of bisexuality and of sadomasochism were explicit. It was almost as if Wonder Woman and her girl friends really enjoyed being whipped, tightly iron-chained, and cruelly tortured with leather ropes and crushing chastity belts. Of course, she always freed herself, beat the men to a pulp, carried her weak boy friend, Steve, to safety, then embraced, hugged, kissed, and necked it up with her female friends the Holliday Girls.

Wonder Woman was the female mirror image of Superman, and her commercial success almost equaled his. The characterization was unique, the stories intriguing and interesting, and the art was almost in the Art Nouveau style—without perspective, two-dimensional, and handsome.

During the early nineteen fifties William Gaines of E. C. Publishers created a group of horror and science-fiction comic books that were superb, wild, mad, political, and beautiful, and today there are collectors who just collect E.C.'s. Gaines employed the very best artists. The art has a distinctive style that easily separates it from all other comics, and many of the stories are extremely well written. Many critics hate E.C.'s and consider the stories almost carnivorous and repellent, but comic collectors break off into many segments. Some just collect super heroes, Number Ones, and origin books, some just Disneys, while others collect E.C.'s, and others just collect for the beauty of cover art, whether recent or ancient. Beauty remains in the eye of the beholder.

Yet the conflict between appeal and value, beauty and money remains, and the conflict is eventually rigidly resolved in every field of collecting—alas, money always wins. Eventually a few, sometimes no more than six items, are considered to be tops. In comic books it is:

Marvel Mystery Comics, No. 1
Action, No. 1
Whiz, No. 1
Detective, No. 27 (Origin of Batman)
Superman, No. 1
Captain America, No. 1

Today these books command thousands of dollars, and the demand more than exceeds the supply. Perhaps the old advice "Collect better than you can afford, that way you do not become a gatherer" is still the best advice for comic-book collectors and all the other collectors of everything.

Another group of near-comic books that is receiving recognition and increasing interest from comic-book collectors is the "pop-up" books from the mid-nineteen thirties produced by Blue Ribbon Books, Inc., and Pleasure Books, Inc. Open the book and a three-dimensional picture pops up depicting a scene from the story. They were extremely well made and designed and have become increasingly rare. The best are: *Mickey Mouse in King Arthur's Court, Minnie Mouse, Mickey Mouse, Little Orphan Annie, Popeye, Dick Tracy, Terry and the Pirates, Buck Rogers in a Dangerous Mission, Buck Rogers: Strange Adventures in the Spider Ship, Flash Gordon, Tarzan, Puss-In-Boots*, the remarkable 1932 Blue Ribbon *Pinocchio*, and *Jack the Giant Killer*, each with four handsome pop-ups.

A word of caution: The experts on the preservation of paper at the New York Public Library, who are responsible for the well-being of millions of books, are very worried. They have recently mounted a public exhibition called "Books in Peril," and their prognosis concerning the life of comic books, pulp magazines, and Big Little Books is extremely negative. Here are some quotes:

Acidity is the primary cause of paper deterioration. Acidity is a state in which various impurities in the paper (especially lignins) decompose to form several acids, especially sulphuric acid. These acids in turn attack the paper's cellulose fibers. Various agents which act as catalysts for acidic conditions include light, heat, humidity and today's heavy air pollution which contains sulphur dioxide in sufficient amounts to hasten the destruction of pulp paper. . . .

Durable paper is acid free. Pulps are not. The acidic contents slowly "eat" the paper turning it brittle, brown, and it eventually and inevitably crumbles. Nothing can stop the paper from dying: the agents of decomposition are within the paper from birth.

Their opinion is a horror: The paper death of the best comics will occur in the years between 1985 and 1990! That means comics from the 1933 to 1945 period!

Before you begin to collect comics, buy the bible— *The Comic Book Price Guide*, 4th Edition, by Robert M. Overstreet. It is available at bookstores, comic shops, and comic conventions, or it can be obtained directly by writing to Robert Overstreet, 2905 Vista Drive N.W., Cleveland, Ohio 44134. It is the most complete, accurate, thoroughly researched, and universally accepted price guide to comics available.

Always inspect a comic book carefully to make sure that no inside pages are missing and that the edges of all pages have not turned brown and brittle, the back cover is intact, the spine is not rolled, and the front cover is not a carefully reproduced copy.

Before you begin to collect comics, buy the bible—*The Comic Book Price Guide*, by Robert M. Overstreet. It is available at bookstores, comic shops, and comic conventions, or it can be obtained directly by writing to Robert Overstreet, 2905 Vista Drive N.W., Cleveland, Tennessee. It is the most complete, accurate, thoroughly researched, and universally accepted price guide to comics available.

Always inspect a comic book carefully to make sure that no inside pages are missing and that the edges of all pages have not turned brown and brittle, the back cover is intact, the spine is not rolled, and the front cover is not a carefully reproduced copy.

	Publisher	Date
Ace Comics, No. 1	David McKay Company	1937
Action Comics, Nos. 1–5	National Periodical Publications	1938
Adventure Comics, No. 1	National	1935
All American Comics, No. 1	National	1939
All Flash, No. 1	National	1941
All-Select Comics, No. 1	Timely Comics	1943
All Star Comics, Nos. 1–2	National	1940
All Winners, No. 1	Timely/Marvel	1941
Amazing Mystery Funnies, No. 1	Centaur Publications	1938
America's Greatest Comics, No. 1	Fawcett Publications	1941
Batman, Nos. 1–10	National	1940
Big All-American, No. 1	National	1944
Big Shot, No. 1	Columbia Comics	1940
Black and White, Nos. 1, 16, 20	Dell Publishing	1937
Blue Beetle, No. 1	Fox Features Syndicate	1939
Blue Bolt, No. 1	Novelty Publications	1940
Boy Commandos, No. 1	National	1942
Buck Rogers, Nos. 1–6	Famous Funnies, Inc.	1940
Bulletman, No. 1	Fawcett	1941
Captain America, Nos. 1–5	Timely Publications	1941
Captain Marvel Adventures, No. 1	Fawcett	1941
Captain Marvel, Jr., No. 1	Fawcett	1942
Captain Marvel, Special Edition	Fawcett	1940
Color Comics, No. 1 (Dick Tracy)	Dell	1939
Color Comics, No. 4 (Donald Duck)	Dell	1940
Color Comics, No. 16 (Mickey Mouse)	Dell	1941
Comics on Parade	United Features Syndicate	1938
Crack Comics, No. 1	Quality Comics Group	1940
Crackajack Funnies, No. 1	Dell	1938
Crime Suspenstories, No. 15 (first issue)	E. C. Comics	1950
Crypt of Terror, No. 17	E. C. Comics	1950
Daredevil Comics, No. 1	Lev Gleason Publications	1941
Daring Mystery Comics, No. 1	Timely Comics	1940
Detective Comics, Nos. 1, 27, 28, 33	National	1937
Doc Savage, No. 1	Street and Smith Publications	1940
Donald Duck Black and White, No. 16	Dell	1938
Donald Duck Four Color, No. 9	Dell	1942
Donald Duck Four Color, No. 29	Dell	1943
Donald Duck March of Comics, Nos. 4, 21, 41	K. K. Publications	1947
Famous Funnies, Nos. 1, 2, 3	Dell Publishing/Eastern Color Printing	1933
Feature Comics, No. 1	Quality Comics	1937
Feature Book, No. 1	David McKay Company	1937
Fight Comics, No. 1	Fiction House Magazines	1940

	Publisher	Date
Flash Comics, No. 1	National	1940
Flash Gordon Four Color, No. 10	Dell	1943
Frontline Combat, No. 1	E. C. Comics	1951
Funnies on Parade, No. 1	Eastern	1933
Gift Comics, No. 1	Fawcett	1941
Green Hornet, No. 1	Harvey Publications	1940
Green Lantern, No. 1	National	1941
Green Mask, No. 1	Fox Features Syndicate	1940
Haunt of Fear, No. 15	E. C. Comics	1950
Heroic Comics, No. 1	Eastern	1940
Hi-Spot, No. 2	Hawley Publications	1940
Hit Comics, No. 1	Quality Comics	1940
Holiday Comics, No. 1	Fawcett	1942
Human Torch, No. 1	Timely Comics	1940
Jackpot Comics, No. 1	MLJ Magazines	1941
Jumbo Comics, No. 1	Fiction House	1938
Jungle Comics, No. 1	Fiction House	1940
Kid Comics, No. 1	Marvel Comics Group	1943
King Comics, No. 1	David McKay Company	1936
Leading Comics, No. 1	National	1941
Little Lulu Four Color, No. 74	Dell	1945
Looney Tunes, No. 1	Dell	1941
Mad, No. 1	E. C. Comics	1952
Magic Comics, No. 1	David McKay Company	1939
Marvel Family, No. 1	Fawcett	1945
Marvel Mystery Comics, Nos. 1–20	Timely Comics	1939
Master Comics, No. 1	Fawcett	1940
Mickey Mouse Book	Bibo and Lang	1930
Mickey Mouse Color, No. 16	Dell	1941
Mickey Mouse Magazine, Vol. 1, No. 1	K. K. Publications	1935
Military Comics, No. 1	Quality Comics	1941
Miss Fury Comics, No. 1	Timely Comics	1942
More Fun Comics, Nos. 1, 52, 53	National	1935
Movie Comics, No. 1	National	1939
Mystery Men Comics, No. 1	Fox Features Syndicate	1939
Mystic Comics, Nos. 1, 2	Timely Comics	1940
National Comics, No. 1	Quality Comics	1940
New Book of Comics, No. 1	National	1936
New York World's Fair Comics	National	1939, 1940
Nickel Comics, No. 1	Fawcett	1940
Our Flag, No. 1	Ace Magazines	1941
Our Gang Comics, No. 1	Dell	1942
Pep Comics, No. 1	MLJ Magazines	1940
Planet Comics, No. 1	Fiction House	1940
Plastic Man, No. 1	Vital Publications	1943
Pocket Comics, No. 1	Harvey	1941
Police Comics, No. 1	Quality Comics	1941
Popular Comics, No. 1	Dell	1936
Prince Valiant Feature Book, No. 26	David McKay Company	1940
Prize Comics, No. 1	Prize Publications	1940
Rangers Comics, No. 1	Fiction House	1941
Red Raven, No. 1	Timely Comics	1940
Red Ryder Comics, No. 1	Hawley/Dell	1940
Rocket Comics, No. 1	Hillman Periodicals	1940

	Publisher	Date
Science, No. 1	Fox Features Syndicate	1940
Sensation Comics, No. 1	National	1942
Shadow Comics, Vol. 1. No. 1	Street and Smith Publications	1940
Sheena, Queen of the Jungle, No. 1	Fiction House	1942
Shield-Wizard Comics, No. 1	MLJ Magazines	1944
Shock Suspenstories, No. 1	E. C. Comics	1952
Silver Streak Comics, Nos. 1, 6	Comic House Publications	1939
Single Series, No. 20	United Features Syndicate	1938
Slam Bang, No. 1	Fawcett	1940
Smash Comics, No. 1	Quality Comics	1939
Sparkler Comics, No. 1	United Features Syndicate	1940
Speed Comics, No. 1	Brookwood Publications	1939
Spiderman, No. 1	Marvel Comics	1963
The Spirit, No. 1	Quality Comics	1944
Spy Smasher, No. 1	Fawcett	1941
Star Spangled Comics, Nos. 1, 2, 7	National	1941
Stars and Stripes Comics, No. 1	Centaur	1941
Startling Comics, No. 1, 10, 17	Better Publications	1940
Stuntman Comics, No. 1	Harvey	1946
Sub-Mariner, No. 1	Timely Comics	1941
Super Comics, No. 1	Dell	1938
Superboy, No. 1	National	1949
Superman, Nos. 1–10	National	1939
Superman's X-Mas Adventure	National	1940
Super-Mystery Comics, No. 1	Ace Magazines	1940
Tales of Terror Annual, Nos. 1, 2	E. C. Comics	1951, 1952
Target Comics, No. 1	Novelty	1940
Terry and the Pirates, B&W, Nos. 2, 6	Dell	1937
Thrilling Comics, No. 1	Nedor Comics	1940
Thunda, No. 1	Magazine Enterprises	1952
Tip Top Comics, No. 1	United Features Syndicate	1936
Top-Notch Comics, Nos. 1, 7, 8, 9	MLJ Magazines	1939
Tough Kid Squad Comics, No. 1	Marvel Comics	1942
Uncle Sam, No. 1	Quality Comics	1941
U.S.A. Comics, Nos. 1–10	Timely Comics	1941
V . . . Comics, No. 1	Fox Features Syndicate	1942
Vault of Horror, No. 12	E. C. Comics	1950
Victory, No. 1	Hillman	1941
Walt Disney's Comics and Stories, Nos. 1–35	Dell	1940
Weird Fantasy, No. 13	E. C. Comics	1950
Weird Science, No. 12	E. C. Comics	1950
Wham Comics, No. 1	Centaur	1940
Whirlwind Comics, No. 1	Nita Publications	1940
Whiz Comics, Nos. 1–20	Fawcett	1940
Wings, No. 1	Fiction House	1940
Wonder Woman, No. 1	National	1942
Wonderworld, Nos. 1, 2	Fox Features Syndicate	1939
World's Finest, No. 1	National	1941
Wow Comics, No. 1	Fawcett	1941
Yankee, No. 1	Chesler	1941
Yellow Kid, Vol. 1, No. 1	*The* New York *Journal*	1899
Young Allies, No. 1	Timely Comics	1941
Zip Comics, No. 1	MLJ Magazines	1940

The Yellow Kid, Vol. 1 No. 1. The first comic book, 1899.

Marvel Mystery Comics, No. 1. Origin of Human Torch.

58

Action Comics, No. 1. Origin of Superman.

Detective Comics, No. 27. Origin of Batman.

Superman, No. 1

Whiz, No. 1. Origin of Captain Marvel.

Captain Marvel Special Edition, No. 1.

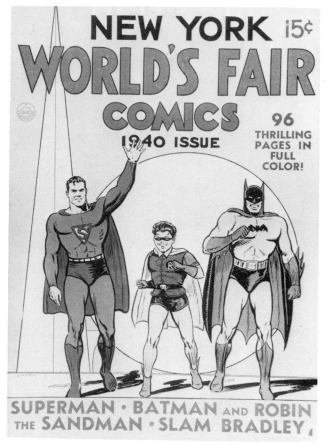

New York World's Fair Comics, 1940.

New York World's Fair Comics, 1939.

New York World's Fair Comics, 1939, back cover.

Daredevil Comics, No. 1.

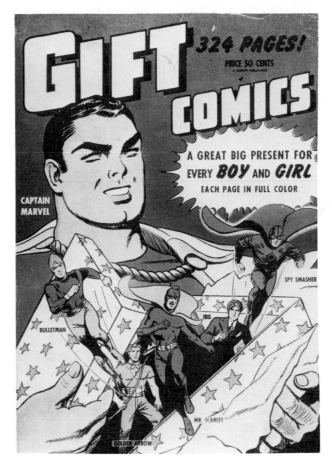

Gift Comics, No. 1.

Military Comics, No. 1.

Young Allies, No. 1.

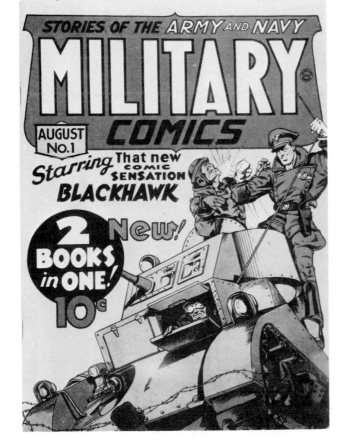

Select, No. 1.

Pep Comics, No. 1.

Flash Gordon Four Color, No. 10, front cover.

Flash Gordon Four Color, No. 10, back cover.

All American Comics, No. 1.

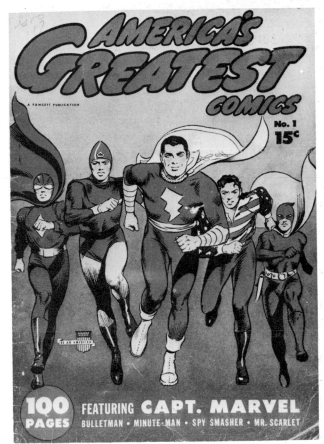

America's Greatest Comics, No. 1.

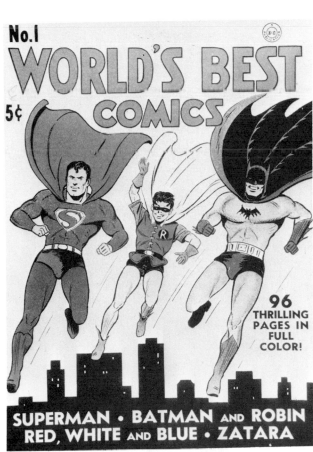

World's Best Comics, No. 1.

Wonder Woman, No. 1.

Top-Notch Comics, No. 1.

Target Comics, No. 1.

Minnie and Mickey Mouse pop-up books.

Little Orphan Annie and Popeye
pop-up books.

Popeye and Little Orphan Annie
pop-up books.

Dick Tracy and Terry and the
Pirates pop-up books.

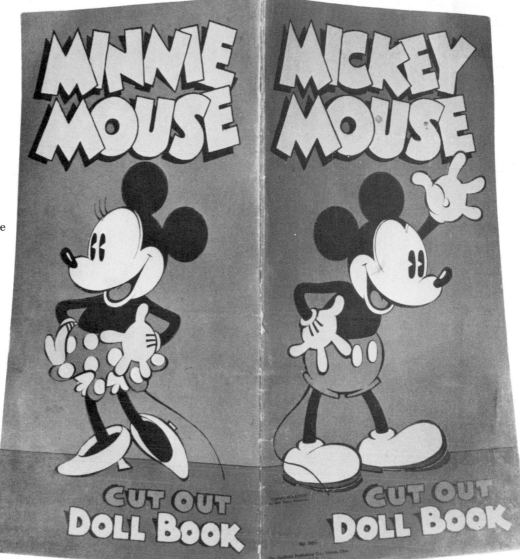

Mickey and Minnie Mouse
Cut Out Doll Book.

Terry and the Pirates and Dick
Tracy pop-up books.

3
Comic-Character Toys

The market for comic-character toys was created by the popularity of particular newspaper comic strips. As a Yellow Kid or Mickey Mouse increased the circulation of newspapers or attendance at local movie theatres, toy manufacturers realized that a profitable vacuum had been created just for them. They bought exclusive licenses and in turn provided a much needed source of income for the newspaper syndicates, movie studios, and cartoonists. The basic pattern and rules of the game were set by a shrewd businessman and excellent artist, R. F. Outcault, whose popular Yellow Kid was licensed to sell toys, cigars, cigarettes, chewing gum, candy, cookies, and almost anything. He realized that the large circulation of the newspaper's comic page created a public demand by association: a presold market. His successful track record with The Yellow Kid led to his later creation of Buster Brown.

One of the first comic-character toys was the cast-iron, hand-painted Yellow Kid in the Goat Cart. Its design was an exact reproduction from the Sunday comic page. The manufacturers were attracted to cast-iron toys because the costs of sand-casting molds, materials, and labor were low. Also, cast iron could survive the rough shipping methods of that time.

From the early and small beginnings of comic-character-toy manufacturing a new industry was to emerge that grew to worldwide proportions. It created new millionaires as well as a popular American industrial sculptural art of superb and imaginative designs. In the eye of the passionate collector of comic-character toys, there is a particular beauty: a combination of color, form, and style that is unlike any other.

Until recently comic-character toys were ignored by toy collectors, but now, all of a sudden, the market has caught fire, resulting in more and more collectors, higher and higher prices, and fewer and fewer toys available. Because this market is new, evaluation is in a state of flux. But the total picture is coming into clearer focus as collectors and dealers determine values in the give-and-take of the marketplace.

Here, as in almost every area of collectibles, the goal is to find the toys in mint condition. This means without any parts missing, without dents or paint scratches or the beginnings of rust. The hope is always to find the toy in its original box, which would have protected it from natural elements and children's fingers. Astute collectors have the patience to wait, to find the toy in mint in the box, knowing that this means that the same item never has to be collected twice. Buying a Toonerville Trolley with a wheel missing in the hope of finding the wheel somewhere, someday, is an odds-against-you hope. Then what do you do with the incomplete toy that you paid a high price for should you find one later in mint condition? You will probably have to sell it at a loss; you'll have "collected twice." This is why a toy in the original box commands twice the price.

In addition, many of the boxes were beautifully decorated and often are more handsome than the toy itself. Also, the box may carry the only information about the toy that can be found, such as the manufacturer's name and sometimes its date. The box is also a good guarantee that the toy inside is not a phony reproduction, since the boxes are never reproduced. The box costs require high-volume production, which the small-collector's market cannot absorb.

It is this basic fear of being swindled by reproductions that has generated some of the interest in the later lithographed tin wind-ups. There is a built-in protection: unlike the cast-iron toys, tin wind-ups cannot be reproduced in small volume. The metal must be preprinted in the flat in large quantities before being formed by expensive dies and tools. These costs are so great that heavy volume is absolutely necessary to amortize these start-up expenses, and the collector market is much too small to absorb that volume. Today, there is no mass public market for tin toys because the United States of America has passed a law outlawing them, claiming that the sharp edges are dangerous to young children. Since tin wind-ups cannot be reproduced and cannot be sold even if they could be reproduced, the collector realizes that he is protected against reproductions but that the current supply must eventually disappear.

Inflation is another factor. Most comic-character tin wind-ups were manufactured during the nineteen twenties and thirties, when labor and material were cheap. But even then the toys had to be made in the millions to absorb the tooling costs and to sell retail at the depression prices that Mom and Dad could afford. The truth is that each toy was a commercial gamble, and a Louis Marx manufacturer or a Kay Kamen distributor were insane—reckless, passionate, courageous gamblers who were damn lucky not to go broke during the worst years of our worst depression.

In the following interview with the Henry Ford of the toy industry (*Fortune* magazine, January 1946) Louis Marx demonstrates how grim and deadly the toy market was during those years:

Marx contrives to run his factories by letter and telephone. . . . He spends a mere $2,400 a year for advertising and employs no outside salesmen whatever: his customers come to him. They are mainly the buyers of the nation's chain, mail-order and department stores. They come originally for the same two reasons that Bernie Gimbel came on a first visit a dozen years ago: they wonder about the man who has sold their competitors such stalwart low priced and popular toys, and whether they can have some of his products for their own stores. . . . Because he is interested in mass production and therefore mass distribution, the answer is sometimes a regretful "No."

As Bernie Gimbel puts it: "Louis has a touch of genius. Any item he makes is a good one, substantial and with the utmost value for the customer. He won't accept second place in his industry, he has to be at the top."

Marx manufactures about 275 different toys each year. Of these, some forty five are already selling so well that he dares not touch them. The others are selling, but require perhaps a "face lifting," such as a new color to keep them up to the volume that Marx would like. [This is the reason why there are so many variations of individual collectible toys, such as the three variations of the Amos 'n' Andy walking figures.]

But twelve are usually brand new Marx creations, and it is his skill at landing an average of seven of these twelve in what he calls, "The Red Hot Hit Class" that gives him the position of leadership in the industry. Any of Marx's twelve new toys can cost him as much as $100,000 to develop. The process on a complicated toy might run as follows:

Marx decides to bring out a super-duper Bulldozer wholesaling at $1.20 which he will retail at $2.00. Dies, molds, and special equipment, all of which he will try to make in his own toolrooms, will cost him about $85,000. To justify tooling up in this manner; Marx hopes to sell 750,000 bulldozers, with an initial run of 288,000. But this initial run requires another $65,000 for special pinions, rubber belts, colored cartons and other features, bringing the total initial investment to $150,000. If he manages to sell only the first run of 288,000, he will make $25,000. However, if the toy goes well and he sells a full million, he will make from $100,000 to $150,000. A second million will earn him $200,000. Going into the third million, which Marx often does, he would find he could profitably sell his bulldozer for 80 ¢ instead of $1.20. At this point he would reach one of two decisions. He might let the bulldozer go for 80¢, thus stimulating a nationwide flurry of special sales of "Famous Marx Bulldozers" now only a $1.29. Or he might add about 30¢ worth of bulldozer in the form of gadgetry and retail for $2.00. Marx says that his profits run from 7 to 12 percent and he tries to average 10 percent.

Chain and department store buyers, who are not a sentimental race, call him extremely fair. Marx reciprocates with a high opinion of his customers' practicality: "You don't sell toys by treating buyers to drinks. They have to feel your stuff will walk off their counters." Since Marx has to stake so much of his money and reputation on a new toy, he spends a vast deal of thought in devising each one. The yearly process begins in earnest toward the end of January, when he starts planning for the following Christmas. Ideas for new toys come to him in numerous ways. Children like to play with facsimiles of familiar things about them: If Marx decides that a sizable number of the 25 million children in the U.S. are ready for a filling station, he will do a filling station. The one he did a few years ago was a great success. Soon after that he had a failure with an airport, not enough children were airport conscious.

Incidentally, the one time Marx defied custom of introducing a major new mechanical toy only at Christmas, the results were unhappy. He crowded the counters one spring with the Amos 'n' Andy Fresh Air Taxicab. The toy sold so fast that he got set to make three million. Around a million and half, sales began to fall: another half million; the toy was through.

"When I make a mistake," Marx explains with glum frankness, "It is usually a whopper."

And these costs were those of 1946, before inflation began to wreak havoc within the toy industry! This insider view should help to explain to the toy collector the history of the tremendous financial risks that influenced the manufacture of the toys that he seeks today. True comic-character toys and dolls had a presold market created for them through the popularity of the comic strips and movie cartoons, but large royalties had to be paid for these rights, and this in turn increased the retail price of the toys. Today, the toy industry cannot absorb the up-front and production royalty costs; therefore, the amount of comic-character

merchandise (with the exception of Disney merchandise) is rapidly decreasing.

Another problem was the wind-up mechanism in all of the toys. It had to be as cheap as possible to produce but sufficiently dependable to sell the toy by creating attractive animation, and it had to work often enough to prevent the toy's being returned to the store. Lucky collectors who find the old toys in their original boxes can be sure that the motors will work or else can be easily repaired, because these are "dead stock" that didn't sell and never reached the careless fingertips of children.

These are just some of the problems that faced all of the manufacturers of comic-character toys during the golden age from 1920 to 1940. And it was these problems that forced the manufacturers to seek lower material and labor costs in Japan and Germany. In fact, a large percentage of American comic-character merchandise was not made in the United States, and the foreign designer, unfamiliar with the American comic, created his own variation. Here Orphan Annie had no eyeballs, but the celluloid and tin toys manufactured in Japan and Germany did have them because foreign designers assumed they were missing and put them in as a correction!

To avoid these mistakes the companies hired the original cartoonists to design the toys and the packaging. Berndt designed the Smitty wristwatch and put his signature on the box. Segar did the same for the Popeye watches and toys. But it was the astute John Dille, publisher of "Buck Rogers in the 25th Century," who hit upon the idea to work the toys into the comic strip as semisubliminal advertising to stimulate sales. The cartoonist, Dick Calkins, made certain that exact replicas of the Daisy Manufacturing Company's Model XZ-31 Rocket Pistol was always in our space hero's hand and that he always wore in his travels to other worlds a Daisy Model XZ-34 Buck Rogers Helmet. It worked, and sales of the merchandise shown in the daily and Sunday strips soared. The helmet was a high-profit item and received additional pushes by its being depicted on other toys. The popular 1934 Marx Buck Rogers tin wind-up rocket ship had both Buck and Wilma in Daisy's headgear. The irony is that Marx, who didn't believe in advertising, was in fact providing free advertising for a competitor's item on his own toy!

One of the difficulties for all toy collectors is the sorry fact that the manufacturers seldom saved any of their catalogs, sample toys, or records. It simply never occurred to them that someday those cheap comic toys and dolls would become high-priced collectibles. Therefore, a Walt Disney 1934 merchandise catalog itself commands a high price, and point-of-sale cardboard advertising displays that pushed the merchandise at the toy counter are avidly sought because they are beautiful in themselves, rare, and provide authentic documentation for the passionate collector.

One joy of the collecting passion is to discover in a flea market at a low price or in a midwestern grandmother's attic a "new-old toy" of Orphan Annie, Mickey Mouse, Betty Boop, Buck Rogers, or Amos 'n' Andy that competitive collectors have never heard of or seen before. Then follows the added (sadistic) pleasure of "leaking" the news through oblique sources to hated rivals:

Dear Mel:

I desperately need your help and hope that you can take the time from your busy schedule to provide an expert's opinion concerning a Mickey Mouse toy that I recently found in a small town in Germany. I have never seen or heard of it before, and I am writing to you for your opinion because, as everyone knows, you have the finest Disney collection in the world and the most knowledge. This Mickey Mouse lithographed tin wind-up toy is only twenty-four inches in height, has cast-iron feet and hands, and has the early rodent look, and his ratlike teeth are quite scary. There are two separate wind-up motors inside that enable him to dance either the Charleston or the Black Bottom while winking his pie-shaped eyes and swinging his tail to the music emanating from the small music box inside his pot belly, while singing a Kurt Weill lyric in fluent German. Lithographed on his ass is: "Walt E. Disney 1930," and the manufacturer was the famous Schuco Company. I know this because it came in the original decorated box.

All I have is one question. I paid $5.23 for it. Do you think I overpaid? Enclosed are photos. I am certain that you have several of these in your fine collection, which everyone knows is most certainly a better one than mine, and can therefore easily provide an answer to my question.

Extremely sincerely,

Maurice Fawcett Mazzeo, Jr.

Maurice Fawcett Mazzeo, Jr.

P.S. I hope it doesn't annoy you that the flap on this envelope is badly torn, but I almost forgot to enclose additional photos of the mate: a Minnie Mouse Schuco toy matching the Mickey that I bought at the same time. Unfortunately its box has a large tear on the side, but I took it anyway because it came with a huge electric animated advertising display with Mickey, Minnie, Donald, Pluto, Horace, Clarabelle, and Goofy doing a German vaudeville ethnic Tango; a Walt Disney German merchandise catalog from 1928 to 1934 depicting in color every Disney item made in Europe during this period; and a junkheap of old animation sketches, master studio art, and original black-and-white Mickey Mouse daily and Sunday comic-strip art—all signed by some artist called Ub Iwerks.

This is the collector's three-o'clock-in-the-morning happy fantasy dream. Sometimes it comes true . . . almost.

But back to reality. And reality among comic-character-toy collectors has to begin with Mickey Mouse. On September 19, 1928, Walt Disney's *Steamboat Willie*, the first Mickey Mouse cartoon, opened at Manhattan's Colony Theatre and was an instant success. Since then Mickey's credits have included character roles in over 140 movies, sponsorship of at least 5,000 different products, 400 comic strips with a mass circulation of 48 million, and books selling a total of 300 million copies. He's been immortalized in wax at Madame Tussaud's, and during World War II his name was the password for the D-day landing. The sales appeal of Mickey Mouse merchandise spread all over the world, and recently the celebrated novelist James Michener called Mickey "one of the most disastrous cultural influences ever to hit America." But he has his defenders, and one of his most important defender-collectors is the fine artist and sculptor Ernest Trova, who opined in *Life* Magazine's 1968 article "Happy 40th Mickey!"

I don't relate to Mickey as a rodent but as a comic character of the grand proportion. Along with the swastika and the Coca-Cola bottle, Mickey Mouse is the most powerful graphic image of the 20th Century.

So the opinions differ, but the facts are documented history. From the very beginning an ocean of merchandise, toys, dolls, games, anything and everything that could be bought for a boy or girl inundated the world of children with the beautiful early graphics of Mickey and Minnie. Toymen listened to the sweet music of the depression cash registers of the nineteen thirties and increased the demand. Design, manufacture, and distribution became worldwide, and fortunes were made in the darkest years.

The driving energy and commercial abilities of one man were largely responsible. His agreement with Walt Disney involved more than just the commercial rights to control and license Disney merchandise; it was a meeting of minds. They shared a basic business philosophy of "throwing every penny of profit back into the pot." Disney had the courage to do this with his movies, and Kay Kamen did the same for the merchandise. Under Kay Kamen's direction the profits from the merchandise exceeded the profits from the cartoons and may have just kept the studio above the level of bankruptcy. Disney and Kamen worked well together; both were courageous, driven, single-minded gamblers who gambled well and won. Sensing the boom and riding it, Kamen quickly established a network of sales offices, licensed manufacturers, importers, distributors, showrooms, a flow of new products well designed, and advertising, marketing, and promotional programs to back them up. To Stockholm, Copenhagen, London, Berlin, Paris, Milan, Dublin, and even Sidney, Australia, and Auckland, New Zealand, it spread, caught on, and caught fire.

Inside toy merchandising there are two different approaches. The most costly is to design a new toy specifically for the comic character. This is costly because money must be spent on designers, prototypes, tools, dies, colored cartons, materials, labor, and administrative expenses. The other way is to take all those noncharacter toys that are rusting in the warehouses by the thousands, stick a Mickey Mouse label on them, junk the boxes, pack the bum toys into beautifully decorated Mickey Mouse cartons, give the salesmen an increased commission percentage, and move out the dead merchandise. Let Mickey Mouse, the super toy salesman, turn your rusting junk into glittering gold. To the everlasting credit of Walt Disney and Kay Kamen, they never took the "stick a Mickey label on the toy approach" in the early and best years. The designs were studio inspired and studio controlled, and the toy designers could go to the movies to see what a Mickey, Minnie, Pluto, Horace, Clarabelle, or Donald looked like. And they must have done this because as the animated cartoon graphics changed, so did the toy Mickeys.

Among advanced Mickey Mouse collectors (often called "Mouse Junkies" since they live for the next fix and must find at least one new toy a week to stave off suicide), there are three different periods of design. The years 1928 to 1932 could be called the Ub Iwerks period. He was *the* artist. "That's an Iwerks Mickey" means that it looks like the Mickey from the first film *Steamboat Willie*. He has a mouthful of mean teeth, a ratlike face, and a big nose and long tail. Perhaps the finest toy of this period is the Mickey Mouse hurdy-gurdy, shown in color. Here a mean, toothy Mickey in tin pushes a hurdy-gurdy that plays as he walks, and on the sides is an almost devil-like Mickey with a pitchfork. To this date only two examples of this fine toy have ever been found.

During this period many of the toys were made in Germany, and they were beautifully designed and executed. The early Mickey Mouse films were very popular with German children, and a large variety of toys, dolls, and games were made available by the German toy industry. Adolf Hitler eventually stopped all the decadent Disney stuff, since he wanted Hitler youth to be as strong as *Kruppstahl*. The short-lived German Disney production ended about 1934, and Stieff dolls, Rosenthal china porcelain Mickeys, and tin wind-ups made in Germany are rare, expensive, and much sought after by Disney collectors.

At the same time Kamen established contact with the Japanese toy makers, and the results were exquisite bisque figurines. Cheap labor allowed them to be hand painted and well made. Many were large in size, and the most valued are those in which the arms are movable. In some the quality of the sculptural art surpassed the material and the subject. The Japanese also produced in large quantities celluloid Mickeys and Minnies in the form of dolls, rubber-band-powered "nodders" in which the heads moved, and combination celluloid, wood, and tin wind-up toys. Celluloid has a charming unplastic look that is cherished by many. Unfortunately, celluloid toys are rare because they were easily crushed in a child's tightened fist and would burn easily. U.S.A. toys are no longer made in celluloid because of the fire hazard to children.

The boom years of the golden age of Disney toys were 1933 to 1938. "That's a thirties Mickey" among collectors means wedge, pie-shaped eyes, a pot belly, a long mouselike tail, and the look of a happy rodent. Nineteen-thirties Disneyana was made in large quantities all around the world, was carefully design controlled by the Disney organization, and is the basis of Disney collecting. Usually these items are marked

"Walt Disney Enterprises" or "Walter E. Disney" and can be quite easily distinguished from the later period.

The period from 1939 to the present day represents a complete change in the graphics. First, they changed the name in 1939 to Walt Disney Productions, and "That's a forties Mickey" or "It's marked Walt Disney Productions" among advanced collectors is the kiss of death. The consensus is that a forties Mickey looks more like a lovable little boy than a rodent. The pie-shaped eyes were filled up with black circles, the tail was chopped off, and he was put on a diet and lost that charming pot belly. And worse, they put him into a Harry Truman Hawaiian sport shirt and porkpie hat. And much worse, the merchandise began to be made cheaply and looked cheap. Walt Disney Productions can set the retail Sears, Roebuck and Woolworth prices, but it is the collectors who determine the prices for Disneyana. A nineteen-thirties Mickey in the original box may command $300, while a similar nineteen-forties Mickey is often lucky to fetch $30. So appealing is the thirties Mickey graphics that some current toy designers are using it anyway, and it does result in more jingles at the cash register, the early graphics are that pleasing and powerful.

The artistic problem in depicting a Mickey or Minnie Mouse can be compared to the discipline of the Japanese watercolorist. In this traditional form he is allowed just a few strokes of his brush to create the most simple image of a bird, a chicken, or a flower. Pure Mickey, derived from the early films, poses the same difficult problem: The best Mickey is the least Mickey, and the least Mickey is the most difficult to draw. Ub Iwerks did the best; few have equaled him since. It looks easy but it is not.

Back to fantasy. If only Walt Disney, Kay Kamen, and Louis Marx could have gotten it all together during the nineteen thirties, what wonderful toys could have been created! But alas, Louis Marx, the great designer of toys and comic-character toys, was never licensed by Disney. Marx produced some of the finest tin wind-ups, but never Disneys, and this may be the reason why there were so few tin Mickeys. The hurdy-gurdy, the Lionel Mickey Mouse Circus toy train, Mickey Mouse Drummer, Mickey Mouse Saxophone Player, and the Schuco Donald Duck represent the few and the best.

The FBI has a Ten Most Wanted Criminals list. What are the ten most wanted Disney collectibles? Certainly, if the ten most advanced Disney collectors were locked into one room and forced to reply, they would come out with eleven different lists, and in their heart of hearts the true answer would be everything! If the Blue Fairy waved her magic wand and said take ten, would you accept these?

1. Mickey Mouse hurdy-gurdy
2. Mickey Mouse French cast-iron bank
3. Mickey Mouse Lionel Circus toy train
4. Santa Claus and Mickey Lionel handcar
5. Donald Duck and Pluto Lionel handcar
6. Mickey and Minnie Mouse Lionel handcar
7. Donald Duck Schuco tin and cast-iron wind-up
8. Mickey Mouse Schuco tin and cast-iron wind-up
9. Mickey Mouse Drummer or Saxophone Player
10. Mickey and Minnie Mouse Dancing on the Piano

All in mint condition in the original decorated boxes, autographed by Walt Disney, with electric animated store displays and . . . and . . . and—all you need is that Blue Fairy and her magic wand!

There were and still are many Mickey Mouse toys that are not. They are called "knock offs." They looked like Mickey but do not carry the name or the imprint of Disney and were never licensed for production. The same is true for Mickey's look-alikes, particularly Felix the Cat and Ignatz Mouse. Comic-character toys almost always carry the character's name and the licensor and often the date; again, finding them in the original boxes assures authenticity.

Second only to Mickey Mouse in popularity and the number of worldwide licensees was an old man without any teeth in his mouth, thin in the waist, always chomping on a corncob pipe, dressed in something resembling a sailor's suit, always ready for a fight, and the comic world's first advocate of health food, namely spinach. Popeye was the first of the super heroes. Marx could not get Mickey and in revenge created the Marx Merrymakers Band (which some collectors consider the best near-Mickey tin wind-up ever made; it is pure Art Deco, Negro minstrel, and near-Mickey—a "crossover"). But he could and did get the OK from King Features Syndicate for the Sailor Man, but not an exclusive. The Chein Company, an excellent toy manufacturer, and other companies also produced Popeye toys. The material used in these tin toys was similar to the coated metal used for grocery-store cans of food, well protected against rust and the elements. In fact, many of the toys were made from recycled food cans. This is why many of the early tin wind-ups never show signs of rust or deterioration and are a joy to the mint collector.

Popeye was created in 1929 by E. C. Segar as an added character for his popular comic strip "Thimble Theatre" and of course became Olive Oyl's boy friend. The earliest Popeye toys were wooden toys with weighted movable legs that would walk down an inclined ramp and were called "walkers." In 1932 Chein created "Popeye in the Barrel" which used the Chein barrel bank as an adaptation for Popeye's mid-section in order to economize. During this period the political cartoonists depicted John Q. Citizen as a stripped taxpayer clothed in a barrel—all that he had left—and the Popeye in the Barrel toy was in that vein of popular political humor. Its reception was enthusiastic, and Chein followed through with fully original toys, such as the all-metal walking figures of Popeye and Barnacle Bill.

But it was in 1936 that Marx created one of the most imaginative comic-character toys ever: Big Fight Popeye the Champ. Its base is a square metal prizefighting ring with all the characters lithographed in bright colors on the four sides. Posts project up from the four corners with ropes connecting them, forming the ring. Celluloid figures of Popeye and his archenemy Bluto are mounted on a circular disc. Wind it up, release the clutch, and as they rotate on the disc, they slug it out. Suddenly the bell rings ending the round, and one or the other gets knocked out on the ropes and you can never predict which. It's like a gambling machine, and conceivably bets could be wagered!

Part of Popeye's general appeal was linked to the social ethos of the nineteen thirties: Kids were manlike if they could use their fists, and dads encouraged their young males to stand up and fight the other kids on the block. Prizefighting and wrestling were popular and accepted sports then. Popeye was always ready to fight and at the beginning of each fight would take severe punishment before the can of spinach was gulped. In the language of the streets, "He could take it like a man." Chein produced a full-figure toy of Popeye punching a prizefighter's punching bag and later a ten-inch-high chalk figure of the sailorman with fists clenched, feet spread apart, and chin jutting out begging for a haymaker that is pure sculpture: a clear communication of who and what Popeye was.

Popeye's commercial appeal justified the mass production of other interesting toys, such as Popeye in the Airplane, the very rare Popeye in the Rowboat, and Popeye with the Parrot Cages. Almost always, he was alone, but one rare and fine exception was another Marx toy, Popeye and Olive Oyl Jiggers. It is sometimes called among collectors Popeye and Olive Oyl on the Roof. The design and many of the parts are derived from earlier Marx Negro toys. The base is a small four-sided houselike structure with beautifully lithographed scenes of all the characters in trouble and in action. On the top of the roof are full figures of Popeye and Olive Oyl with an accordion. Wind it up and they dance a jig. This toy was made in 1936, when poor people were still dancing in the streets for pennies. Sometimes the characters on the cardboard box are depicted differently from the toys inside. On the box Popeye is wearing a top hat, but on the toy he is wearing his traditional cap. Do not be misled into doubting the authenticity of a comic toy because of this difference. It merely means that the carton designer went his own creative way and the toy designer his.

How does a Popeye collector differ from a Disney collector? After viewing many collections across the U.S.A., one is struck by the selective difference. The average Popeye collector is a strict single-character collector: all he collects is Popeye, all he wants is Popeye, with perhaps a few pieces of Wimpy and Olive Oyl. But the Disney collector is a multicharacter collector who collects not only all of the Disney characters from Mickey Mouse to Joe Carioca but also those that are graphically related. Mickey looks much like Felix the Cat and Ignatz, so the toys and dolls of Felix and Ignatz are also collected. Betty Boop is part of the same family, so Disney collectors include her too.

The third type of comic-character-toy collector has a wider catholicity of taste and collects the toys of all of the comic characters in cast iron, lithographed tin wind-ups, composition dolls,* and paper goods. Because of the growing scarcity and popularity of comic items from the nineteen twenties and thirties and the need for trading material (many collectors don't want money anymore and will only trade) strict single- and multicharacter collectors are joining this group.

As old-toy collecting approaches zero supply, more

---

* Composition means that the doll parts were made from a mixture of sawdust and glue poured into metal molds. The separate parts would be dipped into a glaze that would provide a smooth suface for painting. The parts would then be painted with enamel to various color specifications.

and more of the collectors of the three groups are looking toward the Oriental contributions of excellent toys. "Made in Japan" used to mean poorly made imitations, and Americans looked down on them prior to World War II. Now many toy collectors are including these toys in their collections. But because of their sour reputation, most were destroyed, and until recently the charm and excellent workmanship of many of the "Made in Japan" items were ignored. Not so today. Now there are many avid collectors who have a considerable quantity of "Made in Occupied Japan" toys. Unlike their prewar ancestors, these toys were very well made and are in short supply because they were produced for only a few years after the surrender of Japan in 1945, under the watchful eye of the United States occupation authorities.

At that time Japan was attempting to recover from the terrible effects of the war. Labor was cheap, and most of her toys were created for the export market. Toys with the "Made in Occupied Japan" label had to overcome the residue of hatred remaining from the war and the bad reputation remembered from the prewar toys. Therefore, an extra effort was made to achieve a high quality of workmanship and imagination between 1945 and 1949, the years of the occupation.

During the nineteen fifties Japan produced the most marvelous battery-operated toys ever imagined in the mind of man, and there are many astute collectors who have been gathering them into their nets quietly and cheaply.

These are the general parameters of comic-character-toy collecting today, but in a field this new the values can change quickly and without much notice.

Although the nineteenth-century cast-iron toys are still the blue chips of the toy world, the ease of cast-iron reproduction has struck terror into the hearts of new would-be collectors and caused them to turn more and more to the lithographed tin toys, so it is the older, rarer comic toys that command their time and money. This is the most important area today, and its dimensions are being made and measured in a curious fashion. From New York to Los Angeles; Bellevue, Washington; Ypsilanti, Michigan; Minneapolis, Minnesota; Yonkers, and Beacon, New York; the experts—advanced comic-character-toy collectors—run a sub-rosa market via the telephones and parcel post. Buying, selling, haggling, trading, talking, teaching each other, informing each other of new discoveries found at local flea markets and antique stores, these very silent ones determine the hierarchy of values, dealer and collector prices, and the particular reasons for the desirability of certain of the older toys. It is a semisecret society in which equals talk in a slanted language to equals who understand the words. Unlike in the field of comic books, there are no widely distributed price guides that can give instant knowledge to the outsider. There are no authoritative books at your local public library—yet—no night-college courses or lecture series. The new collector is an outsider without a knowledge of current values. They call him a "fish" because he is easily hooked into buying their own earlier mistakes, which they can unload at profitable prices, and because he is easy prey for the hawkish dealers. Below the "fish" is the "garbage can," so named because he will buy your garbage and take it away. It is only after he has bought the worthless that he understands why it is worthless, and at that point his education begins.

The new collector must understand that a few years ago the comic-character toy was bought simply because it was high camp, a conversation piece that generated laughs on the cocktail table, or because it was just plain funky and cost only a few dollars. But today many of these toys are approaching the thousand-dollar mark, and this dramatic rise in prices, coupled with the general ignorance of the values, has attracted the shrewd, money-oriented auction houses, and their toy auctions are increasing in frequency and sharpness. They have brought in with them their many years of manipulative experience, which warrants a few words of caution.

"The Knocker Team" consists of two men who will work you over separately. John Smith looks at your toys and asks the prices. Whatever the prices are, he screams in outrage that they are too high and then "knocks" the merchandise as being inferior, points out the faded paint, the scratches and dents, and states flatly that pieces are missing and the toy is incomplete. He may then offer you half your asking price, and you, believing him to be more expert than yourself, come down in price. He then identifies himself as a dealer and requests a dealer's price, since he "must make a profit." You come down again, and he takes a second look at the toys and in dejected tones says, "No. These toys are in such bad shape I don't think anyone will buy them at your high prices, and I've just heard a rumor that a warehouse has just been tapped in Brooklyn where hundreds of these toys have been found in mint condition in the original boxes, which is certainly going to collapse the market price. Sorry, but I'm not in business to lose money." He walks out. He has cracked your selling price and put you into a state of panic. That's his job. Fifteen minutes later his buddy Jim Jones walks in, knowing you are willing to sell for less than half. "I own a discount store in Jersey and want to add a line of cheap toys for Christmas. How much?" You quote a low price, then he flashes a roll of bills and asks, "How much off for cash?" Down you go lower. He buys and gets a receipt. You've been had, hustled, conned.

"The Knock-Out Ring" is another device that works well. You have consigned your toys to an auction house for sale to the highest bidders. A group of dealers approach the auctioneer and express interest in the lot. He will listen because dealers account for as much as 80 percent of his total business. The goal is to "knock out" the lot at very low prices to the ring. The group agrees to a "kipper," not to bid against each other in a sale, so that one of them can purchase the entire lot of .toys at a low price. After the sale, the members of the ring, using sealed bids, reauction the toys among themselves in a "knock-out" sale and divide the profits. The auctioneer gets his cut because he has made certain that advertising of the auction appeared on the last page in fine print in the *Northeast Podunk Monthly Gazette*, the direct-mail advertisements were all sent by mistake to Fairbanks, Alaska, and none of the major toy collectors were notified of the auction, to eliminate high retail bids. Should they inquire after the auction, "Where are the toys now?" the helpful auctioneer will forward the names and addresses of the friendly dealers and pick up a double commission after the retail sale.

"Auction Fever" is just the reverse. The auction house buys your lot of toys and will put into the catalog the slanted truth: "Property from the estate of T. C. Collector, sold by the order of the Crooked Snake Auction Company, Ltd., London, New York, and Zurich." They do not state that they own it. They have a list of the major collectors and invite them all to the auction, knowing that many are rich competitive enemies who will pay any price to prevent the toy from ending up in the other guy's collection. In the audience they place shills who help to bid up the price and increase the "auction fever," and after the auction you find out what the reserve prices were, now understand how you have been had, and quietly but firmly contemplate and compare the least painful ways of suicide.

What do they know that you don't know? More important, what do they know that they don't want you to know? Simple: the most important toys, their names, and what they look like. They know that the demand is intense and that the price they could get is almost as high as the sky.

The most sought-after comic-character toy today is hardly known at all by the general public. It is called The Hi-Way Henry. It was made in Germany probably during the late nineteen twenties or early thirties. Hi-Way Henry was the creation of the cartoonist Oscar Hitt. He designed the toy from his strip and arranged to have it produced by a contract manufacturer, which is the reason for the manufacturer's name now appearing on the toy. It is the funkiest and funniest comic toy of them all. It is a small lithographed tin car with an old bearded man hunched over the steering wheel and his fat wife in the backseat. Their laundry is drying on a clothesline on the roof, their pots and pans are lashed to the back of the car, the radiator cap has popped up, and the head of their dog sticks out from the crank-handle insert. It is rare to find the toy complete because there were so many different parts; usually the pots and pans are missing. It came with the following poem inserted:

The Hi-Way Henry

Out on the highway rain or shine
This funny bus you'll always find,
Six million of these cars they say
Start out on every holiday.
With stove and clothes line all intact,
They "step on it" and leave the pack,
And thump and bump along the road,
Regardless of the heavy load.
And then when dusk begins to fall
Into their back seat beds they crawl,
Until the dawn of another day,
When they resume their merry way.
And so the cartoonist, Oscar Hitt
Has made this into a comic strip
That runs in papers far and wide,
For folks who read life's funny side,
And, we in turn, have made a toy,
That's sure to bring a lot of joy,
To every little girl and boy.

Opinions will vary among comic-character-toy collectors about the correct pecking order of the following, but not about their importance and not about Hi-Way Henry being absolute number one.

During Charlie Chaplin's worldwide popularity a presold market was created for anything and everything Charlie, particularly toys, and in the nineteen tens and twenties the best were being made in Germany. The Charlie Chaplin tin and cast-iron wind-up is a spectacular example of German craftsmanship. It is a full figure of the world's favorite tramp eight and a half inches in height, complete with derby and swinging cane. It is made in two separate sections: upper half and lower half, connected in the middle. Wind him up and the upper half wobbles back and forth like a pendulum as he walks. The sculptured sheet metal is an excellent depiction of him, the internal motor is of the highest quality, and the oversized circus-clown shoes are made from cast iron. It is certainly one of the finest examples of comic-character toys. Another is the Whistling Charlie, also made in Germany, hand carved from wood, with a clockwork mechanism plus bellows. Charlie's head moves from side to side while he whistles "How Dry I Am."

The cartoonist Fontaine Fox created the very popular comic strip, "Toonerville Trolley," which appeared in over three hundred daily and Sunday newspapers. Movies, books, games, and toys were created directly from it. Fox became extremely wealthy and decided to design, manufacture, and market his own toys, and during the nineteen twenties and thirties he contracted with German manufacturers to produce the highest-quality toys that could be made and sold profitably. Powerful Katrinka was very fat, very strong, and one of his most humorous creations. This toy was made in two varieties: one in which she demonstrates her strength by lifting the popular Jimmy in one hand, and the even more desirable toy in which Jimmy sits in a wheelbarrow while Powerful Katrinka raises and lowers him with just one hand.

But Fox's most famous creation was not any of the characters, it was a machine: The Toonerville Trolley That Meets All Trains. The Toonerville Trolley entered the language and became a household expression describing second-rate railroad transportation. The toy was made in Germany in 1922, and each one was numbered. It was a one-to-one copy right out of the comic strip, driven by the "Skipper," who revolves the brake to give it an erratic motion. Other adaptations also appeared, such as a less attractive American version, a cast-iron Toonerville Trolley manufactured by the Dent Hardware Company in Fullerton, Pennsylvania, and distributed by George Borgfeldt & Company; a small pot-metal version; and an even smaller one that could be found inside a box of Crackerjacks.

Oscar Hitt and Fontaine Fox were typical of cartoonists so wealthy that they could control the design and quality of manufacture of their own toys derived from their strips with no middleman-businessman to insist on compromises. This may have been the central reason for the success of these toys. Another example of the same direct relationship is the Maggie and Jiggs tin wind-up. George McManus created Maggie and Jiggs in 1913 in "Bringing up Father." It became one of the most popular and widely read strips ever created, and it was inevitable that a toy from it must appear. The basic dramatic conflict was the continual husband and wife warfare between henpecked Jiggs and his strict wife Maggie, and the toy illustrates this conflict beautifully. It was manufactured in 1924 by the German toy company Nifty. It attempts to create a real fight between them: she attacking him with a rolling pin, he defending himself with his cane. Back and forth it moves in jerky movements, husband and wife swinging away at each other. It consists of two full figures handsomely lithographed, with their names in bold print, on separate two-wheeled platforms connected by a thin strip of spring steel. Underneath one platform is a clockwork mechanism that makes the toy start, stop, and go backward and forward as they swing away, creating the illusion of a family fight to the death. Underneath Maggie's feet is a mean-looking dog, obviously on her side, ready to bite her hubby. The toy is seven inches in length and is a fantastic theatrical show.

On August 5, 1924, Little Orphan Annie and her dog Sandy, drawn by the fine cartoonist Harold Gray, were introduced by the New York *Daily News*. In those days orphans and dogs loyal to orphans created instant sympathy, and the strip was an immediate success. Gray used the strip to convey his particular brand of right-wing politics, which resulted in thousands of cancellations of newspaper subscriptions. But despite the protests of editors that the purpose of a newspaper comic strip was to increase circulation, not destroy it, he continued to be a prophet of gloom and doom and a self-appointed instructor in political and social morality. Despite the popularity of the character, there never were very many Orphan Annie toys.

During the early nineteen thirties Louis Marx brought to the market Little Orphan Annie Skipping Rope. It was five inches in height and lithographed in bright colors, with a red dress and her orange curls. Her name was printed on her belt and her creator's name is on the back of her shoes. The action of the toy is wild: wind her up and she skips rope. Underneath her feet are four small gears that allow the wire rope to pass around her and underneath her feet. Along with her came Walking Sandy, her faithful dog well known for his "Arf! Arf!" reply to all of her questions. He was five inches in length, with four power-operated legs, Orphan Annie's schoolcase in his mouth, and a large "Sandy" collar around his neck. He was lithographed in orange and black and came in a brightly decorated box that can be folded into a doghouse. The box was decorated with Annie and Sandy performing circus acts.

This pair did not escape the talented hands of the Japanese, and they created one of the earliest items. Orphan Annie and pooch are in celluloid mounted on two separate metal platforms with wheels. They are connected with a string. Wind up Annie, and Sandy follows wagging his head. There were many dolls depicting this famous pair but very few wind-up toys, which are avidly sought.

It should be understood that rare often means very rare, because for many of these toys there are no more than a half dozen that have been saved and put into private collections. For some there may be only one existing example, such as Henry and Henrietta, Travelers. Carl Anderson created this popular comic strip of the nineteen thirties, and several toys were designed by Anderson for the market. Henry and Henrietta, Travelers was made in Japan in 1934 and combines celluloid, lithographed tin, and wire forms into a complicated toy that must have been difficult and expensive to mass-produce. Our bald-headed Henry and his girl friend look sad. He is carrying a trunk, and they are apparently running away from home. He and she are seven-inch-high molded celluloid figures. Wind up the motor hidden in the trunk and a wheel at the bottom moves Henry and Henrietta forward, while their legs go up and down, giving them the appearance of walking. The trunk is printed with labels from Paris, Tokyo, London, Boston, Chicago, Rome, Liverpool, and other strange and foreign places. The box for the toy depicts it in an abstract Japanese watercolor approach and is a magnificent work of comic art.

Another very rare toy is the Smitty Scooter, made by Louis Marx. Smitty was the world's most famous office boy, created by the cartoonist Walter Berndt in 1922. Millions followed his exploits, and the toy became a typical Marx success. The colors are bright orange, black striping and red handle and wheels. Smitty is dressed in nineteen-twenties fashion, with high-laced shoes, long stockings, short pants, bow tie, cap, and, unlike the comic strip, his eyes are empty circles, giving him an Orphan Annie look. The figure of Smitty is removable so that it can be played with separately, and the motor that drives it is the standard Marx unit of that period. It is eight inches in height and approximately five inches in length. The quality

of the lithographic printing on the metal is excellent, and the reason for the toy seldom being found in a rusty condition is that the reverse side of the metal is heavily painted to prevent deterioration.

The most popular radio program in the history of American broadcasting was *Amos 'n' Andy*, created and played by Charles Correll and Freeman Gosden, who were whites but had Negro imaginations. Witty, funny, original, it captured America. From 1929 to 1935 listening to *Amos 'n' Andy* became a national craze. It had a nighttime audience of 40 million listeners, a third of the population of the country. Even President Hoover set aside his work each weekday evening at 7:00 P.M. in order to listen, and Correll and Gosden had a long visit at the White House in a command performance.

In 1932 the craze had become so great that department stores, saloons, and restaurants had put in radios so that their customers could listen to the program between seven and seven fifteen, Monday through Friday. Movie theatres had to stop their films in midreel at seven o'clock, put a radio out onto the stage, and tune in *Amos 'n' Andy*, otherwise the customers would have stayed home to listen. Pepsodent toothpaste sponsored the program and watched its sales triple in just a few weeks; it started on a nationwide hookup August 19, 1929, and probably saved the National Broadcasting Company from bankruptcy. Amos 'n' Andy had come up north to Harlem from a small town in Georgia to make money in the taxicab business and got caught in the web of George (Kingfish) Stevens, whose credit rating was "Triple Z: Be careful when he pays cash." Between them they created voices for 550 different characters, including Lightnin', Brother Crawford, Fred Gwindell, Algonquin J. Calhoun, and Henry van Porter.

Amos Jones and Andrew Hog Brown started the "Fresh Air Taxicab of America Incorpoplated," "Rates cab sold to them by the Kingfish for their entire life savings of $360. The program is long gone, but the Amos 'n' Andy Fresh Air Taxicab created by Louis Marx is one of the most avidly sought comic-character toys. It was certainly one of the best and most imaginative of the Marx designs. The cab is decorated in bright orange and black with childish scrawls, such as "Fresh Air Taxicab of America Incorpoplated," "Rates ask Amos," "Check and doublecheck," "License applied for time after time." Amos sits hunched over the steering wheel while Andy sits like a king on the throne in the rear, smoking a cigar stub. Next to Andy is a mean-looking white dog. To be complete there should be a hand crank jutting out of the crankcase and a golden horseshoe radiator cap. These two parts are usually missing. From front bumper to back it measures eight inches and from the top of Amos's derby to the bottom of the worn-out tires it is five inches. There are two known variations: the one with the headlights does not have the inscription, "Andy Brown Prez Amos Jones driver" on the door; the one without headlights does. Wind it up and it moves forward, then suddenly stops and jiggles from side to side like a shaggy dog shaking off water. It's really a comic toy and invariably makes people laugh out loud. The box is pure fantasy.

The Amos 'n' Andy walking figures were brought to market in 1930 and were controversial even then. In those days ethnic jokes were part and parcel of the vaudeville tradition, but these toys went too far, and there were protests. On the box Amos is drawn near apelike, with projecting teeth, thick lips, and multiple cheekbones, and Andy looks like a monkey with a cigar in his mouth. The tin faces are very black, with thick red lips, and the back of the head sections have curly Negro hair in print. Worse, wind up these walking figures and they "shuffle" like a chimp trying to walk like a real human being. As the letters of protest poured in, Marx made a quick change. He lightened the faces from deep black to light brown and made the features less apelike. A later version had Andy with a swinging cane, and the eyes moved up and down. They wholesaled for $12.25 for a dozen pairs and eventually were packaged in a new box entitled "Check and Double Check," capitalizing on their first Hollywood movie.

There were many other Negro toys, so many in fact that that comprises another complete category of toy collecting. Some of the most prominent collectors of them are blacks themselves, who see a funky quality that is appealing. Both Marx and Strauss were the leaders and popularized them during the nineteen twenties and thirties. Alabama Coon Jigger, Jazzbo Jim, The Charleston Trio, The Chicken Thief (a black caught stealing a chicken by a dog biting his leg) were popular. And in those days of legal firecrackers a cherry bomb was widely advertised as a Nigger Chaser. Ham and Sam, the Minstrel Team was produced by the Ferdinand Strauss Corporation in 1921 and is one of the best examples of toys depicting Negroes in caricature. One plays the banjo and the other bangs away on the piano, and they are dressed in the early minstrel costumes. Other sharply dressed minstrel characters are printed on the piano and stool.

Wind it up and they play and dance. The popularity of band toys caused a continuous stream of production from Marx, Strauss, Lehman, and Unique Art, from Hot and Tot to Marx Merrymakers, Li'l Abner and His Dogpatch Band, and Howdy Doody.

The Marx Merrymakers Mouse Band is one of the most beautiful of all the Marx toys. The mechanical operation and configuration is similar to the black bands, but here the Negro characters are replaced with highly stylized figures of mice. The mice look very much like Mickey Mouse, and it is reputed that Marx could not get a license from Walt Disney in the nineteen thirties so this was his answer. It is a "crossover," because Disney collectors recognize its close resemblance, Negro-toy collectors see Negro mice, and its Art Deco design makes it a must among Deco collectors. As in many Marx toys, there were variations. The most wanted one is the band with the violinist perched on top of the piano and a handsomely lithographed vaudeville backdrop inserted into the back of the piano. On it, two wild mice dance to the music of a cat playing the tuba! The box is very Art Deco and a most wanted item.

Li'l Abner and His Dogpatch Band was brought to market at the end of World War II by Unique Art Manufacturing and was a great commercial success. It was one of the last tin toys in which the individual figures were sculptured with creases, wrinkles, and folds, giving them a three-dimensional, lifelike appearance. This is a costly, labor-intensive process because the sheet metal is predecorated in the flat and the forming dies have to be machined and remachined to align the flat lithography into the correct dimensional positions. Toy after toy has to be formed into prototypes for the junk pile before the alignment is correct and the dies can be heat-treated into a hard surface for mass-production forming. Today, the high wages of tool and die makers make this process almost impossible.

The creator of "Li'l Abner" was and is the controversial Al Capp, who started as the assistant to Ham Fisher, creator of "Joe Palooka." In 1934 he began "Li'l Abner" and caught the imagination of the American public. It was situation comedy mixed with satire, and the names Daisy Mae, Sadie Hawkins Day, the Schmoo, Kickapoo Juice, Lord Cesspool, and others became household words. The toy is the usual band design, with the figures of Pappy, Mammy, Li'l Abner, and Daisy Mae seated at the piano. It is very colorful and the box is beautifully decorated.

Little Max Speshul #1 was another handsome toy

made after the Second World War. It was inspired by Ham Fisher's "Joe Palooka." Little Max was an angelic, always good little boy who idolized Joe. It was made in a very small quantity by Sal Metal Products. Many years ago kids used to take wood crates, nail a wood plank to the bottom, and add old roller skates for wheels, and they had a homemade scooter. This is what Max is riding, and on the sides are pictures of Joe Palooka, his manager, Knobby Walsh, and the prize ring. It is exceptionally well made and quite rare. On the back of the box is a comic strip involving Joe, Knobby, Humphrey, and Max in a drive to buy U.S. Bonds to fight postwar inflation. It's quite a piece of history.

Dagwood the Driver is typical of the many automotive comic-character toys that were produced during the nineteen twenties and thirties. It is a "crazy car" and goes back and forth while Dagwood's head turns round and round. Printed on the metal are all of the favorite characters of "Blondie": Daisy their dog, Cookie, Blondie, Baby Dumpling, and Mr. Dithers. The toy was marketed during the mid-nineteen thirties, when the strip was at its height of popularity. The two large wheels in the center are motor driven and are located at the center of gravity of the toy, permitting the crazy gyrations. Again, the shrewdness of Marx was in knowing that a presold market existed.

And what a market! "Blondie" was one of the most popular of all newspaper comic strips. It was created by Chic Young on September 6, 1930, and appeared in 1,623 newspapers in sixty countries, and millions of readers were devoted fans. Few readers today are aware that Dagwood Bumstead began comic-strip life as the playboy son of J. Boling Bumstead, a foul-tempered railroad tycoon; or that Blondie was formerly Blondie Boopadoop, a gold-digging flapper. But it was Joseph V. Connolly who changed it all. He was the manager of King Features Syndicate and suggested to Young, "Why don't you have them marry? You know more about married life than flighty dames." And so, on February 13, 1933, Blondie and Dagwood were married, and Chic Young lived happily ever after. Happily? During the bottom of the depression years his annual income rose from $22 a week to $300,000 a year!

Charlie McCarthy in His Benzine Buggy was another Marx "crazy car" that entered a presold market. It was produced in 1938 during the height of the radio and movie popularity of Charlie McCarthy and Edgar Bergen. There is Charlie in top hat, tuxedo, and monocle in his black luxury car ready to "Mow you down." It is a handsome, well-made toy that measures seven inches in both length and height and is fun to wind up and watch.

The McCarthy Strut was produced at the same time and was a great commercial success. It was over eight inches in height, a full tin figure of our wooden friend; wind him up and he walks toward you, while his mouth goes up and down like a real ventriloquist's dummy. Both toys were packaged in colorful boxes with pictures of Charlie and Edgar in their formal show-biz attire.

Moon Mullins and Kayo on a Handcar was based on Frank Willard's very popular comic strip and was basically fashioned from the standard design of a railway handcar, with flat, tin, lithographed figures of Moon Mullins on one end and his small, derby-hatted sidekick, Kayo, at the other end helping to operate the vehicle. Marx manufactured two slightly different versions: One had a black tin base with Kayo standing on top of a box of dynamite that was a wind-up floor toy. The other one had a heavy yellow metal base and operated on a circular railroad track. Both toys used a powerful clockwork motor for propulsion. The fantastic box certainly helped sell the toy. It has Moon and Kayo on the handcar out of control speeding along, aimed at a mean-looking bull standing on the railroad track and about to collide with the box of dynamite. Both are holding on to their derbies, scared to death, expecting the worst of disasters!

Joe Penner and His Duck Goo Goo, also produced by Marx, capitalized on the popularity of this ex-vaudevillian turned radio comedian of the mid-nineteen thirties. It was a wild time of crazy fads, and Penner's famous phrase "Wanna buy a duck?" swept the nation. He came on the scene quickly and went out just as fast, but the wind-up toy remains as a most wanted collector's item. It is a full figure of Joe walking, holding on to a basket full of ducks in one hand and collaring a full figure of Goo Goo in the other, while smoking a cigar as his hat tips up and down. He wears a checkerboard jacket, red tie, and bell-bottomed trousers. It is a humorous, colorful toy and belongs in anyone's comic-character-toy collection.

The Lone Ranger Hi-Yo Silver, produced by Marx in 1938, is one of the few well-designed lithographed tin toys ever made for the masked rider of the plains. The colors are bright and the metal is formed into realistic creases, folds, and wrinkles that suggest expensive preparation. Silver is supported on his hind legs and tin tail, while his weirdly dressed master is in blue trousers, red shirt, and scrolled leather boots, with a six-gun in one hand while he operates a motor-driven lasso in the other.

Superman Racing the Airplane is one of the few Superman toys and one of the last well-made toys prior to World War II. It was manufactured by Marx in 1940, just before metal became short in supply as foreign and domestic defense contracts were being filled. It is a small wind-up lithographed toy only five inches in length, and Superman races the propellor aircraft, obviously chasing the mean-looking bad guy in the cockpit. Part of its value to collectors is that it is the only three-dimensional figure of Superman ever made in metal and, of course, there wasn't much time between his beginning in late 1938 and Pearl Harbor to make many Superman items in metal.

Felix the Cat on the Scooter was just one of many Felix toys produced in the nineteen twenties and thirties, but it is important because it is one of the finest renditions of Felix, is a lithographed metal wind-up of a well-known movie and comic-strip favorite, and is very rare. It was made by Nifty Company and imported and distributed by George Borgfeldt & Company, is eight inches in length and a very sturdy toy. "Felix" is printed on his tail, and he has that mean look as if he is going to run you down with his scooter and just keep on going.

Felix the Movie Cat sparkler is another Nifty-Borgfeldt production from the same era, equally rare and in demand. Push up the bar at the bottom, a wheel turns, flints scrape, and sparkles emerge from his eyes. It was a popular toy, and similar sparklers were made for Mickey Mouse and Amos 'n' Andy. The box has superb graphics: Felix is chasing an Ignatz-looking terrified mouse who knows he is going to be eaten alive in one gulp. Copyright by Pat Sullivan, the creator of Felix, is on the box and all of the toys.

Howdy Doody Clock-A-Doodle is one of the most interesting, and well-made post–occupied-Japan toys. Our hero swings back and forth, providing pendulum power to drive a quick-operating clock that chimes at every quarter hour. It is handsomely lithographed with all of the characters from Flub-a-Dub and the Princess to Clarabelle and Howdy Doody himself. It was brought to market by the Kagran Corporation in a very small quantity and quickly disappeared. Howdy Doody is beautifully formed in three dimensions, and the design, beauty, and quality of the toy makes it one of the finest that can be added to any comic-character-toy collection.

The Captain Marvel Lightning Racing Cars is another example of well-made postwar toys. It is comprised of a set of four racing cars, all in different colors, with individual wind-up keys, wooden wheels, and adjustable steering mechanisms. On the side is Captain Marvel in a horizontal flying position with his right fist extended, ready to punch the evildoer at over a hundred miles an hour. It was manufactured under contract to Fawcett Publications in 1948 and was packaged in a beautiful pop-up box for counter display.

There were many other comic-character tin wind-up toys from the golden years of newspaper comics, difficult to find, expensive to buy today, and magnificent in the eye of the collector-beholder. There were the handsome dolls of Mickey Mouse, Felix the Cat, Betty Boop, and Shirley Temple, in cloth, composition, and celluloid, which are increasing in popularity and are rapidly becoming a separate branch of doll collecting; there are the magnificent early cast-iron comic toys that command huge prices in the collector's marketplace, such as Andy Gump in the 348 Car, manufactured by Arcade.

Lastly, there are the undiscovered comic toys hidden in attics and cellars, waiting to be known again, to be discovered by the avid hunter and restored to pristine condition. The newspapers in America are dying, and dying even faster are their comic strips. A popular era of simple fun and fantasy is drawing to a close. But these beautiful examples of American comic sculptural art will remain, and perhaps future generations of Americans will begin to see the beauty that delights the eye of today's comic-character-toy collector.

COMIC-CHARACTER TOYS:
SUGGESTED LIST OF COLLECTIBLES

In collecting comic-character toys a word of caution. Buy better than you can afford, that way you don't become a "gatherer." Your collection is finer and your equity safer in ten great toys than in a thousand broken, rusty pieces of junk. Don't buy toys with parts missing because they are cheap and you hope to find the part. You're gambling against house odds a thousand to one, and you'll lose. Avoid rusty toys, because the rust spreads like Dutch Elm disease. On the other hand, if the motor is broken and the toy itself is in good condition, grab it; motors can be easily fixed. Leave it alone; never repaint or try to have visual parts that are missing remade and replaced; just let it be. Try to collect them in mint condition in the original boxes. Yes, it is an impossible dream today, but by establishing this internal discipline you will be amazed that dealers will recognize you as a mint collector and will therefore offer you their finest pieces, and you will be paying more but getting the best of their wares. Lastly, don't hesitate in a rising market. If you find a great one and your collector's "third eye" tells you it's great, buy it. As the saying goes, "He who hesitates is lost." In this explosive area of collectibles, availability is more important than price.

	Manufacturer	Date
The Hi-Way Henry	Oscar Hitt	1922
Charlie Chaplin tin and cast-iron wind-up	German	1914
Powerful Katrinka (with Jimmy in the wheelbarrow)	Fontaine Fox	1923
Powerful Katrinka (lifting Jimmy)	Fontaine Fox	1924
Toonerville Trolley tin wind-up (Also made in an American-version tin wind-up, and in cast iron, pot metal, tin Crackerjack premium, and a glass candy container.)	Fontaine Fox	1922
Maggie and Jiggs tin wind-up	Nifty Co.	1924
Barney Google and Sparkplug	German	1924
Smitty Scooter	Louis Marx	1920s
Amos 'n' Andy Fresh Air Taxicab	Louis Marx	1930
Amos 'n' Andy Walking Figures	Louis Marx	1930
Ham and Sam, the Minstrel Team	Ferdinand Strauss Corp.	1921
Little Orphan Annie Skipping Rope	Louis Marx	1930s
Walking Sandy	Louis Marx	1930s
Merrymakers Mouse Band	Louis Marx	1930s
Orphan Annie and Sandy celluloid and tin wind-up	C. K. Japan	1930s
Henry and Henrietta, Travelers, celluloid and tin wind-up	C. K. Japan	1934
Henry on the Elephant's Trunk celluloid wind-up	C. K. Japan	1934
Moon Mullins and Kayo on a Handcar	Louis Marx	1930s
The Yellow Kid in the Goat Cart (cast iron)	R. F. Outcault	1898
The Yellow Kid on an Easter Egg	R. F. Outcault	1898
Happy Hooligan Walker	Chein Co.	1932
Happy Hooligan Roly-Poly	F. B. Opper	1920s
Buster Brown and Tige on Seesaw hand-painted tin wind-up	German	1910
Buster Brown camera	Kodak	1910
Andy Gump in the 348 Car (cast iron)	Arcade	1928
Andy Gump in 348 Car Tootsietoy*	Dowst Manufacturing	1932
Uncle Walt in Roadster Tootsietoy*	Dowst	1932
Smitty and Herbie on Motorcycle Tootsietoy*	Dowst	1932
Moon Mullins in Paddy Wagon Tootsietoy*	Dowst	1932
Kayo on Ice Wagon Tootsietoy*	Dowst	1932
Uncle Willy and Mamie in Boat Tootsietoy*	Dowst	1932
Buck Rogers Tootsietoys**	Dowst	1937
Flash Blast Attack Ship**	Dowst	1937
Venus Duo Destroyer**	Dowst	1937
Buck Rogers Battle Cruiser**	Dowst	1937
U.S.N. Los Angeles**	Dowst	1937
Cast figures of Buck Rogers and Wilma Deering**	Dowst	1937
Buck Rogers 25th Century Rocket Ship	Louis Marx	1934

* These were sold individually and as a set, The Funnies Set Number 5091. They are now among the most sought-after Tootsietoys.
** These were also sold individually and as a set.

	Manufacturer	Date
Buck Rogers Rocket Police Patrol Ship	Louis Marx	1939
Flash Gordon Rocket Fighter	Louis Marx	1939
Flash Gordon Space Pistol	Louis Marx	1936
Popeye the Sailor (also known as Popeye in the Rowboat—very rare!)	Hoge Manufacturing	1935
Big Fight—Popeye the Champ	Louis Marx	1936
Popeye and Olive Oyl Jiggers	Louis Marx	1936
Popeye in the Barrel	Chein	1932
Popeye walking figure	Chein	1932
Barnacle Bill walking figure	Chein	1932
Popeye With Punching Bag doll	Chein	1932
Popeye doll (wood)	Chein	1932
Popeye statue (chalk)	King Features Syndicate	1933
Popeye ramp walker	C. K. Japan	1929
Wimpy ramp walker	C. K. Japan	1929
Popeye in the Airplane (Popeye Eccentric Airplane)	Louis Marx	1930
Harold Lloyd on the Telephone	German	1930s
Dagwood the Driver	Louis Marx	1935
Charlie McCarthy in His Benzine Buggy	Louis Marx	1938
The McCarthy Strut walking figure	Louis Marx	1938
The Lone Ranger Hi-Yo Silver	Louis Marx	1938
Joe Penner and His Duck Goo Goo	Louis Marx	1934
Superman Racing the Airplane	Louis Marx	1940
Superman doll (wood)	Ideal	1939
Superman Krypto Ray Gun	Daisy Manufacturing Co.	1939
Li'l Abner and His Dogpatch Band	Unique Art Manufacturing	1945
Little Max Speshul #1	Sal Metal Products	1948
Captain Marvel Lightning Racing Cars	Fawcett Publications	1948
Howdy Doody Clock-A-Doodle	Kagran Corp.	1953
Dick Tracy Police Station	Louis Marx	1948
Aggie, Reg'lar Fellers Girl	Nifty	1923
Mr. Peanuts	Planters Peanuts	1939
Ignatz Mouse on Tricycle	Chein	1932
Ignatz Mouse stuffed doll	Knickerbocker	1931
Krazy Kat stuffed doll	Knickerbocker	1931
Felix the Cat on the Scooter tin wind-up	Nifty	1931
Felix the Cat pull toy	Nifty	1931
Felix the Cat Bowler	Nifty	1931
Felix the Movie Cat sparkler	Nifty	1931
Speedy Felix	Nifty	1931
Felix Wagon	Nifty	1931
Felix the Cat wood dolls	Schoenhut	1932
Felix the Cat composition doll		1920s
Betty Boop "Nodder" wind-up	C. K. Japan	1930
Betty Boop dolls	Ideal and Fleischer	1930s
Betty Boop radio	Hudson-Ross	1932
Betty Boop and Bimbo racer	Keeneye, Inc.	1932
Bimbo stuffed doll	Dorco	1932
Mickey Mouse hurdy-gurdy	German	1930
Mickey Mouse cast-iron bank	France	1930
Mickey Mouse Circus toy train	Lionel	1935
Mickey and Minnie Mouse handcar	Lionel	1935
Santa Claus and Mickey handcar	Lionel	1935

	Manufacturer	Date
Donald Duck and Pluto handcar	Lionel	1935
Donald Duck tin and cast-iron wind-up	Schuco	1935
Mickey Mouse tin and cast-iron wind-up	Schuco	1930s
Mickey Mouse Drummer (tin)	Nifty	1931
Mickey Mouse Saxophone Player (tin)	Nifty	1930
Mickey and Minnie Dancing on the Piano	Marks Bros.	1934
Mickey and Minnie Tumbling Circus	George Borgfeldt & Company	1931
Mickey Mouse sparkler	Nifty	1931
Mickey and Minnie celluloid dolls	Nifty	1931
Mickey Mouse Spinner	Nifty	1931
Mickey and Minnie Mouse velvet dolls (heights: 4¼″, 6½″, 8¼″, 10½″, 12½″, 16¾″)	M. Stieff and Co.	1931
Mickey Mouse velvet hand puppet	Stieff	1931
Mickey Mouse velvet doll on tricycle pull toy	Stieff	1931
Mickey Mouse "Nodder" wind-up	C. K. Japan	1930
Donald Duck walking figure	C. K. Japan	1935
Mickey Mouse bisque (9″ height, both arms movable, on integral base)	C. K. Japan	1933
Mickey Mouse radio	Emerson	1933
Snow White radio	Emerson	1938
Three Little Pigs radio	Hudson-Ross	1933–1934
Snow White and the Seven Dwarfs, Mickey Mouse, Donald Duck, The Big Bad Wolf, The Three Little Pigs, and Pluto the Pup molded-rubber figures	Seiberling Latex Products	1937–1938
Mickey Mouse Ball trapp game	Migra, France	1934
Climbing Mickey Mouse	Dolly Toy Co.	1932
Donald Duck, Pinocchio, Joe Carioca wind-ups	Migra	1950s

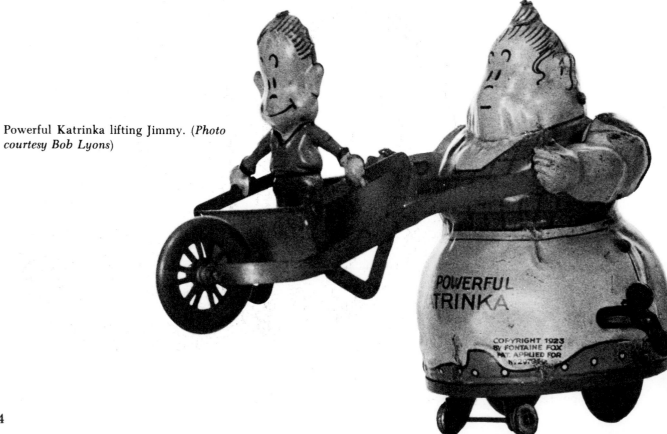

Powerful Katrinka lifting Jimmy. (*Photo courtesy Bob Lyons*)

The Yellow Kid in the Goat Cart, 1899. Probably the first of the comic toys.

Happy Hooligan roly poly; and the Yellow Kid on an Easter Egg.

They're Toy Salesmen De Luxe—
THOSE CHEERY

The popularity of our comic population swells each succeeding year. Their great by-product, use of their name on merchandise, has become an industry in itself. Herewith, TOYS AND NOVELTIES presents a complete back-stage picture of the men who guide this important work—the first time such a resume has ever been presented to the toy trade

Celebrity's Classics

Quick to find a way to capitalize on the color film vogue was Celebrity Productions, 723 7th Avenue, New York. Their former effort was Willie Wopper, but now production is concentrated on adapting tried and true fairy tales to the screen. Among the early releases are the

New Sinbad Book
Book to Film to Book

Grimm and Anderson classics. After the film is released, back goes the movie version into book form, dressed up in modern style and priced in the popular brackets. Toy departments find it easy to sell.

•

Columbia: Scrappy's Home

Go getting promotional leadership makes "Scrappy's" connection with Columbia Pictures franchise department a happy one. Without previous introduction via newspaper strip, Scrappy made his debut on the screen and clicked. Quickly his popularity was put to work by toymakers and today his list of licensees ranks among the longest in the field.

Scrappy is brainchild of Charles Minz, who has the aid of a hundred folk in producing the animated cartoon. All drawings of Scrappy are kept simple, thus youngsters find it easy to copy his likeness. On that premise, Columbia's alert franchise department scored with an

idea to make up cartoon lessons with Scrappy as chief model. Already 5,000 public schools, 1,500 childrens' camps and scores of department stores have accepted the idea.

A hookup with this promotion is found in paint sets and drawing books featuring Scrappy. Contests are being run to single out proficiency among the young artists.

One national magazine group invites children to write letters on, "Why I like Scrappy," gives prizes in the form of merchandise featuring the smiling little cartoon character. Again, a nationally known chocolate maker recently began to market chocolate cakes under Scrappy's name, and has begun to distribute a million Scrappy magazines featuring merchandise wearing Scrappy's license.

A back to school promotion for fall is expected to produce additional popularity for this young star.

The Columbia office at 729 7th Avenue, New York, features a unique co-operative plan whereby licensees of Scrappy can plan tieups of the film in towns where it is shown, thus helping dealers move their goods. The plan paves the way for local newspaper co-operation and thus provides a three-way smash that insures cash register results.

Go-Getter Scrappy
Easy to Draw, Easy to Sell

Dille's Boy of Future

John F. Dille, boss of an aggressive syndicate operating out of Chicago, is himself father to the idea behind the creation of Buck Rogers, famous newspaper and radio participant in 25th Century adventure. With Buck, Dille originated an entirely new field for manufacturers pro-

Buck Rogers Atop World
Ace Imagination Stimulator

ducing toys and youth merchandise. The imaginative appeal of the 25th Century is distinctly a new new note in youth merchandising.

Last year many sales records were set by Buck Rogers merchandise and 1935 gives promise of surpassing last year's achievements.

Buck Rogers is the hero of millions of American youth in the daily newspaper strip and Sunday color page in the newspapers of America.

Buck Rogers — and his companion, Wilma Deering — broadcast throughout the United States and Canada on the Columbia chain, providing a daily scientific thrill adventure, enthusing youngsters, winning parental applause because of the adventure's wholesome type.

Mr. Dille has received thousands of letters from parents and hundreds from school teachers applauding Buck Rogers.

•

Drake's Fellers

In his Flatiron building office in New York, Charles N. Drake leans back to term "Reg'lar Fellers" the perfect trade name phrase. There is reason to agree

24

FOLK OF THE FUNNIES

Wholesome Fellers
Twenty-Five Million Friends

with him, for the gay little crowd of neighborhood tikes have stepped out of Gene Byrnes' syndicated cartoon to boost sales in a wide variety of toy lines, as well as in children's wearing apparel and other goods made for youngsters.

Reg'lar Fellers has won its popularity on comic pages solely. The strip is familiar to readers through fifteen years of history. Today it runs in more than 200 newspapers throughout the world, and Drake opines that some twenty-five million adults and children follow it daily. Reason for this lasting popularity, as put forth by Mr. Drake, is Gene Byrnes' genuine humor and naturalness, plus freedom from vulgarity and cheapness.

•

Tribune Crowd

Long experienced in successful promotion work, A. M. Loewenthal, president

of Famous Artists syndicate, 35 East Wacker Drive, Chicago, has grouped a powerful list of prominent folk, both fictional and real, under his direction. Headliners are the familiar faces seen in strips of the Chicago Tribune—New York News syndicate. Among these are hotcha Harold Teen, style monger Winnie Winkle and brother, Perry, true-hearted Orphan Annie, raucous Moon and Kayo Mullins, loveable Walt Wallet and his Gasoline Alley clan, heart-warming Smitty and Herby, futile Andy Gump and the hard-hitting sleuth, Dick Tracy. Also in the Famous Artists fold are enrolled Joe Palooka, the Lone Ranger, and such personalities as Max Baer, Jack Dempsey, Clyde Beatty, Jackie Cooper.

Such an army of popular idols is a force to be reckoned with, and there is no mystery as to why Famous Artists has been adding steadily to its list of licensees.

•

Kamen and Mickey

Favorite cartoon plot with young and old is that in which poor Minnie Mouse, clutched in the cruel grasp of a hairy villian, is carried off to meet a bitter fate—only to be rescued, nick of time, by brave, kind little Mickey. Champion life and virtue saver is Mickey, and so natural is the rescuing instinct in him, he continued to work at it when invited into the toy trade.

Toymakers and merchants everywhere knew how Minnie Mouse felt when the depression assailed them as the beast did

Glad-Handing Mouse
Rescues Any and All

her. They learned, too, that hilarious feeling of relief when rescue came at the hands of Mickey, who upped sales when all seemed lost.

The industry can point to many instances where, single-handed, Mickey Mouse drove off lurking receivers with the same vigor he exerts in fending Minnie from Big-Bad Bill. Today, more than 80 U. S. toymakers swear allegiance to Mickey's banner, and his flag flies over about 120 more factories through Europe, Canada, Australia.

Most pretentious of Mickey's merchandising exploits is the loan of his name and likeness to a diamond bracelet that retails for $1,200. But Mickey is no snob. His shining face may be seen in homes of slum children as well as on Park Avenue and the Drive. A recent triumph is the Mickey Mouse Magazine, first published quarterly, but now a monthly, by popular demand.

Back of the scenes, directing Mickey's snap-dash rescue work, is Kay Kamen of the Walt Disney enterprises, 729 Seventh Avenue, New York. Unmindful of the bromidic warning against putting all the eggs in one basket, Kamen has built his world-wide organization on a single character, Mickey. True, the Disney inkpot and facile pen produce other members of Mickey's family (Minnie, Pluto Pup, Donald Duck, Horace Horsecollar, Clara, Cluck, Three Little Pigs). But Mickey stays far enough ahead to keep it a one-man show.

Glad is Mickey to help anyone with promotion of his wares. Outstanding, perhaps, as a single promotion feature is New York's annual Thanksgiving parade wherein one of Manhattan's leading department stores displayed the genial mouse in proportions fifty feet high. Co-operating in this standout feature were a prominent rubber company and a famous designer of marionettes. Kay Kamen's office contains artists, publicity promotion men, decorators, all ready to aid dealers with sales stimulating plans and campaigns.

Under Lowenthal's Wing
Tribune People—heart warming, courageous, modish, loveable, raucous, futile—but business getters all

Buster Brown takes a picture of his dog, Tige, with his own camera.

Mickey Mouse drummer. Minnie dances to his tune on the box.

Lionel Mickey Mouse handcar.

• Lionel Discharge from Receivership Proves Real Drama in Business

> **Federal Judge Proclaims Redemption of Leading Train Makers "Most Successful in History of New Jersey Courts"; Famous News Commentators on Radio Single It Out as Day's Business Achievement; Nation's Greatest Newspapers and News Weeklies Feature Story on Front Page and Comment Editorially —Receivers Pay Claims of $296,197 and Turn Back to Company Assets of $1,900,000.**

THE curtain has just rung down on perhaps the outstanding romance of the vanishing business depression. The principal actor is the Lionel Corporation, makers of Lionel Trains, and so conspicuous was its performance in extricating itself from receivership that Federal Judge Guy L. Fake in the United States District Court at Newark was moved to comment that it "was probably the most successful receivership in the history of the New Jersey courts." In discharging the Lionel Corporation from receivership, the court praised the management and vision of the receivers, Worcester Bouck and Mandel Frankel. The receivers paid $296,197 in claims and turned back to the

company assets of $1,900,000, putting the Lionel Corporation in one of the soundest positions of all manufacturing institutions, volume considered.

But the salient details give but a faint glimpse of the drama that preceded and followed receivership.

When the Lionel Corporation went into receivership in May, 1934, it did not "bog down." If anything, receivership served as a spur to its initiative, creative genius and imagination. Under the direction of Mr. Caruso, in charge of all production, the factory set to work and evolved the first authentic scale model of the Union Pacific's famous streamline train. That caught the imagination and business foresight of the trade, and orders for this model rolled in on Lionel. Not only that, but it dramatically improved its entire train line, introducing new combinations, new motors, new colors, new values and enhancing the salability of the line immeasurably. How accurately the Lionel

management had read the desires of trade and public alike can be seen in the history of sales. Lionel has been in business for more than 35 years, but never in its history has it enjoyed so great a December sales volume as in 1934.

But the climax to all its thinking came in August. It completed a contract with Walt Disney, the father of Mickey and Minnie Mouse, whereby it would produce these national joy-bringers in mechanical and electrical toys. The idea of Mickey and Minnie Mouse pumping away on miles of track was a smashing triumph. An action toy centered around this beloved couple swept the toy world. Orders for this toy, which retailed at a dollar, exceeded 350,000, and although the great Lionel factories at Irvington, N. J., worked night and day seven days a week, their production was not equal to the vast tide of demand.

Produced for the holiday trade, the Lionel Mickey and Minnie Mouse toy has

turned into a brisk all-year-round seller, and in many stores is the life of the toy department.

"Now we have gone one step further," said Mr. Cowen, president of the company. "For years there have been candy rabbits, chocolate rabbits, fluffy rabbits for Easter, but never a real rabbit toy. So we conceived the Peter Rabbit Chickmobile. This toy consists of a Peter Rabbit on a car, pumping it madly as it races around a circular track or across a straightaway. On the forepart of the car is a quaint basket which can be filled with Easter eggs. This ingenious and amusing toy enables the toy department to partici-

pate for the first time in the profits from heavy Easter spending. The Peter Rabbit Chickmobile has been received as enthusiastically by the trade as Mickey and Minnie Mouse and orders are pouring in."

In the story of Lionel's ingenuity the newspapers, magazines and radio commentators found human material to send to the four corners of the earth. Scarcely had Judge Fake's words become official record than Lionel's story was front page news.

Both Lowell Thomas and Edwin C. Hill took time out on the radio from discussing world affairs to talk about Lionel's Mickey and Minnie Mouse, and its streamline train. Into more than 20,000,000 homes was broadcast Lionel's enthralling business story.

For 1935, Lionel has plans as dramatic, as fascinating as those which rode the leader of the toy train industry out of receivership and to its greatest sales peak since 1930, which was its banner year.

• Halsam's New 1935 Lines Ready for Display

When the Halsam Products Company contracted with the Walt Disney Enterprises for the exclusive use of Mickey Mouse characters on their Block, Checker and Dominoe lines, and showed a line of 50c and $1.00 numbers last year, it was in line with their established policy of constantly striving to give their trade up-to-the-minute newness and exclusiveness.

Mickey Mouse blocks met with such enthusiastic buyer reception and proved such popular sellers that Halsam has extended this line to include several numbers in the lower price retail ranges.

This is but one of the many new features that Halsam is bringing out for this year's trade, all of which will be on display at their salesrooms in the Toy Center Building in New York City.

New Toys and Toy News

Mickey saves Lionel from bankruptcy. *Toys and Novelties*, February 1935.

Mickey and Minnie dance on the piano while Horace and Clarabelle help with the music.

Donald Ducks in metal, celluloid, and cast iron.

Mice in celluloid.

Mickey Mouse ball trap game, with Horace, Clarabelle, Pluto and, of course, Minnie. From France.

The Most Sensational Seller in Years!

MICKEY MOUSE

All Velvet including the profits!

	Doz.		Doz.
88/1411—4¼″ Felt	$4.25	88/1430—10½″ Velvet	$19.80
88/1416—6½″ Velvet	$7.80	88/1436—12½″ Velvet	$27.00
88/1423—8¼″ Velvet	$13.50	88/1448—16¾″ Velvet	$42.00

Velvet Hand Mickey Mouse, 79/88/424, 8½″, $ 7.80 Doz.
Record Mickey Mouse, 88/420, 7″, $18.00 "
PULL TOY

TERMS: NET 30 DAYS

In Stock for Immediate Delivery

Our line of newest creations is most comprehensive, including Kangaroo with young, Siamese Cat, Dicky Bear Rattler —just a few of the many innovations.

Send for our latest catalogue describing the leading line of animals.

MARGARETE STEIFF & CO., INC. 44-60 East 23rd Street NEW YORK CITY

Toys & Novelties Nov 1931

Popeye Cowboy
The One Man Rodeo

Here is a 50c retailer that's going places this year if the Toy Fair response is a sound indication! Popeye is tossed up and down as the nag gallops along with plenty of sound, action and sales appeal.

Write for 1937 Catalog

FISHER-PRICE
East Aurora, New York
Suite 417, Fifth Avenue Building
New York City

Chein Forges Ahead

J. Chein & Co., well known through the manufacture of their line of "Hercules" Metal Toys, which includes such items as the "Peggy Jane" sail boat, Ferris wheels, jazz bands and trucks, are

also producers of trick match boxes, sparkling-toys, etc. They are now also showing a very big line of Popeye, Krazy Kat and Ignatz Mouse characters in the form of mechanical and wood jointed toys retailing from 10c to $1. Popeye is known to the children throughout the United States through the Popeye cartoon published in the syndicated daily

Toys & Novelties Nov 1932

and Sunday newspapers. Krazy Kat and Ignatz Mouse also appear in the cartoon sections of the syndicated newspapers, the former appearing on the screen as well.

They are also making an electrical demonstration for their No. 255 Popeye Bag Puncher and No. 256 Popeye Heavy Hitter.

Toys & Novelties Nov 193

Advertisements for the beautiful Stieff dolls: Popeye Cowboy, Popeye With Punching Bag, and Ignatz Mouse on Tricycle.

94

Mickey Mouse velvet dolls from
M. Stieff and Company.

Giant Mickey Mouse bisque with
movable arms and two smaller mice
toothbrush holders.

Mickey Mouse Toreador and
Ferdinand the Bull.

Mickey wooden jointed doll, pencil box,
noisemaker, and pencil sharpeners.

Pinocchio and Joe Carioca wind-up dolls from V.B. & Cie, France.

Climbing Mickey Mouse, bank, flashlight, barometer, and a rare, early toothy metal Mickey from Spain.

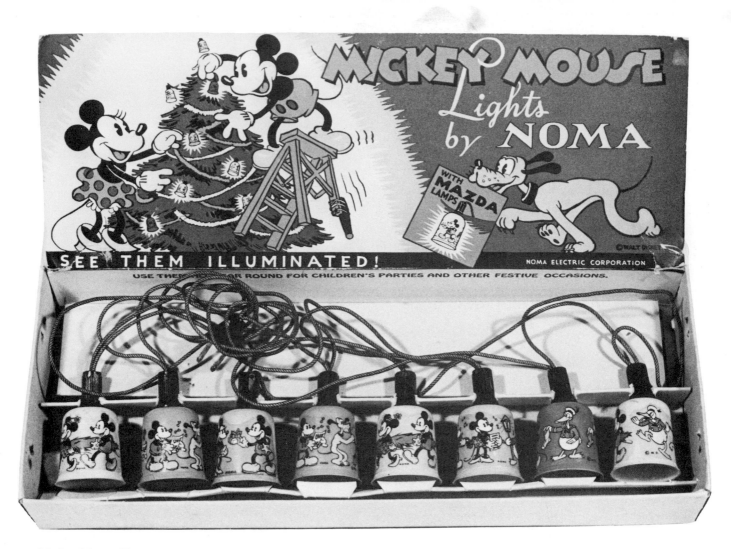

Mickey Mouse Christmas-tree
lights.

Mickey Mouse radio, 1933; and the
rare Three Little Pigs and Big Bad
Wolf Radio.

A Radio by the Three Little Pigs

The famous "Three Little Pigs" have
decided to have a radio of their very own
design, so that children from six to sixty
can enjoy the pleasure and amusements
that they create. No more struggles for
the radio set between children who want
to listen to juvenile programs and parents
who want adult entertainment.

A radio receiver designed expressly for
the children's room, with three little pigs

cavorting on the grille, has been produced by Hudson-Ross, Inc., of Chicago.
Although compact and extremely low-
priced, this new children's radio combines
unusually fine reception with simplicity
of operation.

Now let the sirens scream and the villains be confounded to their heart's content—in the children's room. Papa can
relax in comfort in the living room and
enjoy his baseball scores or his lectures
on relativity.

The Seven Dwarfs by Seiberling, handsomely molded into solid-rubber figures.

Donald in the Boat; and Minnie Pushing a Baby Carriage. Photograph courtesy of Bob Lyons.

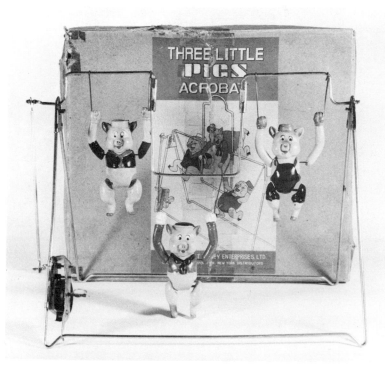

Three Little Pigs Acrobats.

Advertisement for Mickey and Minnie Mouse toys. George Borgfeldt & Company, January 1931.

Advertisement for Ignatz Mouse and Krazy Kat dolls. Knickerbocker Toy Company, August 1931. Notice the close family resemblance to Mickey Mouse.

Popeyes—in the Barrel, on the Roof (Popeye and Olive Oyl Jiggers), on the Delivery Motorcycle; and Wimpy and Barnacle Bill walking figures.

Popeye the Sailor, called by collectors Popeye in the Rowboat. Perhaps the rarest and most wanted of all Popeye toys.

Popeye in the Airplane. Photograph courtesy of Bob Lyons.

Chalk figure of Popeye, ten inches in height. A striking pose.

Charlie Chaplin tin and cast-iron wind-up walking figure; Whistling Charlie, and Charlie in celluloid.

The Toonerville Trolley tin
wind-up with the "Skipper"
driving. Cast Toonerville Trolley in
pot metal.

Little Orphan Annie Big Little
Book; a very Art Deco celluloid
brooch with Annie and Sandy;
Little Orphan Annie Dime Bank;
Walking Sandy (with his doghouse);
and Little Orphan Annie Skipping
Rope.

Annie and Sandy on wind-up
platforms in celluloid.

Superman group: Wood jointed doll by Ideal; Superman racing the airplane; dime bank; wrist watch; and *Superman*, No. 1.

Henry and Henrietta, Travelers; Henry on the Elephant's Trunk; celluloid wind-up; and a molded Henry rubber doll.

Moon Mullins and Kayo on a Handcar; and the Smitty Scooter.

The Amos 'n' Andy Fresh Air
Taxicab and walking figures.
Louis Marx, 1930.

Ham and Sam, the Minstrel Team.

Marx Merrymakers Mouse Band, a combination of Negro minstrel, Mickey Mouse, and Art Deco.

Barney Goodle and his famous horse, Sparkplug. Tin wind-up by Nifty and jointed wood dolls by Schoenhut, 1924.

Li'l Abner and His Dogpatch Band.

Little Max Speshul #1. That's Joe Palooka and his fight manager, Knobby Walsh, on the side of the scooter.

Dagwood the Driver; and Harold Lloyd on the Telephone.

109

The McCarthy Strut walking figure and the Charlie McCarthy in His Benzine Buggy.

Joe Penner and His Duck Goo Goo; and the Lone Ranger Hi-Yo Silver.

110

Felix the Cat on the Scooter tin wind-up; "Worried" Felix celluloid doll; Felix composition doll, jointed and twelve inches in height; Felix the Movie Cat sparkler.

Advertisement of Felix the Cat toys. *Toys and Novelties*, January 1931.

Howdy Doody Clock-A-Doodle. Wind it up and Howdy Doody swings on his swing, Flub-a-Dub eats, and the clock hands speed around and chime at every quarter hour. The lithography is superb and colorful.

The complete set of Captain Marvel (The Big Red Cheese, to comic-book collectors) Lightning Racing Cars.

The Betty Boop "Nodder." Wind her up and a rubber motor "nods" her hand from side to side. Two Betty Boop dolls, each wearing handsome Betty Boop necklaces made in Czechoslovakia during the early nineteen thirties.

The Lone Ranger and his pal
Tonto, with handmade clothes and
cast-iron pistols. Twenty inches in
height and pure 1938 doll
craftsmanship.

Aggie, Reg'lar Fellers Girl; Bugs
Bunny cast-iron still bank; and a
rare Mr. Peanuts wind-up walking
figure.

Dick Tracy Police Station. Wind it
up and the Dick Tracy car roars out
from the station with siren
screaming.

The Flash Gordon Space Pistol, a
handsome, abstract design. Pull the
trigger and a siren sounds.

Andy Gump in the 348 Car, in cast iron by Arcade. The smaller one is a Tootsietoy. Photograph courtesy of Bob Lyons.

Lionel Donald Duck Rail Car and Lionel Santa Car with Mickey Mouse in His Gift Pack. 1935-1936.

The very rare and handsome Barney Google and Sparkplug Scooter Race, 1924, with Walking Felix watching.

Mortimer Snerd car, Popeye wood-jointed doll by Ideal and Popeye Express.

4
Comic-Character Timepieces

It's not just the Mickey Mouse Watch. In fact, inexpensive comic-character timepieces began almost one hundred years ago. They originated in the United States and Germany. These animated-dial clocks were extremely popular and depicted Negroes with rolling eyes, the daring young man on the trapeze, ladies with fans or playing mandolins, shoeshine boys plying their trade, an old man feeding his pet poodle while he performs tricks, and many other fascinating subjects.

The earliest dated clock of this type was made by the Waterbury Clock Company and was patented September 11, 1877. Curiously, it was this same company that produced the first Mickey Mouse Watch fifty-six years later. These animated-dial clocks are fun to watch and were very cleverly made. But the mechanisms were difficult to repair, and since it was a cheap, inaccurate clock, they were thrown away; therefore, they are difficult to find and command very high prices.

Most had single animation, but some had two or more figures moving on the dial. Some were alarm and some were nonalarm, but all were called "tin-can clocks" because their cases were shaped like tin cans. They are difficult to find in good condition because the dials are paper, printed in bright colors that easily fade, stain, and are susceptible to browning and crinkling at the edges. Most of the cases were made from brass and crack due to the hardness in the original

forming process or dent easily because of the thin metal used. Although Junghans in Germany and Waterbury in the United States produced a wide variety, few have survived. Museums, clock collectors, and particularly toy- and mechanical-bank collectors, those interested in "things that move," are the most avid searchers and seekers.

It was these clocks that began the manufacture and marketing of character timepieces, mostly for children, and they are closely related to the toys of the period. The most rare and most wanted among collectors is the unusual Junghans Man on the Trapeze Clock. The figure of the trapeze performer offers a variety of trapeze tricks, which is different from the other animated types that present single action, repeated and continuous. Sometimes he pauses, sometimes he does a single somersault, and when the clock is fully wound, he may do a double somersault. It is fascinating to watch, and as one becomes hypnotized, it appears that *he* is making the decisions, not the intermittent clock mechanism inside.

The Bixby's Best Clock is equally rare, stamped on the back, patented March 2, 1886. It was one of the first animated-dial clocks to include advertising and is called among collectors a "crossover" because it is wanted by several different groups of collectors: advertising, clock, toy and mechanical bank, which increases the heat of competition. It is a beautiful period piece depicting a fashionably dressed young man and his girl friend having their boots shined. The brush of the shoeshine boy moves back and forth, while in the background a young shoeshine girl shines the well-dressed lady's boots, and a large bottle of Bixby's Best Shoe Polish is shown.

During this period the Germans were intrigued by the very existence of a black person. There were none in Germany, so they imagined their own, with Aryan features but jet black skin, in advertising, games, toys, packaging, the graphic arts, and, of course, animated-dial clocks. The one shown is the Negro Mammy Clock. It has a loud alarm, her eyes roll back and forth in delight, and she is dressed in white pearls, gold earrings, a red bandanna, blue dress, and a wide red-lipped, white-toothed smile—very wild and colorful!

Occupational clocks were also quite popular before the turn of the century. The Waterbury Clock Company in 1887 produced the Druggist Clock, which has a handsome full-color dial showing the interior of an early druggist's shop. The druggist, with handlebar moustache and string tie, is busy grinding with a mortar and pestle. Seth Thomas, a long-familiar name in American watchmaking, contributed the Blacksmith Clock, which has a bearded blacksmith, hammer in hand, pounding on his anvil.

Lady With Mandolin is a very early German clock set in an ornate wooden case and has an antique and charming appearance that would enhance the decor of any home.

But these are just a few of the many different animated-dial clocks that were made. There are almost no records other than the clocks themselves, since most of the companies have long departed from the marketplace and seldom had catalogs or used advertising. Waterbury, Junghans, Seth Thomas, Ingraham, and Ansonia produced the majority of them prior to the turn of the century, later to be followed by Lux and United Clock Company. Clock manufacturers have always comprised a fragmented industry of many small factories and just a few large one and the small seldom put their name on their creations. While watching and enjoying the animation of these early character timepieces one can imagine the delight experienced by the designer as he also watched the first movements of his ingenious mechanism bring to life the Negro mammy, the shoeshine boy, the blacksmith, the druggist, and the daring young man on the flying trapeze.

In 1880 two brothers, sons of a Michigan farmer, came to New York and started a business marketing a variety of inexpensive articles for which they sensed a popular demand. Most popular was the line of Waterbury animated-dial clocks. All of the items that they merchandised had, however, a common feature —they all sold for a dollar. Since the Waterbury clocks sold well at that price, they decided to try to make a rugged and accurate pocket watch at the same price. Up to that time, watches had always been expensive, since they required a considerable amount of hand labor.

Robert Ingersoll, aged twenty-one, and his brother Charles, aged fifteen, bought the smallest pocket watch they could find, redesigned the case to a dial diameter of two inches, and tried to get it manufactured. Eventually the Waterbury Clock Company, impressed with their clock salesmanship, and who were producing a small pocket watch of a similar kind, accepted an order from the Ingersolls for 12,000 pocket watches—but only on the condition that they were to be taken and paid for within one year.

The first Ingersoll pocket watch, which they called the Universal, was brought to the market in 1892 and it sold with a large watch chain for a dollar and a half. They sold the 12,000 watches in one year, with much difficulty. Three years later, Robert Ingersoll achieved his ambition to mass-produce a pocket watch for a dollar. Robert Ingersoll, super salesman, had achieved a considerable marketing feat. He had introduced into a field formerly dominated by craftsmanship and hand finishing the principle of mass production of identical and interchangeable parts. He saw the potential market for his dollar watch and he was certainly one of the pioneers of the mass-marketing principle—the selling of large quantities of the same item, at a low fixed price, for a small unit profit.

In order to convince the public that they were getting their money's worth and to assure them that their watches could be repaired in case of a failure, he guaranteed them for a year. He took the responsibility for any fault of workmanship or material, and his guarantee was in the form of a circular disc of paper slipped into the back of the watch. Each disc contained the guarantee, Robert Ingersoll's signature, and the number. And yes, there are collectors who just collect "watch papers."

In 1893 the Ingersolls exhibited at the Chicago World's Fair, and the first commemorative pocket watch was presented: the Chicago World's Fair Watch. It was a poor attempt, with no decoration on the dial and a roughly embossed back, but it sold well and so did their other watches. Ninety thousand in that year, and only two years later sales totaled the million mark.

Robert Ingersoll's first sales trip to England was in 1899, during which he secured an order from Symond's London stores for 1 million of his dollar watches, which were completely sold out in three years. Included in this order was the South African War Souvenir Watch, with a colored pictorial dial showing Queen Victoria, the Prince of Wales, and several war leaders. There is only one in the world that has been saved, and that is in the Ingersoll museum in London.

Sales went well, and a branch was opened in Chicago, and in three years it increased its volume of business twenty-four fold! These successes decided the Ingersoll brothers to open an office in London, and from the first year sales grew from 12,000 to over 3 million, and their advertising proclaimed: "Ingersoll —the watch that made the dollar famous!" A considerable advertising campaign was begun with full-page advertisements in magazines and in the penny weekly papers, but the most prominent feature of the sales campaign was the introduction of point-of-sale advertising supplied in showcards, watch displays, and signs offered directly to the retailer. Robert Ingersoll told his customers: "We will sell our watches for you"— and he did. The direct response from his advertising was considerable, and his salesmen started taking really big orders. By the end of 1906 the total number of Ingersoll watches sold is recorded at 15 million. The Waterbury factory in Connecticut, producing Ingersoll watches, had grown to nearly twenty times its original size and covered a floor area of ten acres.

In 1901 at the Pan-American Exposition in Buffalo, New York, the first well-designed American commemorative pocket watch was introduced by Ingersoll. The North American and South American continents were pictured as angelic women holding hands joining the continents in friendship, and the metal back was deeply embossed with a similar design. They are very rare, difficult to find, and are prized among collectors. In 1904 at the St. Louis World's Fair another well-designed American commemorative watch was introduced by Ingersoll. The colorful flag of the fair was on the dial and on the back, die-embossed, was the Cascades building, the outdoor triumph of that fair. It sold well, and the selling of commemorative watches and the introduction of new models at expositions and fairs became a standard

merchandising tool for the company, culminating in the very first introduction to the public of the Mickey Mouse wristwatch, pocket watch, electric and wind-up clocks at the Chicago World's Fair in 1933.

But it was at the St. Louis World's Fair that the very first comic-character watch was born. Buster Brown originated as a comic strip in 1902 created by Richard Fenton Outcault and achieved immediate popularity. Buster was a mischievous kid, who with his sister Mary Jane and his dog Tige, were the favorites of all who read the funnies. Outcault, who patterned these cartoon characters after his own son, daughter, and dog, set up a booth at the St. Louis Fair and sold to any merchant who came along the trademark rights to Buster Brown. The prices apparently ranged from $5 to $1,000, depending on the cartoonist's whim and the size of the company involved in the transaction. He had tried a similar pattern in marketing the trademark for The Yellow Kid, an earlier creation. But here it went wild! The result was a deluge of Buster Brown products, ranging from harmonicas, toys, games, banks, to soap, and including a soft drink, coffee, wheat flour, and even apples.

A Buster Brown nationwide sales promotion began, with groups of midgets, dressed like Buster in Little Lord Fauntleroy clothes and accompanied by dogs that looked like Tige, touring the country between 1904 and 1915. They played to audiences in rented theatres, department stores, on the vaudeville circuits, and in shoe stores. John A. Bush, a rising young sales executive with the Brown Shoe Company, saw the value of the Buster Brown name as a juvenile-shoe trademark. He persuaded the company to purchase the rights to the name from Outcault, and the brand was introduced to the public in 1904 during the St. Louis World's Fair. The Brown Shoe Company— which was named for its founder, George Warren Brown, and not for Buster—promoted the brand on a national scale and today there are over 2,500 Buster Brown Shoe Stores throughout the U.S.A.

Robert Ingersoll immediately visualized a new market: inexpensive pocket watches for children. It was a quick deal: Bush and Ingersoll and Outcault. Ingersoll would manufacture, Outcault would design the face, and Bush would give away a watch with a pair of shoes (working the wholesale cost of the watch into the retail price of the shoes).

Generations of boys and girls, fans of Buster, acquired these watches and treasure them to this day as nostalgic heirlooms. The popularity of the Buster Brown Pocket Watch has never stopped. The Buster

Brown Textile Company (not related in any way to the Brown Shoe Company) recently purchased a Buster Brown Wristwatch in large quantities for nationwide distribution, and the Buster Brown Shoe empire is pursuing a similar course. The first comic-character pocket watch is a highly prized collector's item today because it was the first and because it is a "crossover." Collectors of advertising memorabilia also want it because encircling the colorful figures of Buster and Tige is: "Buster Brown Blue Ribbon Shoes for Boys and Girls."

In 1929, the Ansonia Clock Company manufactured a plain silver and black watch for Buster Brown Shoes, and as late as 1971 the most beautiful of all the Buster Brown watches was made. The face of the watch was "picked up" from a 1908 colorful advertising button that depicted a devilish Buster and a wicked Tige. It was packaged with a pendant chain and wristband and could be used as a pocket watch, pendant, or wristwatch. It was marketed in department stores, and eventually the design was adopted by the Buster Brown Shoe Company and became a point-of-sale clock harmonizing with their new nostalgic decor in their stores. (It is a beautiful watch; I know, I designed it for them!)

But back at Ingersoll important changes were taking place. Growth became super growth! The young salesmen who once were permitted to buy 12,000 watches as a first order with difficult terms bought the factory. In 1914 Ingersoll bought the New England Watch Company, which had been previously known as the Waterbury Clock Company. By 1918 Ingersoll owned four factories. By the end of World War I the company had made over 50 million watches, and they were trading with customers speaking twenty languages.

Among their well-known purchasers were Mark Twain, J. Pierpont Morgan, Thomas Edison, and Glenn Curtis, the flyer; even Theodore Roosevelt remarked that when he went to Africa on a hunting trip he was recognized as the man who came from "the land where Ingersolls are made." Between 1918 and 1922 a line of alarm clocks was added, and the simple pin-lever movements developed for them became the prototypes for the later Mickey Mouse and Big Bad Wolf clocks. These movements were so reliable that during World War I they were approved and bought by the United States and English armed services.

In 1922, however, the connection between the Ingersolls and the manufacturer was severed. The Waterbury Clock Company bought Robert H. Ingersoll & Bro. and continued the business as the Ingersoll-Waterbury Company. Robert, who had not enjoyed the best of health, died six years later in Denver, Colorado, but Charles Ingersoll outlived him by another twenty years and was killed in an automobile accident in 1948. In London the Ingersoll Watch Company Limited went on merchandising as before and developed a chain of shops in which both retailers and the public could purchase the full range of Ingersoll watches.

Accurate facts concerning the history and origin of the fabulously successful Mickey Mouse watches are difficult to find, because a flood in the Waterbury area in the mid-nineteen fifties washed away all of the factory's records and the Disney Archives were started as late as 1951 and little was saved previous to that date. Worse, although Ingersoll Ltd. in London has a museum, a letter from them dated January 9, 1974, runs:

> It was nice to hear from you again but I am sorry to say we have had a series of rather unfortunate mishaps. The new advertising manager cleared out all the old files and destroyed much correspondence, and was also very careless in his arrangements concerning our collection.

Unfortunately, this is typical of almost all companies that produce comic-character collectibles: they save nothing. The primary sources of information are the collectors, catalogs, and advertisements.

The most definitive source has always been the reporter on the spot. As stated in *Playthings Magazine*, August 1933, by their "News . . . Notes" reporter:

MICKEY MOUSE TELLS TIME

Mickey Mouse, who has proven himself as able a contributor to toy department volume as he has an accomplished and delightful artist on the moving picture screen, now turns up in a new role as official timekeeper for childhood. On a new line of Mickey Mouse timepieces brought out by Ingersoll-Waterbury Co., Waterbury, Conn., Mickey's own hands tell the time. In doing so they get into a hundred amusing positions. They give animation to the Mickey figure printed on the dial. . . . So ingeniously have these watches been conceived and so attractive is the Mickey personality that there is little doubt that these new watches and clocks bid fair to be high on the list for fall and Christmas sales in toy departments. Already many of the leading department stores are displaying full lines and have found it necessary to re-order not once, but several times. Already there is a forecast of really important volume. Ingersoll reports that production has reached more than five thousand pieces a day, and that production is considerably behind orders, though it is hoped that production can be stepped up within the next several weeks.

There are four pieces in the Mickey Mouse line. A pocket watch and fob retailing at $1.50; a wrist watch at $2.75; an electric clock at $1.50 and a spring wound clock at $1.50. All are packed in typically Mickey Mouse cartons exploiting the full popularity of Walt Disney's famous characters, Clarabelle Cow, Pluto the Pup and Horace Horsecollar. Arguments between the toy buyers and jewelry buyers as to which department this merchandise rightfully belongs are already on the horizon. In fact they have come and gone in several stores—the settlement being that both departments will carry them, resulting in increased business all around. Some indications of the rapidity with which Mickey Mouse timepieces are finding a place in the American public's big warm heart is apparent in the sales figures at the Ingersoll exhibit at the Century of Progress Exposition. Ingersoll has established a miniature factory there, so that people may step up to order a watch, see it made and have it delivered while they wait. A special world's fair watch is the watch being manufactured. But sales of Mickey Mouse watches at the same counter are approximately three times greater.

Ingersoll learned from their success with the Boy Scout watches. They obtained an exclusive contract in perpetuity, forever! and worldwide from Walt Disney Enterprises. They worked an up-front money deal from Sears, Roebuck, which paid for the initial expenses of development, inventory, and advertising. Then, of course, they sold to everyone anywhere.

In terms of design they had also learned to package the watches in attractive boxes that would catch the eye and use related point-of-sale displays. Similar to the Boy Scout watch, they used die-stamped character hands; Mickey Mouse's long arms with yellow gloves were used to tell time, along with a circular, rotating second hand with three small Mickeys on it for animation. As in the movies, Mickey moved!

The Mickey Mouse wristwatch, pocket watch, wind-up and electric clocks were Ingersoll's first attempts at providing a complete line of character timepieces. It was successful beyond their wildest dreams and may have prevented their bankruptcy during the dark depression days. The demand was so great that weeks before Christmas, retailers were completely sold out. Adults wore them because the reliable pin-lever movements were accurate and, developed during World War I for the Army and Navy, they were cheaper than ordinary adult watches, and they were considered chic long before the expression high camp had been invented.

The wristwatch, today called Mickey Number One among collectors, was circular, had beautiful nineteen-thirties Mickey graphics, with well-proportioned Mickey hour and minute arms and the delightful, rotating three-Mickeys-chasing-one-another second hand. Attached was a beautiful metal-link band with our hero on the first two links, or a leather band with two stapled-on Mickeys.

Later, production had "Made in U.S.A." (as a precaution against possible Japanese reproductions) on the face; the earliest ones did not, making them the more desirable for collectors. They were made primarily for children, but artists, writers, and stage and screen personalities wore them also, and there were astute collectors of Mickey Mouse watches even in 1933.

Boys in the thirties went to school wearing white shirts, ties, shined shoes, and suits with vests. Therefore, a kid's pocket watch was not absurd. The pocket watch had the same face design as the wristwatch and was sold with an attached watch fob. The back of the watch had a die-debossed figure of Mickey, two circles near the rim, and the legend: "Ingersoll Mickey Mouse." This was done to discourage cheaper Japanese production, prevent unauthorized reproductions, and to make the timepiece more attractive.

A word of caution, because of the high prices an original Mickey Mouse pocket watch commands today: Before you buy one, turn the watch over; if it doesn't have the die-debossed back, it is a counterfeit. The crooks cannot afford the cost of a debossing die and still make a profit. Try to buy one in the original decorated box because this would also guarantee its authenticity, since the cost of duplicating the boxes is astronomical. In fact, new collectors should follow the rule of collecting character watches *only* in the original boxes, to guarantee authenticity and mint condition.

Among "Mouse junkies," the Mickey Mouse Electric Clock in the original box is considered to be the finest expression of Disney commercial comic art. One was sold recently for $1,000. The box has a red background with all the members of the group—Mickey, Minnie, Pluto, Horace, and Clarabelle—and a large pop-up flap of Mickey holding a sign reading, "Ingersoll Mickey Mouse Clock." The clock is green, four and one-quarter inches square, the top and sides have a paper decal with all of the characters, and the rotating second hand is a cut-out two-inch-high metal Mickey that is one of the best artistic renditions of Mickey Mouse ever made commercially.

The wind-up clock utilized the same box as the electric clock, with decal and case, but the face has a ratlike Mickey with a large circular rotating second hand with the three Mickeys eternally chasing one another. These four timepieces comprised the entire first line of Ingersoll Mickeys and are a must find among character-watch collectors.

Perhaps the rarest of all Mickeys is the small desk clock with the same design as the wind-up clock, but only about two inches square and with a very Art Deco base. It must have had a very short production run, since only one of these has ever been found.

Although the clocks sold well, Ingersoll discovered that they had made one mistake—no alarm. So in 1934 they produced the first Mickey Mouse alarm clock, and the Sears, Roebuck catalog of that year described it:

> No trick getting up mornings with Mickey Mouse on the job to waken you. Mickey Mouse with his head wagging tells time with his hands. Genuine Ingersoll clock, 30 hour movement.
> Mickey Mouse Alarm Clock....$1.39

This was the Mickey Mouse "Wagging Head" Animated Alarm Clock. It had the first circular case, and a special movement was developed for the animation of the head. Very few have been found, probably because the works were difficult to repair, and since the price was cheap, most were thrown away.

The fantastic public demand throughout the United States for Mickey Mouse timepieces caused Ingersoll-Waterbury to remember Ingersoll Ltd. in London. In order to penetrate the world market in a time of high tariff walls, Ingersoll Ltd. was authorized to produce the "English Mickeys." It seems that the English designer could not make up his mind concerning the best Mickey portrayal, so there are variations, but the basics remained: wristwatch, pocket watch, wind-up and electric clocks. At the bottom of each watch face is the word "Foreign" to differentiate from the U.S.A. product.

Two different English Mickey pocket watches were made: the first had a very ratlike, overweight Mickey in a running position and the second had one of the most beautiful pictures of Mickey Mouse ever put on the face of a watch or on anything. Here, Mickey has a five-o'clock shadow, a big grin, a long tail, and is dressed to the nines in upper-class English fashion and sporty orange gloves. The watch faces are made from a high-gloss paper, and the rotating second hand has the three Mickey Mouses chasing one another. The graphics for both are superb, but there are no die-debossed backs. The wristwatch had the same design as the pocket watches, but unlike its American cousin, did not have a decorated wristband. The wind-up clocks were manufactured in two different Mickey styles, but the case, decorative decal, and the movements were the same and quite similar to the U.S.A. Ingersoll originals.

These English Mickeys are extremely rare and very high priced when found. None have been found in the colorful Mickey Mouse decorated boxes. The Ingersoll Ltd. museum in London has two of the pocket watches, only one of the wristwatches has been found, and perhaps six of the clocks are known to be in private collections. Perhaps the most important reason for their worldwide success was that they were the right product at the right time: they were introduced when the Mickey Mouse fad was spiraling due to the popularity of the movies and newspaper cartoons. Two million watches were sold in two years! And this was during the lowest point of the worst depression the world has ever known.

Success generated success and new designs. In the mid-nineteen thirties the Mickey Mouse Lapel Watch was introduced, and among "Mouse junkies" this is considered to be the most beautiful and desirable of all of them. It was a sporty watch intended to fit in the breast pocket of your 1935 double-breasted gangster-style suit. The button on the end of the cord would slip into the buttonhole in the wide lapel, and the watch would dangle down into the pocket. The case was black, and on the back was a handsome picture of Mickey Mouse with a happy expression on his face, running forward to greet you. The colors were bright and the proportions perfect. The face had a smaller Mickey with a long tail and a similar expression of innocence and happiness combined. It was packaged in a blue box with a large colorful picture of Mickey and with a similar cardboard easel-type watch stand.

A companion wristwatch, called the Mickey Mouse Deluxe, appeared and had an oblong case that was chrome plated. The rendition of Mickey was the same as on the lapel watch. The second hand now consisted of the same circle design but with only one mouse on the dial. Among astute collectors the box is wanted more than the watch because the poses of Mickey are great. The front of the box has Mickey Mouse in top hat and cane, wearing his own watch, looking much like Fred Astaire; turn it over and inside is Mickey, tipsy, in the early morning hours after a night on the town, tipping his hat. A later edition of the Deluxe was designed particularly for girls and had a metal wristband with charms attached—figures of Mickey, Minnie, Donald, and others.

These are the most sought Mickey Mouse watches. The pocket watches were discontinued after 1938, and the production of all novelty watches was stopped by the government in 1942, though they were still shown in the Sears, Roebuck and Montgomery Ward catalogs during the war but were stamped "Non-Essential." In the same year U.S. Time Corporation bought the Ingersoll-Waterbury Clock Company and transferred them to a new plant in Middlebury, Connecticut. During the war many American soldiers wore them and at the end of the war sold them to Russian soldiers for $1,000 each, the highest price ever paid for a Mickey Number One!

In November 1946 U.S. Time resumed the manufacture of Mickey Mouse watches. Just clocks and wristwatches, no pocket watches, and the graphics are dubbed by Mouse collectors as "Forties Mickeys." They changed Mickey Mouse from a rat into a little boy. Gone was the pot belly, the pie-cut eyes, the tail, the unique expression that was derived from the early movies. It is ironic that even the name had been changed from Walt Disney Enterprises to Walt Disney Productions. In the early nineteen thirties it was "enterprising," but in the late thirties and early forties it

became just "production." Postwar production consisted mostly of wristwatches in the oblong cases and the Deluxe models that had been adopted in 1937. Gone was the charming, rotating second hand with the chasing Mickeys, and the "U.S. Time" trademark replaced the very well-known "Ingersoll." Nevertheless, the watches were popular in the postwar period, and more than 600,000 were made in 1947 and a million more in 1948 in the Middlebury factory and the new factory in Little Rock, Arkansas. By 1957 the 25-millionth Mickey Mouse watch was sold, and Walt Disney was given a solid-gold Mickey Mouse watch that had been made for him in the Middlebury factory.

Design went from bad to worse. In 1960 Mickey Mouse was removed from his own watch, and only the name "Mickey Mouse" appeared. A market survey concluded that children would not wear the watches with Mickey Mouse's picture on it because other kids would ridicule them and call them babies. This watch is the least collectible of all.

In 1968 a counterrevolution occurred. It was the year of Mickey's fortieth birthday, and Walt Disney Productions solicited various magazines to do a feature article. *Life* Magazine said yes, and in October "Happy 40th Mickey" appeared. A torrent of mail descended on the Walt Disney office in New York. (My name appeared under the picture of my Mickey Mouse collection, and I received two full sacks and had to unlist my phone number!) Timex brought out a new Mickey Mouse wristwatch with Mickey Mouse's nineteen-forties picture on it with thirties-style hands on a wide Mod band. It was 1933 all over again, and the watch sold in the millions. It was soon followed by an electric Mickey wristwatch, assorted clocks, and a beautiful large Minnie Mouse wristwatch (which is considered a collector's item of the future because it is the first: there never was a Minnie Mouse wristwatch in the thirties).

As a result of all this publicity, the early watches became high-camp collectibles. Soupy Sales, Carol Burnett, and Johnny Carson zoom-lensed them on nationwide television, and the rush up into attics and down into cellars to find that old Mickey Number One began. In 1971 Elgin National Industries obtained the worldwide rights from Walt Disney Productions for Disney-character timepieces and through their Bradley division is currently marketing a complete line of wristwatches, pocket watches, and clocks. It was lucrative for Elgin because the contract included an exclusive franchise to have the only retail watch stores in Disneyland and Disneyworld, and they could sell their standard timepieces as well. And, for a short time during the recent stock-market crash, their stock soared just because of Mickey Mouse! The white heat of demand, however, brought out the crooks, and unauthorized Mickey Mouse versions appeared, and Disney's army of lawyers with the help of local policemen went to battle to protect their licensees.

Collectors hoped that Elgin would reproduce the thirties-style Mickey, and so did Elgin, because their market surveys showed that the public would prefer it. But the contract stated that Walt Disney Productions would supply and approve all artwork. Perhaps to reinforce the legal strength of their copyright, WDP insisted on the nineteen-forties style. But thirties Mickeys were breaking out all over, particularly on millions of T-shirts all over the world. Cash registers rang up a thirties-style tune, and Elgin was permitted to put the early Mickey Mouse graphics on some of their watches. So Mickey is back today where he began yesterday. Consumers dictated the art they wanted with the force of their money. Although Seiko in Japan and Bayard in France and many contract manufacturers throughout the world have manufactured a wide variety of Mickey timepieces, today only Bradley remains. It is hoped that the Mickey Mouse watch is institutionalized and will go on and on forever, but only time will tell.

While the American wage earner was trying to keep the wolf away from the door during the depression year of 1934, Disney released the very popular film *The Big Bad Wolf and the Three Little Pigs*. It was in color and so was the flood of merchandise that followed. Again, Ingersoll designed a group of timepieces, worked them into the Sears mail-order catalog, priced them reasonably, and packaged them attractively: a wristwatch, an animated alarm clock, and an animated pocket watch. Although today's collectors call them Big Bad Wolf Watches, Disney never did. They used the victims' names and not that of the villain. The Big Bad Wolf was really scary and controversial, because in the original film he was portrayed in one short segment as a Jewish peddler (since then that section has been cut out), and there was protest. Earlier there had been the Fagin-like character called The Shyster, who appeared with Peg Leg Pete in the comic strips and, of course, robbed orphans, but was always foiled by Mickey Mouse. So the timepieces were named The Three Little Pigs

Alarm Clock, Pocket Watch, and Wristwatch, respectively, on the very beautifully designed boxes that contained them. But this conservative display of commercial good taste didn't stick, because the mail orders that came into Sears were for Big Bad Wolf watches. So Sears was forced to change the name in their catalogs and advertisements.

To complete this group of three in the original boxes is a collector's dream! With each tick of the pocket watch the Big Bad Wolf winks in near-psychotic hunger at the Three Little Pigs. The weird winking eye combined with his sharp teeth and open mouth, and the terrified pigs, all on a bright red background, is pure nightmare. Die debossed on the back of the watch is:

MAY THE
BIG BAD
WOLF
Never come to
your door
Walt Disney

plus a brick wall with a steel door secured with iron hinges! A leather strap attached to the watch sports an aluminum watch fob depicting the pigs on piano, flute, and violin playing their song "Who's Afraid of the Big Bad Wolf." All . . . all for $1.39!

The wristwatch pictures a wolf without hope. The three pigs are dancing on his head, and one is beating his bulbous nose with his violin, out of range of his sharp teeth. It has a metal wristband, the left link is an open-toothed wolf trying to bite his way through the watch to the link on the right side containing three terrified pigs.

The Ingersoll Three Little Pigs Alarm Clock is animated, and the ferocious jaws of the Big Bad Wolf open and close with each tick of the clock, while his yellow gloves on hairy arms tell the hour and minute. The case and dial are bright red, and the little pigs are shown in lifelike colors. The same clock movement is used that was developed for the Mickey Mouse "Wagging Head" Alarm Clock. The pop-up box is even more rare than the clock. The pigs are dancing in safety above the open jaws of the wolf, and three of the sides of the box depict scenes from the movie. They comprise a spectacular trio, but one word of caution: keep them away from sunlight; the red background on the dials fades into a pink-white quickly, and the money value of the timepiece drops straight down.

In 1934 a new Disney character appeared for the first time in *The Wise Little Hen* and achieved instant popularity: Donald Duck. Ingersoll and Disney assumed that success would also be instantaneous and as big as Mickey's, but for some undetermined reason Donald Duck merchandise never made it big. Ingersoll produced only two items, the Ingersoll Donald Duck Number One wristwatch, which had the same movement as the Mickey Mouse Number One, worked Mickey Mouse into the watch using the three-mice-chasing-one-another second hand, and attached the original Mickey Mouse wristband. The production run must have been very small since so few have been found.

It wasn't until 1939 that the Donald Duck Pocket Watch appeared, and even that had a decal picture of Mickey Mouse on the back to help push it past the cash register. It was advertised as the Mickey-Donald Watch and is dated on the face "1939." The only Donald Duck Alarm Clock known was manufactured in France by the Bayard Company, which stopped its production in 1969. After World War II, U.S. Time produced several versions of the New Donald Duck Wristwatch, a Daisy Duck, and even a Louie Duck Wristwatch, but these never equaled Mickey in sales.

The girls were not to be ignored, and the hope was that the new films *Snow White, Cinderella,* and *Alice in Wonderland* would spur sales. Alas, the boxes were better designed than the watches. The Cinderella Wristwatch is attached to a beautiful glass slipper (plastic, of course) held with elastic inside a handsome box that portrays scenes from the movie, but the watch face is of poor design. The earliest Snow White Wristwatch is better in that it has in full colors a dainty Snow White lifting her skirts in a curtsy. Inside, the box is a reproduction of a movie cel used in making the film and is quite attractive. *Alice in Wonderland* was not a money-maker for the studio, and the Alice watch is rare because few were made. It was an animated watch, with the Mad Hatter rocking back and forth on the second hand. Alice is well depicted in full color, and it is an attractive collector's item.

In 1948, for Mickey Mouse's twentieth birthday, Disney and U.S. Time offered ten different watches that were designed by Disney's staff and packaged in a birthday-cake box that showed Mickey Mouse holding a heavy birthday cake, while all the other famous characters danced around him: Pinocchio, Jiminy Cricket, Bongo, Joe Carioca, Daisy Duck, Donald Duck, Dopey, Bambi, and Pluto. All ten were displayed in a large cartoon box, the Ingersoll name was prominently displayed (even though by now it was no more), and time was told on each by the arms, hands, and ears of all the characters. For the first time the straps were made of a washable vinylite plastic so that mothers could wash away the dirt, and Pluto had radium ears to help you tell time in the dark. It was the last complete group of comic characters to be made together and was an astounding commercial success. But from 1948 to 1968 comic-character watches were not popular, and sales went straight downhill.

New production methods meant new concepts in design. The injection molding of plastics meant a Pluto clock in the shape of Pluto, and it is one of the most impressive of all the Disney timepieces. It is a large clock shaped like a squatting Pluto, with luminous eyes that roll up and down, a long tongue that also moves, and in the middle of his belly the molded clockface tells time with two bones for the hour and minute hands. It is really a well-designed piece of comic sculpture. This electric clock was manufactured by the Allied Manufacturing Company in 1956 and is considered by many Disney collectors to be one of the best Disney clocks ever made.

During this same period the Bayard Company in France distributed a complete line of Disney alarm clocks that were animated. These included Mickey Mouse, Donald Duck, Pluto, The Lady and the Tramp, Pinocchio and the best of that group, Snow White and the Seven Dwarfs. Even though millions of Disney-character timepieces were worn on wrists, carried in pockets, and put on night tables next to beds, they are hard to find today. Perhaps because we associated them only with outgrown childhood, perhaps because they were not economical to repair, whatever the reasons, it has become increasingly difficult to start a new collection. Even more difficult to find are the other comic-character watches, because they were produced in much smaller quantities.

One example that is hard to find is Popeye, the first of the super heroes created by E. C. Segar in 1929. In 1934 the New Haven Clock Company obtained the rights from King Features Syndicate to use Popeye. They had been aware of the success Ingersoll and Ingraham were having with character watches and decided to plunge in. The popularity of this spinach-eating sailor with his thin-as-a-rail girl friend, Olive Oyl, grew so great that Popeye was second only to

Mickey Mouse in the number of licensed manufacturers. This position is maintained to this day. The original Popeye Wristwatch had an oblong chrome-plated case and a colorful profile view of the sailor, with his muscled, tatooed arms turning to tell the time. Between his legs was Wimpy chasing a hamburger, and many of the other characters are shown on the face. The box is a superb illustration of comic packaging design, drawn and signed by the creator of the strip, Segar, who always completed his signature with a half-smoked cigar butt. "In time for some spinach?" asks Bluto. "Yam always on time since I got this yere watch," replies Popeye, displaying his own watch on his wrist.

The 1934 Popeye Pocket Watch is even better because it is larger and the details and the colors are more distinct. All of the characters from "Thimble Theatre" who preceded Popeye in the early twenties are depicted on the rim. Our sailor strides the watch face with a long spread of his legs, and his tatooed arms tell the time. The second hand is round and turns in a fashion similar to the Mickey Mouse design and has Wimpy eternally condemned to chase a hamburger that has just fallen from his hand. This watch is very rare because it was made in 1934 only. In 1935 a second Popeye Pocket Watch replaced it, and alas, all of the characters from "Thimble Theatre" were gone and so was the brightness of the colors. This was done to make time telling easier.

The most beautiful of all the Popeye timepieces and the most rare is the alarm clock produced by the New Haven Watch and Clock Company. The case is of lithographed metal, made much like the tin wind-up toys of the period. On the rim is a beautiful full portrait of Popeye and Wimpy, and they are also on the base. The face has our sailor friend in a running position, and his arms tell the time. But it is the back of the watch that makes this a triumph. On the back is a country scene with a young apprentice cartoonist leaning his drafting board against Popeye's knee, drawing our hero, who is obviously sitting for his portrait. Even the bottom of the base has four characters from the comic strip. Again, the artwork was prepared by the artist and is signed "Segar."

Popeye was a favorite around the world, and Smiths in England manufactured a Popeye Alarm Clock that was animated. It has a bright-colored, comic-strip-style face, with Popeye being struck in the head by a clock pendulum, and underneath the fallen hero Sweetpea is wagging his head back and forth. This was produced circa 1970 in England, distributed by Bradley Time in New York in a very small production run, and is very difficult to find.

The last of the Popeyes is one of the most attractive ever made. It is a wristwatch manufactured by the Sheffield Watch Corporation in 1971, along with a Felix the Cat and Porky Pig. It was copied from the New Haven design and improved. Again the sailor man in a running position, with flesh-colored arms telling the time, but carrying a can of spinach with excellent proportioning and bright colors. The box is super. It has all of the characters in full color and has the title: "The Collector's Timepiece." It is.

Comic-character pocket watches were popular from 1933 to 1940 and went out of fashion after the war. Three of the most beautifully designed were Betty Boop, Tom Mix, and Buck Rogers.

Betty Boop was a product of the Fleischer Studios in New York and was the sexiest star of the animated movie cartoons. Her popularity was instantaneous, and Max Fleischer, the originator, pushed her profitably into toys, games, dolls, and related character merchandise. Pocket watches were made for boys, never for girls, since in those days girls didn't wear pants or vests and didn't have pockets. So the Betty Boop Pocket Watch is the only one ever made with a female person on it. It was manufactured by Ingraham and was advertised in the Montgomery Ward mail-order catalog of 1934. The face has a very sex-oriented Betty with a mini skirt and full-length yellow pantyhose sitting on the second-hand area. It must have been obvious to the designer that as the phallic shaped second hand turns to an upright position, Betty's getting goosed, which may explain the rather tense expression on her face. The hands are shaped like naked arms and the watch back is heavily debossed with Betty, her dog Bimbo, and a quarter moon in the sky. To be an original it must have the debossed back. Beware of the reproductions that do not.

"Buck Rogers in the 25th Century" began as a comic strip in January 1929, and his popularity and fame spread worldwide. Then, kids had the fantasy of outer space; today they have reality. Then, there was Buck Rogers and his girl friend, Wilma Deering, fighting the villain, Killer Kane, for control of the entire universe in space ships and flying belts with disintegrator pistols from the moon to Mars. Tigermen, Comet men, weird monsters, super scientists with super-secret weapons, good guys versus bad guys zoomed around at 25,000 miles per hour and zapped each other with rocket pistols that you could buy at Macy's for just 50¢ and join in the fight.

Ingraham joined in and designed one of the most beautiful character pocket watches ever made. The Buck Rogers in the 25th Century Pocket Watch appeared in the 1935 Sears, Roebuck catalog:

> Buck Rogers tells time by the stars! Straightaway into the 25th Century Buck Rogers transports every boy and girl, draws his power and lightning like speed from cosmic rays! See the hero Buck Rogers and the heroine Wilma on the dial in brilliant colors. See the famous Buck Rogers rocket pistol for hair raising escapes and rescues. The villainous Tiger Man is on the back of the watch! Selling as fast as Ingraham can make them in a very attractive colorful box . . . $.98.

On the face, our hero is guarding our heroine, Wilma, from an unknown terror that just might be the one-eyed, hairy monster die debossed on the back, who has a large hypodermic needle in his belt and that look of Earth-girl lust on his face! The radio flash hands are made from copper. The story gleaned from an old employee of the company is that the copper hands were cut and filed by hand in order to make work for their skilled watchmakers who were being paid about $8 per week! Look closely at the hands and one can see the rough file marks! The box is pure Art Nouveau and looks like a Louis Tiffany stained-glass window design. There was a Buck Rogers Wristwatch produced by the E. Ingraham Company, but it must have had a very short production run because not one has been found. It is extremely rare and valuable.

Even more rare is the Flash Gordon Pocket Watch that was manufactured in 1939 and sold in U.S. Army Post exchanges just prior to World War II. On it was Flash in bright colors with an animated Hawkman flapping his wings in outer space. The watch and the box were designed by Alex Raymond, the originator and artist of the comic strip and certainly one of the finest artists ever to draw comic art. In 1971 another fine artist, Gray Morrow, designed a Flash Gordon Wristwatch and box, on which his signature appears, for the Precision Watch Company. Even though it is recent, it is also rare because only 200 were made before production was discontinued.

There are other outer-space super-hero watches. A handsome wristwatch was designed by Ingraham for Tom Corbett Space Cadet. A picture of Tom and a rocket ship are on the face, and the wristband is decorated with rocket ships and whirling planets. It came mounted on a cardboard vertical rocket ship ready to take off. The Rocky Jones Space Ranger Wristwatch is typical of the handsome comic-art design of space-character watches: rocket ship, planets, and space-suited hero in bright colors, with a decorated wristband and a beautifully designed box. One of the most interesting, and quite rare, is the Buzz Corey's Space Patrol Wristwatch manufactured by U.S. Time. A rocket ship is shown on the face leaving the planet Earth and heading for the heavens, and inside the box is a plastic outer-space compass to chart our hero's way.

Perhaps the most ornate, complicated, and rare outer-space pocket watch ever designed was manufactured by Ingersoll Ltd. during the mid-nineteen fifties. Dan Dare is the Buck Rogers of England and is one of the most popular comic strips in that country. The Dan Dare Pocket Watch is the only double-animation character watch as yet discovered. The background of the face consists of a strange sun-lighted planet with a yellow-sand surface and bright red mountains. At stage right is a terrifying sharp-toothed flying dinosaur about to attack our hero. But Dan is protected by a pink space suit, white helmet, and moving rocket pistol that shoots at the monster, while his rocket ship circles in orbit ready to pick him up should that weird creature prove just too tough for our fearless outer-space Englishman. The energy drain of two movements—rocket ship and pistol—is just too much for the mainspring, and the watch has to be wound about every three hours. On the die-debossed back is an eagle with the word "Eagle" beneath the claws, an authorization from the Eagle Comics Company.

In 1938 a strange visitor from the planet Krypton rocketed to our Earth. Inside was a baby, much like any other Earth baby, and it was discovered and adopted by a typical middle-class suburban couple called Kent. They named him Clark, and he astounded the whole town with his superhuman strength. He grew to manhood and committed his life to fighting evil and crime. Pure in heart, faster than a speeding bullet, the quickest quick-change artist ever to do his thing inside a telephone booth, Superman struck the imagination of everyone on this planet. The next year World War II began and so did shortages of materials for nonessential items, such as toys and comic-character merchandise. Therefore, there are few prewar Superman collectibles. One of the few is the Superman Wristwatch, manufactured by the New Haven Watch and Clock Company in 1939. It has a large picture of Superman on the face in bright red and blue, with fists on hips ready for any fight. The decorated box has a handsome full figure of our super hero, complete with red boots and cape and the campy legend "True Time Appeal For the Man of Steel!" It was distributed by the Everbrite Watch Company and sold for $2.95. Bradley Time Company obtained the rights and produced one of the last of the comic-character pocket watches in the late nineteen fifties. It was Superman, flying like the rare bird he was, high over the skyscrapers of downtown America. Their last effort was an animated wristwatch of recent vintage that has a large rotating Superman second hand and is quite popular among collectors.

Macy's has Gimbels, and Superman had Captain Marvel. He was drawn by a fine comic artist, C. C. Beck. In 1948 Fawcett Publications authorized the formation of the Captain Marvel Watch Division of the American Merchandising Company, and wristwatches were produced for Captain Marvel, Captain Marvel Junior, and Mary Marvel. Pictures of our new heroes appeared on the watch faces and attractively designed boxes enclosed them. There was also a Captain Marvel Pocket Watch that is quite rare.

Batman, despite his flying speed, arrived late. It was in the nineteen sixties that the Gilbert Clock Corp. produced a Batman wristwatch. No hero on the face, but a die-cast ominous bat wing encapsulated the watch. At the same time Bradley produced a short run of Batman clocks, again unfortunately without a pictured dial but set into an attractively designed plastic case with a large, evil-looking Batman, looking more bat than man.

Related to the space heroes were the cowboy heroes: They were always morally right, never drew blood or got killed, and always won with lasso or six-gun.

Tom Mix was one of the most popular of the cowboy heroes of screen and radio. In the early thirties cowboys were respected more for their prowess with a lasso than a six-gun, and every imaginative American under the age of ten was practicing with any hunk of rope he could find. (Concurrently, Will Rogers was doing his lasso act on the stage of the Ziegfeld Follies.) During 1933–1934, Mix's popularity was so great that Ingersoll gambled on it and produced a handsomely designed animated pocket watch and wristwatch.

The pocket watch has Tom Mix seated on his reared-up horse Tony, while Tom's lasso whirls around a turning second hand on which is the head of a Texas Longhorn steer. (Not only is the Tom Mix Pocket Watch difficult to find, but so is a Texas Longhorn steer; they don't breed them anymore!) The watch back is debossed in a square frame of lasso rope, inside of which is the corny legend:

> Always
> Find time
> For a good
> deed.
> Tom Mix

The wristwatch has a similar design, and word of mouth has it that there was also an animated Tom Mix Clock, with Tom riding Tony, but none has ever been found.

During the same golden era of the nineteen thirties the first of the singing cowboys appeared, complete with guitar, horse, and lasso: Gene Autry with his horse Champion of the Flying "A" Ranch. The first wristwatch appeared in the thirties, with Gene on Champion in bright colors and radium hands to help tell time in the dark. The box and watch stand showed an overweight cowboy, a very young Gene Autry on a Champion struggling to stand upright despite his heavy rider. The Wilane Watch Company redesigned and reissued the wristwatch in 1948 with a much more colorful design and a thinner but older cowboy Gene. Ten-gallon hat, Pepsodent-toothy smile, a bandolier of rifle ammunition over his shoulder, Mexican-bandit style, cowboy wristband, and an inscription die debossed on the back:

> Always your pal
> Gene Autry

made this a commercial and design success—so successful that the watch was redesigned to include animation. It became the Gene Autry "Six-Shooter" Wristwatch, "fires 120 shots a minute." The second hand became a six-gun and rocked back and forth as if from the recoil of a .44 bullet.

Cowgirls were included, and the Annie Oakley "Six-Shooter" Wristwatch appeared, with nineteen-forties-fashion shoulder pads under her blouse and a hairstyle resembling a horse's mane. These watches were manufactured by the New Haven Watch and Clock Company but were often distributed by other companies, so the boxes and advertising may have different names.

Ingraham produced two wristwatch versions of Roy Rogers and his horse Trigger: the first was square cased, with Roy on a rearing Trigger; the second, round cased, with Roy posing with his horse-buddy, his riding-gloved hand holding Trigger's nose as if in a posed photograph. Bradley Time Company then obtained the rights and produced the Queen of the West Dale Evans Wristwatch for novice cowgirls in a beautiful celluloid-enclosed pop-up box. Dale waves greetings at you from atop her cardboard horse as you approach the Roy Rogers ranch. Bradley also produced a Roy Rogers Pocket Watch with a well-designed face, an older-looking Roy (circa 1959), and Trigger, plus a stopwatch feature that was probably added to help young cowboys check out their imagined horses in the quarter mile.

Hopalong Cassidy, gray-haired cowboy star of movie and TV screens, fathered considerable character merchandise, from guns to cameras to radios. He was so popular and commercially viable that the U.S. Time Corporation made a major investment and obtained the rights to all timepieces. They produced a very handsome Hopalong Cassidy Alarm Clock, Pocket Watch, and Wristwatch. With each came his personal-improvement message:

> Hi Pardner!
>
> Time is the most important thing in your lives. Even one minute wasted is a moment lost that could have been spent in helping you to be a better and happier person. Since time is important to you it is just as important to other people. Wrong as it is to waste your own time, it is even worse to waste the time of your friends. Be prompt and punctual with your appointments. . . . I sincerely hope that this watch will be a means of bringing you great joy, happiness and success by keeping track of every minute of every hour of your most important TIME.
>
> Good Luck
>
> Hoppy

Hoppy was right, and TIME made money for him and U.S. Time Corporation. The watches became very popular worldwide and production continued well into the late nineteen sixties, spurred on, of course, by his television success.

The Davy Crockett craze started with coonskin caps for the kids and spawned millions of dollars worth of character merchandise. Bradley was authorized by Walt Disney Productions to produce the wristwatch, and for collectors it poses a problem. The watch is badly designed, but the packaging is superb and is the superior collector's prize. Although the watch is Bradley, the packaging and guarantee is from U.S. Time, always good in the ideas department. The watch is mounted on an old powder horn in a beautiful box, with Fess Parker (who played Davy Crockett in the movie) on the cover. Behind him are Indians and a typical Hollywood Western fort.

But one of the most ambitious character clocks ever engineered was the Davy Crockett Animated Electric Clock. It was a large brown molded-plastic log cabin; on the left is a small electric clock without decoration, but on the right is a large glass window. As soon as this electric clock is connected, the area behind the window illuminates to reveal Davy Crockett rocking back and forth on his horse, being attacked by a huge bear! The Wild West woodlands provide the scenic background, and the entire display resembles a true-to-nature montage in the Museum of Natural History. It was produced by the Haddon Mfg. Company and was one of the most expensive character clocks ever made, costing almost $40.

New Haven Watch and Clock Company designed the first Lone Ranger wristwatch, and it was distributed exclusively by the Everbrite Watch Company. The pocket watch and wristwatch were introduced in 1939 and were commercially successful. The Montgomery Ward mail-order catalog effected a very wide distribution. The wristwatch was made in a small and large size, one for girls and the other for boys. There was the masked rider on his great white horse Silver, charging at a full gallop. Both the pocket and wristwatches were attractively designed and are fine items to be added to any comic-character-timepiece collection.

Another cowboy watch was a handsome timepiece made in 1949, the Red Ryder Watch. There is Red on his black horse with Lil' Beaver, his Indian sidekick, riding away. Again, the production run may have been small, because so few have been found.

In England's Eagle Comics, their Jeff Arnold is the cowboy equivalent of our Tom Mix–Gene Autry–Roy Rogers, and in the mid-nineteen fifties Ingersoll Ltd. designed a rare and handsome animated cowboy pocket watch. Two-Gun Jeff is seated on his horse, right pistol hand up in the air and the left gun banging away up and down. On the back the Eagle Comics symbol is deeply die debossed.

Yes, there was a Zorro watch, but, in the style of the mid-sixties, only his name appears on the face of the wristwatch. It is attractively packaged around a Mexican sombrero.

These were the cowboy watches that rose to high popularity with the commercial success of these singing, acting, lassoing, gun-shooting heroes—all rare collector's items today.

The Beatles were the inspiration for two extremely handsome timepieces; a magnificent wristwatch and an alarm clock that took their art from the motion picture *Yellow Submarine*. They were produced by the Sheffield Watch Company in bright colors, very mod, very Peter Max, but unfortunately the production run was small and the wristwatch and clock are very difficult to find. The box for the alarm clock was handsomely decorated and depicts some of the best *Yellow Submarine* art. Yes, there was a Dennis the Menace Wristwatch produced by the Bradley Company, and it is quite colorful and the favorite wrist decoration of many of his fans.

The quickness of a fad illustrates several of the problems of collecting comic-character timepieces. There is never continuous production. It was and is always a short production, usually prepared for the Christmas season or to supply a fad of the moment. The movements are always cheap pin levers, so as soon as the movement needs repair, the watch is usually thrown away. Worse, very few jewelers are willing to repair them because of the excessive time and effort required. Much worse, the watch and clock industry is narrowing down to a few large multinational companies with highly advanced mass-production machinery take makes the short-run production of character watches unprofitable. Perhaps the only comic-character watch that will endure is the Mickey Mouse, since Mickey Mouse is institutionalized worldwide. You can go down to the corner store and buy a comic book—they still print them—to the toy store and buy a comic-character toy—they still make them—next Sunday to the newsstand and collect comic Sunday pages . . . but no more comic-character watches!

Since value depends upon supply and demand, and there is no longer a supply, any increase in demand from new collectors will increase competition and the value of existing collections, They are beautiful miniatures, like nineteenth-century cameos and the tiny portraits of the kings of France—well worth collecting.

CHARACTER TIMEPIECES:
SUGGESTED LIST OF COLLECTIBLES

	Manufacturer	Date
Animated Clocks:		
Man on the Trapeze	Junghans	1880 approx.
Negro Mammy With Rolling Eyes	Junghans	1886
Negro Banjo Player	Junghans	1885 approx.
Druggist Clock	Waterbury Clock Company	1887
Bixby's Best Shoe Polish	Waterbury	1886 approx.
Blacksmith Clock	Seth Thomas	1895 approx.
Lady With Mandolin	Junghans	1885 approx.
Lady With Fan	Junghans	1885 approx.
Comic-Character Timepieces:		
Mickey Mouse Electric Clock	Ingersoll	1933
Mickey Mouse Wind-up Clock	Ingersoll	1933
Mickey Mouse Pocket Watch With Fob (must have die-debossed back to be an original)	Ingersoll	1933
Mickey Mouse Wristwatch	Ingersoll	1933
Mickey Mouse Wagging Head alarm clock	Ingersoll	1934
Buster Brown Pocket Watch	Ingersoll	1908
Mickey Mouse Miniature Table Clock (very rare)	Ingersoll	1934
Mickey Mouse Lapel Watch	Ingersoll	1937

	Manufacturer	Date
English Mickey Mouse Pocket Watch #1 (does not have die-debossed back)	Ingersoll Ltd.	1933
English Mickey Mouse Pocket Watch #2 (does not have die-debossed back)	Ingersoll Ltd.	1933
English Mickey Mouse Wristwatch	Ingersoll Ltd.	1933
English Mickey Mouse Wind-up Clock	Ingersoll Ltd.	1933
English Mickey Mouse Electric Clock	Ingersoll Ltd.	1933
French Mickey Mouse Alarm Clock	Bayard Co., France	1936–1969
Three Little Pigs (Big Bad Wolf) Alarm Clock	Ingersoll	1934
Three Little Pigs Pocket Watch (must have die-debossed back to be an original)	Ingersoll	1934
Three Little Pigs Wristwatch	Ingersoll	1934
Donald Duck and Mickey Mouse Wristwatch	Ingersoll	1936
Donald Duck Pocket Watch (one model has decal of Mickey Mouse on back)	Ingersoll	1939
Donald Duck Wristwatch	Ingersoll	1947
Daisy Duck Wristwatch	Ingersoll	1948
Huey Duck Wristwatch	Ingersoll	1949
French Donald Duck Alarm Clock	Bayard	1969
French Pluto Alarm Clock	Bayard	1969
French Snow White Alarm Clock	Bayard	1969
Snow White Wristwatch	Ingersoll	1940
Pluto Wristwatch	Ingersoll	1948
Pinocchio Wristwatch	Ingersoll	1948
Cinderella Wristwatch	Ingersoll	1950
Alice in Wonderland Wristwatch	Ingersoll	1950
Popeye Alarm Clock	New Haven Watch and Clock Co.	1932
Popeye Pocket Watch #1 (does not have die-debossed back)	New Haven	1934
Popeye Pocket Watch #2 (does not have die-debossed back)	New Haven	1935
Popeye Wristwatch	New Haven	1935
Popeye Wristwatch	Sheffield Watch Co.	1971
English Popeye Alarm Clock	Smiths	1968
Pluto Electric Clock	Allied Manufacturing Co.	1956
Davy Crockett Animated Electric Clock	Haddon Manufacturing Co.	1954
Davy Crockett Wristwatch	U.S. Time	1954
Bugs Bunny Electric Clock	Richie Prem	1950
Bugs Bunny Alarm Clock	Richie Prem	1951
Bugs Bunny Wristwatch (must have carrot-shaped hands to be an original)	Richie Prem	1951
Woody Woodpecker Wall Clock	Columbia Time	1950
Woody Woodpecker Alarm Clock	Columbia	1950
Woody Woodpecker Wristwatch	E. Ingraham Co.	1950
Charlie McCarthy Animated Alarm Clock	Gilbert Clock Corp.	1938
Buck Rogers in the 25th Century Pocket Watch (must have die-debossed back to be original)	Ingraham	1935
Buck Rogers Wristwatch	Ingraham	1935
Flash Gordon Pocket Watch	Ingersoll	1939
Flash Gordon Wristwatch	Precision Watch Co.	1971
Tom Mix Pocket Watch (must have die-debossed back to be original)	Ingersoll	1933
Tom Mix Wristwatch	Ingersoll	1933

	Manufacturer	Date
Betty Boop Pocket Watch (must have die-debossed back to be original)	Ingraham	1934
Buster Brown and Tige Pocket Watch (does not have die-debossed back)	Ingersoll	1908
Buster Brown and Tige Pocket Watch (does not have die-debossed back)	Ansonia Clock Co.	1929
Buster Brown and Tige Pendant Pocket Wristwatch	Huckleberry Time Co.	1971
Buster Brown Wristwatch	Brown Shoe Co.	1974
Hopalong Cassidy Pocket Watch	U.S. Time Corp.	1950
Hopalong Cassidy Alarm Clock	U.S. Time	1950
Hopalong Cassidy Wristwatch	U.S. Time	1950–1967
Roy Rogers Alarm Clock	Ingraham	1951
Roy Rogers Pocket Watch	Bradley Time Co.	1959
Roy Rogers Wristwatch	Ingraham	1951
Dale Evans Wristwatch	Ingraham	1951
Gene Autry and Champion Wristwatch	Wilane Watch Co.	1935
Gene Autry Wristwatch	Wilane	1948
Gene Autry "Six-Shooter" Wristwatch	New Haven	1951
Lone Ranger Pocket Watch	New Haven	1939
Lone Ranger Wristwatch	New Haven	1939
Annie Oakley "Six-Shooter" Wristwatch	New Haven	1951
Superman Wristwatch	New Haven	1939
Superman Pocket Watch (does not have die-debossed back; beware of reproductions)	Bradley	1959
Tom Corbett Space Cadet Wristwatch	Ingraham	1951
Rocky Jones Space Ranger Wristwatch	Ingraham	1954
Captain Marvel Pocket Watch	Fawcett	1945
Captain Marvel Wristwatch	Fawcett	1948
Mary Marvel Wristwatch	Fawcett	1948
Dan Dare Pocket Watch	Ingersoll Ltd.	1953
Jeff Arnold Pocket Watch	Ingersoll Ltd.	1953
Dick Tracy Pocket Watch	Bradley	1959
Dick Tracy "Six-Shooter" Wristwatch	New Haven	1951
Dick Tracy Wristwatch	New Haven	1937
Smitty Wristwatch	New Haven	1935
Orphan Annie Wristwatch	New Haven	1934
Orphan Annie and Sandy Wristwatch	Hi-Time	1972
Smokey Stover Wristwatch	Hi-Time	1972
Brick Bradford Wristwatch	Hi-Time	1972
Li'l Abner Saluting American Flag Wristwatch	New Haven	1947
Li'l Abner With Laughing Mule Wristwatch	New Haven	1947
Schmoo Pendulum Clock	Lux	1950
Howdy Doody Wristwatch	Ingraham	1954 approx.
Howdy Doody Wristwatch With Movable Eyes	Patent Watch	1954 approx.
Robin Hood Wristwatch	Viking	1938
Joe Palooka Wristwatch	New Haven	1947
Porky Pig Wristwatch	Ingraham	1949
Porky Pig Wristwatch	Sheffield	1971
Felix the Cat Wristwatch	Sheffield	1971
Hoky Poky Magician Wristwatch	Acco	1949
Puss-N-Boots Wristwatch	Nuhope	1949
Batman Clock	Bradley	1969

	Manufacturer	Date
Batman Wristwatch	Gilbert	1969
James Bond 007 Wristwatch	Gilbert	1970
Beatles Wristwatch	Sheffield	1968
Beatles Yellow Submarine Alarm Clork	Sheffield	1969
Charlie Chaplin Pendant Pocket Watch	Huckleberry	1971
Buck Rogers Pendant Pocket Watch	Huckleberry	1971
Dennis the Menace Wristwatch	Bradley	1969
Uncle Wiggily Wristwatch	Schapiro	1973

The beginning—animated character clocks from the nineteenth century: Negro Mammy With Rolling Eyes, Bixby's Best Shoe Polish, and Man on the Trapeze.

Lux animated clocks from the early nineteen thirties: Happy Days clock celebrating the repeal of Prohibition, the Organ Grinder and the Monkey, and the Negro Shoeshine Boy.

The Tortoise and the Hare, an early English comic-character clock that helped children learn to tell time.

Buster Brown pocket watches advertising shoes, 1908 and 1929. The first comic-character pocket watches.

Ingersoll Mickey Mouse wind-up and electric clocks, wrist and pocket watches are featured in this "Leadership Sale" at Macy's, New York, 1934. Note the low! low! prices! Photo courtesy of Henry Mazzeo, Jr.

Mickey Mouse electric clock with pop-up box (Ingersoll, 1933) and the very rare Mickey Mouse desk clock.

News . . . Notes

The New Ingersoll Mickey Mouse Watch

Introduction of the Mickey Mouse timepieces as reported in *Playthings* magazine, August 1933, at the Chicago Century of Progress Exposition.

Mickey Mouse Tells Time

Mickey Mouse, who has proven himself as able a contributor to toy department volume as he has an accomplished and delightful artist on the moving picture screen, now turns up in a new role as official timekeeper for childhood. On a new line of Mickey Mouse timepieces brought out by Ingersoll - Waterbury Co., Waterbury, Conn., Mickey's own hands tell the time. In doing so they get into a hundred amusing positions. They give animation to the Mickey figure printed on the dial, and they establish an indisputable reason why little Mary or young Johnny needs to have a watch right away. So ingeniously have these watches been conceived and so attractive is the Mickey personality that there is little doubt that these new watches and clocks bid fair to be high on the list for fall and Christmas sales in toy departments. Already many of the leading department stores are displaying full lines and have found it necessary to re-order not once, but several times. Already there is a forecast of really important volume. Ingersoll reports that production has reached more than five thousand pieces a day, and that production is considerably behind orders, though it is hoped that this can be stepped up within the next several weeks. There are four pieces in the Mickey Mouse line. A pocket watch and fob retailing at $1.50; a wrist watch at $2.75; an electric clock at $1.50, and a spring-wound clock at $1.50. All are packed in typically Mickey Mouse cartons exploiting the full popularity of Walt Disney's famous characters, Clarabelle Cow, Pluto the Pup and Horace Horsecollar. Arguments between toy buyers and jewelry buyers as to which department this merchandise rightfully belongs are already on the horizon. In fact they have come and gone in several stores —the settlement usually being that both departments will carry them, resulting in increased business all around. Some indication of the rapidity with which Mickey mouse timepieces are finding a place in the American public's big warm heart is apparent in sales figures at the Ingersoll exhibit at the Century of Progress Exposition. Ingersoll has established a miniature factory there, so that people may step up to order a watch, see it made and have it delivered while they wait. A special world's fair watch is the watch being so manufactured. But sales of Mickey Mouse watches at the same counter are approximately three times greater.

PLAYTHINGS—August, 1933

Three Little Pigs animated alarm clock with pop-up box.

138

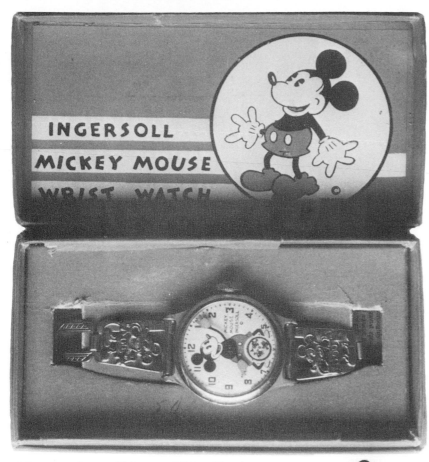

Presenting the world-famous Mickey Number
One Wristwatch! Great rodent graphics! The
metal-link band is more desirable than the
leather band. 1933.

Presenting the original Mickey Mouse Pocket
Watch with Fob. Must have die-debossed back
to be an original. 1933.

A rare English Ingersoll Ltd. 1934 Mickey
Wind-up Clock, Mickey Wagging Head Alarm
Clock, and the Mickey Wind-up Clock.

English Ingersoll Ltd. Mickey Mouse Pocket
Watches, 1933–1934. The Mickeys are quite
wild and the watches are quite rare. They do
not have die-debossed backs.

The rarest of all: the Mickey Mouse Desk Clock, only two and one-quarter inches square, with a very Art Deco base. 1934.

Mickey Mouse lapel watch; perhaps the most beautiful of all.

The Mickey DeLuxe Wristwatch. On the box is Mickey dressed up like Fred Astaire. Notice he is wearing his own watch!

Genuine MICKEY MOUSE Watches

YOUR CHOICE $2.98 EACH

Watch Illustrations ¾ Actual Size

$1.39 IN GIFT BOX

Mickey Mouse Watch and Fob
Unbreakable Crystal

An Improved, Smaller Size, Better Model, Mickey Mouse Watch than the Regular Mickey Mouse Watches sold.

YOUR BOY is really a "do-er of things" when he owns a Mickey Mouse watch. Genuine thin model Ingersoll. On the dial is Mickey Mouse in gay colors telling you the time with his hands. For a second-hand there are three little Mickeys chasing each other in a circle. Mickey's on the back of the watch, too. And when the watch is in his pocket, Mickey's there, chipper as you please, dangling at the end of the "grown-up" looking fob. Nickel plated case. **4 F 1650** Shpg. wt., 6 oz. ... **$1.39**

Mickey Mouse Wrist Watch
Regular $3.75 Value
Big Saving When You Buy at Sears.

Mickey Mouse on a wrist watch! Can you think of anything to please a child more? On the dial is Mickey Mouse in all his glory telling you the time with his hands. For a second hand, three Junior Mickeys chase around in a circle. Two Mickey Mouse characters in enameled colors on the wrist band. Genuine Ingersoll. Chromium plated case, unbreakable crystal. White dial with black figures. Shpg. wt., 6 oz.

Metal Band. 4 F 950..**$2.98**	Leather Band 4 F 951...**$2.98**

Mickey Mouse Alarm Clock

No trick getting up mornings with Mickey Mouse on the job to waken you. Mickey Mouse with his head wagging tells time with his hands. Genuine Ingersoll clock, 30-hour movement. Attractive **red** or **green** finish. State color wanted. 4⅜ in. high. Has 3⅝ in. dial. Shpg. wt., 1 lb. 8 oz.

5 F 8518...**$1.39**

$1.89

Official Boy Scout Watches

... Around the dial are inscribed the 12 scout laws, while the minute hand points to them with this inscription: "A Scout Is." On the hour hand is the scout motto: "Be Prepared." Chromium plated cases and non-breakable crystals. Made by Ingersoll. Shpg. wt., each, 6 oz.

Pocket Watch	Wrist Watch
Official colors on dial and hands.	Official colors on dial and hands. Leather Strap.
4 F 1652	Plain Dial 4 F 912 .... **$3.39**
Thin model.. **$1.89**	Luminous dial 4 F 913 ...... **3.89**

$2.39

Genuine Ingraham
Popular Priced Wrist Watch

Handsome watches in stunning Chromium plated cases. Good timekeeper, too. Ingraham American made. Neat, plain pattern case and band. Raise gilt numerals. Shpg. wt., ea., 8 oz.

Open Link Metal Band 4 F 1700 **$2.39**	Leather Strap 4 F 1701 **$2.39**

WHO'S AFRAID OF THE BIG BAD WOLF

Big Bad Wolf Wrist Watch—$3.75 Value

With each tick of the watch the Bad Wolf's evil eye is winking at the three little pigs on a bright colored dial. Center opening metal wrist band, decorated with Bad Wolf and Little Pigs. Thin model Chromium plated case. Nonbreakable crystal. Stem wind and stem set. Made by Ingersoll. Shpg. wt., 6 oz.

Metal Band 4 F 952 **$2.98**	Leather Band 4 F 953 **$2.98**

Big Bad Wolf Watch and Fob

With each tick of the watch the Bad Wolf winks at Three Little Pigs on bright colored dial. Dangling from black leather strap is a nickel plated fob with Three Pigs in bright colors. Message from Walt Disney on back of watch. Ingersoll, thin model nickel-plated case. Unbreakable crystal. Shpg. wt., 6 oz.
4 F 1651........**$1.39**

Big Bad Wolf Alarm Clock

Three Little Pigs Alarm Clock. Ferocious jaws of Bad Wolf open and close with each tick of the clock. Bright **red** case and dial; little pigs and bad wolf in lifelike colors. Genuine Ingersoll 30-hour movement model. Case 4⅜ in. high with 3⅝-in. dial. Shpg. wt., 1 lb. 8 oz.
5 F 8519........**$1.39**

Great News for the Youngster
Orphan Annie and Dick Tracy Wrist Watches
Made to Sell for $3.95

All the boys and girls are wearing them ... prize them beyond words. American movement. A fully guaranteed timekeeper. Chromium plated cases. Genuine leather strap. Shpg. wt., each, 8 oz.

Orphan Annie	Dick Tracy
Annie's picture in colors on the dial. The ideal watch for the young American Miss who wants the latest. In attractive Orphan Annie box.	Sears is right up to the minute with this genuine American Dick Tracy Wrist Watch. Has an official reproduction of Dick Tracy himself in colors on the dial.
4F1715 **$3.59**	4 F 1714... **$3.59**

Buck Rogers Watch

Given for 1 $1.00 subscription and 35¢ extra

Here's a watch you will be proud to own and to carry. The envy of all your friends. It's a honey for time keeping, and it's guaranteed against defects for one whole year. On its face are your old pal Buck with his rocket pistol together with Wilma, both in bright colors. The minute, hour and second hands are copper representing flash lightning, while the back is engraved with a naturalistic picture of a monster from another world. Specify Prize #302

Great News for the Youngsters!
Now! An Orphan Annie Wrist Watch

Look! Annie's picture, in colors, is on the dial! The ideal watch for the young American miss who wants the latest. American movement. Chromium plated case. Genuine Leather strap. Made to sell for $3.95. Not Prepaid.
4 E 1714—In Orphan Annie Box **$3.67**

Watch Out! Here's Dick Tracy!
He's on Time, as Usual!

Sears is right up to the minute with genuine American made Dick Tracy Wrist Watches! Has an official reproduction of Dick Tracy, in colors, on dial. Chromium plated case. Fine timekeeper, fully guaranteed. Made to sell for $3.95. Shpg. wt., 8 oz. Genuine leather strap.
4 E 1715—Not Prepaid.... **$3.67**

Advertisement from Sears, Roebuck catalog of 1935 with prices for all the timepieces from Mickey to Buck Rogers.

The French Mickey Mouse Wall Clock, about 1933.

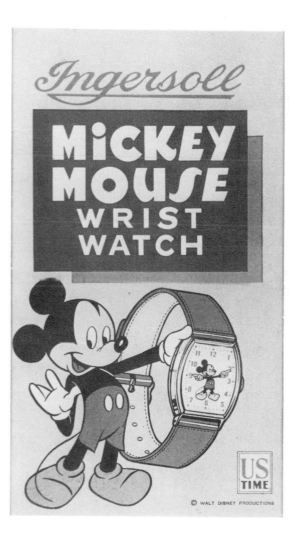

The 1948 Mickey Mouse Wristwatch. The charm of the
early-thirties graphics has been destroyed. He has been
changed from a rodent into a little goodie-boy.

The French Bayard "Wagging Head" Mickey Mouse Clock. The Mickey graphics remained the same from the thirties to 1969, when it was discontinued. The others are forties Mickey Ingersoll clocks.

The Donald Duck Number One Wristwatch had a Mickey
Mouse second hand and band, and the pocket watches also
had Mickey Mouse decals on the back. Donald watches
didn't sell well, so Mickey was put on to help. 1935–1939.

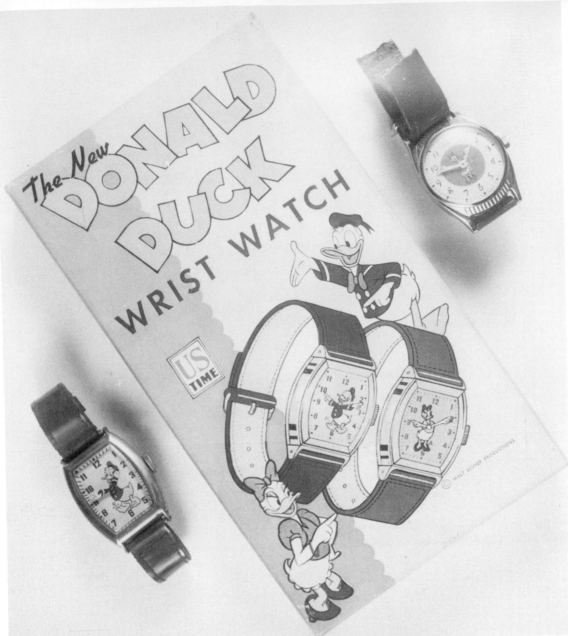

Daisy and Donald Duck wristwatches. 1948.

The Snow White Wristwatch with imitation cel from the movie packed into box.

The Cinderella Wristwatch, packaged with the glass slipper.

French Bayards. These clocks are animated and the designs, particularly *"Blanche Neige,"* are attractive.

The animated Popeye Clock, manufactured in England by Smiths.

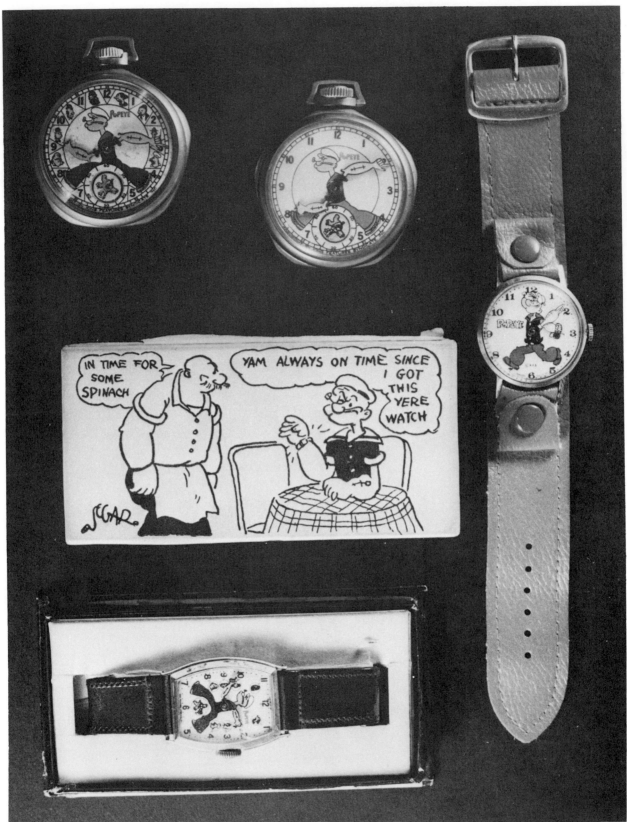

The 1934 Popeye Pocket Watch, with all of the comic characters from "Thimble Theatre," and Wimpy on the rotating second hand eternally chasing a hamburger that has fallen from his fist. The 1935 Popeye Pocket Watch, with all the comic folks removed to make time telling easier. The 1935 wristwatch and box and the 1971 wristwatch.

148

The Buck Rogers in the 25th Century Pocket Watch, only 98¢ at Sears in 1935! The watch and the handsome box are beautifully designed. The back is debossed with a one-eyed outer space monster.

The Tom Corbett Space Cadet wristwatch.

The Rocky Jones Space Ranger Wristwatch.

The Superman Pocket Watch by Bradley Time Co., 1959;
and the Dan Dare English Ingersoll Ltd. Pocket Watch of
1953. This watch has double animation: a moving rocket
pistol and a rotating rocket ship.

The Superman Wristwatch, very popular in 1939.

The Captain Marvel
Wristwatch, 1948.

The Charlie McCarthy
Animated Alarm Clock. The
mouth movement was
designed to resemble Charlie's
own. 1938.

The very rare Bugs Bunny Electric Clock. His ears tell the time, and all his buddies are on the clock.

The Bugs Bunny Wristwatch. It should have hands shaped like carrots to be an original.

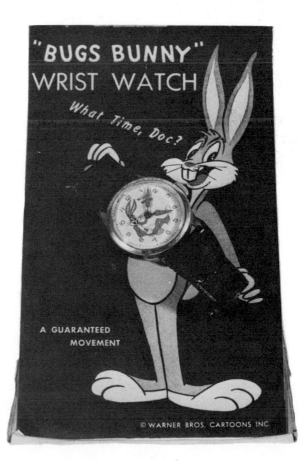

The Woody Woodpecker Wall Clock.

The Woody Woodpecker Wristwatch.

The Dick Tracy Animated Wristwatch.

The Howdy Doody Wristwatch, packaged in an attractive
stand-up box.

A later Howdy Doody wristwatch with movable eyes.

The Porky Pig Wristwatch with colorful box. 1949.

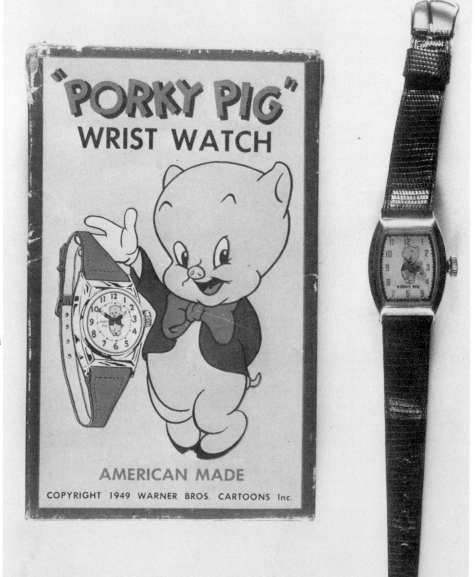

The Shmoo Pendulum Clock and friends.

Li'l Abner animated wristwatches: saluting the waving American flag and watching the "movin' mule."

The Joe Palooka Wristwatch.

The Lone Ranger Pocket Watch and Wristwatch, 1939.

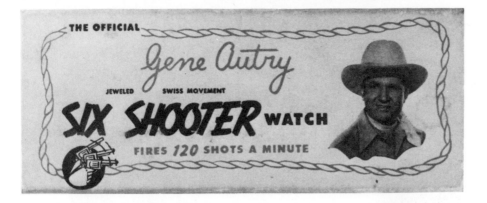

The animated Gene Autry
Wristwatch.

Roy Rogers and Dale Evans
wristwatches.

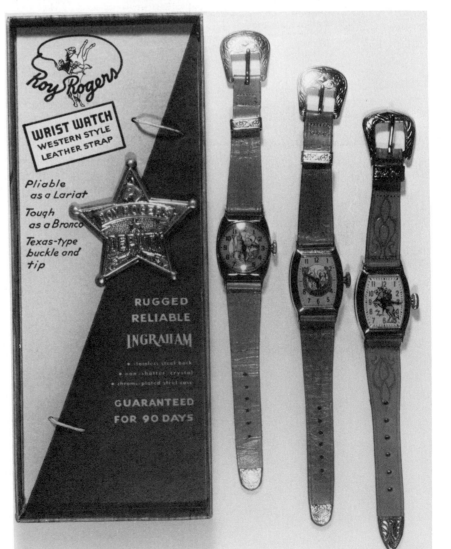

The Hopalong Cassidy Pocket
Watch, Alarm Clock, and
Wristwatch, attractively packaged.

The Davy Crockett Wristwatch.

The Davy Crockett Animated Electric Clock. The horse bucks poor Davy up and down while the bear attacks.

A group of cowboy heroes: Hoppy, Roy Rogers, and England's Jeff Arnold.

The Robin Hood Wristwatch.

The Puss-N-Boots Wristwatch.

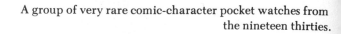

A group of very rare comic-character pocket watches from the nineteen thirties.

Made in Nazi Germany 1938 by Kienzle Watch Company, the very rare Adolf Hitler pocket watch.

Made in the USSR in 1967 to celebrate 50 years of Communism: The Joseph Stalin commemorative clock showing Uncle Joe leading the charge against the Winter Palace with a six shooter!

The Batman Clock and Wristwatch.

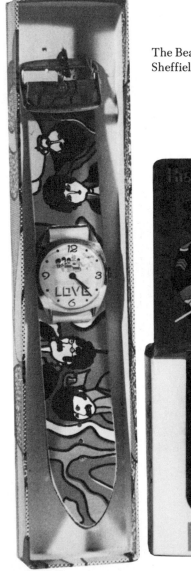

The Beatles Yellow Submarine Alarm Clock and Wristwatch, handsomely designed by Sheffield Watch Co.

The very rare Shirley Temple Wristwatch in the original box, and the recent Orphan Annie and Smokey Stover timepieces.

5

Buck Rogers in the 25th Century – The Fabulous Fantasy

Elsewhere I have set down, for whatever interest they have in this, the 25th Century, my personal recollections of the 20th Century.

Now it occurs to me that my memoirs of the 25th Century may have an equal interest 500 years from now, particularly in view of that unique perspective from which I have seen the 25th Century, entering it as I did, in one leap across a gap of 492 years.

I should state therefore, that I, Anthony Rogers, am, so far as I know, the only man alive whose normal span of eighty-one years of life has been spread over a period of 573 years. To be precise, I lived the first twenty-nine years of my life between 1898 and 1927; the other fifty-two since 2419. The gap between these two, a period of nearly five hundred years, I spent in a state from the ravages of katabolic processes, and without any apparent effect on my physical or mental faculties.

When I began my long sleep, man had just begun his real conquest of the air in a sudden series of trans-oceanic flights in airplanes driven by internal combustion motors. He had barely begun to speculate on the possibilities of harnessing sub-atomic forces, and had made no further practical penetration into the field of ethereal pulsations than the primitive radio and television of that day. The United States of America was the most powerful nation in the world, its political, financial, industrial and scientific influence being supreme; and in the arts also it was climbing into leadership.

I awoke to find the America I knew a total wreck—to find Americans a hunted race in their own land, hiding in the dense forests that covered the shattered and leveled ruins of their once magnificent cities, desperately preserving, and struggling to develop in their secret retreats, the remnants of their culture and science—and the undying flame of their sturdy independence.

World domination was in the hands of the Mongolians and the center of world power lay in inland China, with Americans one of the few races of mankind unsubdued—and it must be admitted in fairness to the truth, not worth the trouble of subduing in the eyes of the Han Airlords who ruled North America as titular tributaries of the Most Magnificent.

For they needed not the forests in which the Americans lived, nor the resources of the vast territories these forests covered. With the perfection to which they had produced the synthetic production of necessities and luxuries, their remarkable development of scientific processes and mechanical accomplishment of work, they had no economic desire for the enslaved labor of an unruly race.

They had all they needed for their magnificently luxurious and degraded scheme of civilization within the walls of the fifteen cities of sparkling glass they had flung skyward on the sites of ancient American centers, into the bowels of the earth underneath them, and with relatively small surrounding areas of agriculture. Complete domination of the air rendered communication between these centers a matter of ease and safety. Occasional destructive raids on the waste lands were considered all that was necessary to keep the "wild" Americans on the run within the shelter of their forests, and prevent their becoming a menace to the Han civilization. But nearly three hundred years of easily maintained security, the last century of which had been nearly sterile in scientific, social and economic progress, had softened and devitalized the Hans.

It had likewise developed, beneath the protecting foliage of the forest, the growth of a vigorous new American civilization, remarkable in the mobility and flexibility of its organization, in its conquest of almost insuperable obstacles, in the development and guarding of its industrial and scientific resources, all in anticipation of that "Day of Hope" to which it had been looking forward for generations, when it would be strong enough to burst from the green chrysalis of the forests, soar into the upper air lanes and destroy the yellow incubus.

At the time I awoke, the "Day of Hope" was almost at hand. I shall not attempt to set forth a detailed history of the Second War of Independence, for that has been recorded already by better historians than I am. Instead I shall confine myself largely to the part I was fortunate enough to play in this struggle and in the events leading up to it.

It all resulted from my interest in radioactive gases. During the latter part of 1927 my company, the American Radioactive Gas Corporation, had been keeping me busy investigating reports of unusual phenomena observed in certain abandoned coal mines near the Wyoming valley, in Pennsylvania.

With two assistants and a complete equipment of scientific instruments, I began the exploration of a deserted working in a mountainous district, where several weeks before, a number of mining engineers had reported traces of carnotite and what they believed to be radioactive gases. Their report was not without foundation, it was apparent from the outset, for in our examination of the upper levels of the mine, our instruments indicated a vigorous radioactivity.

On the morning of December 15th, we descended to one of the lowest levels. To our surprise, we found no water there. Obviously it had been drained off through some break in the strata. We noticed too that the rock in the side walls of the shaft was soft, evidently due to the radioactivity, and pieces crumbled under foot rather easily. We made our way cautiously down the shaft, when suddenly the rotted timbers above us gave way.

I jumped ahead, barely escaping the avalanche of coal and soft rock, but my companions, who were several paces behind me, were buried under it, and undoubtedly met instant death.

I was trapped. Return was impossible. With my electric torch I explored the shaft to its end, but could find no other way out. The air became increasingly difficult to breathe, probably from the rapid accumulation of the radioactive gas. In a little while my senses reeled and I lost consciousness.

When I awoke, there was a cool and refreshing circulation of air in the shaft. I had no thought that I had been unconscious for more than a few hours, although it seems that the radioactive gas had kept me in a state of suspended animation for something like 500 years. My awakening, I figured out later, had been due to some shifting of the strata which reopened the shaft and cleared the atmosphere in the working. This must have been the case, for I was able to struggle back up the shaft over a pile of debris, and stagger up the long incline to the mouth of the mine, where an entirely different world, overgrown with a vast forest and no visible sign of human habitation, met my eyes.

I shall pass over the days of mental agony that followed in my attempt to grasp the meaning of it all. There were times that I felt that I was on the verge of insanity. I roamed the unfamiliar forest like a lost soul. Had it not been for the necessity of improvising traps and crude clubs with which to slay my food, I believe I should have gone mad. Suffice to say, however, that I survived this psychic crisis. I shall begin my narrative proper with my first contact with Americans of the year 2419 A.D.

"Armageddon—2419 A.D."
by Philip Francis Nowlan

Thus began the introduction of Anthony "Buck" Rogers to the world in the August 1928 issue of *Amazing Stories.*

A fabulous fantasy followed that wrapped itself around the imagination of the world. An industry of outer space began within the worst depression the United States had ever known, creating new millionaires who made comic strips, movie serials, radio programs, watches, radio premiums, casting sets, printing sets, space suits, games, roller skates shaped into rocket ships, and a flood of related products.

Amazing Stories added two full-size illustrations to the story with three cartoon panels, which gave Nowlan the idea of submitting the concept to a comic-strip syndicate. In 1929 John F. Dille, president of the National Newspaper Syndicate of America, a forceful, intelligent, and creative businessman, agreed with Nowlan to change this character into a comic-strip hero. Dille assigned Dick Calkins, his best staff cartoonist to draw the illustrations. It was Dille who changed his name to Buck, and there was much opposition to this decision since it suggested a cowboy rather than a space hero. The strip first appeared in January 1929 and became "Buck Rogers 2429 A.D." Each year the strip's title was updated by one year to maintain the 500-year difference. As the popularity grew the name was changed to "Buck Rogers in the 25th Century." During the first two years the theme was pulp science fiction, but gradually it evolved away from that origin and achieved an originality all its own.

The Sunday and daily comic strips created a sensation, adding new words to the language that still remain. Phil Nowlan wrote and Dick Calkins and his aides drew the famous characters of Buck Rogers, his girl friend Wilma Deering, the super scientist Dr. Huer, the villain Killer Kane and his girl Ardala, Black Barney and Buddy, and a host of outer-space monsters and weird machines, providing continuous good-guys-versus-bad-guys conflicts and hair-raising adventures.

And there were the marvelous inventions of the future: rocket pistols, disintegrator guns that could destroy any obstacle, rocket ships traveling at thousands of miles an hour, strapped-on-your-back flying belts, outer-space-to-earth television, the mysterious new element Inertron that created automatic weightlessness and permitted a defiance of gravity. Years later, many came true, such as the instant Polaroid camera, space satellites, outer-space television spy satellites, parachute recovery of space capsules, monorail trains, rocket-powered flying belts, Skylabs, space suits and space walks, atomic bombs and power plants, landing of men on the moon, picturephones, lie detectors, nuclear submarines, and remote-control robots to serve science in handling dangerous experiments.

Where did these ideas come from? Many of John Dille's friends were faculty members in the science departments at the University of Chicago, and he was so impressed with the excellence of that institution that he sent his son Robert there to obtain his education. During the nineteen twenties and thirties it was a brilliant university alive with new concepts and creative minds that eventually resulted in many Nobel Prize winners and the first atomic chain reaction. Since the National Newspaper Syndicate was in Chicago, Dille had easy access to these scientists pursuing the future.

Today Buck Rogers is the synonym for the world of the future—new inventions, the world of outer space, and the heroism and courage of our Earth's astronauts. The stories were really not just for children. Adults enjoyed them, because many were based upon the most advanced but plausible science of the time. They had an aura of accurate prophecy about them that has become fact. "Buck Rogers in the 25th Century" precisely described the bazooka, the jet plane, the walkie-talkie, the infrared ray gun for night fighting, and many other advances that have not yet arrived but are on their way.

In the first strip, January 7, 1929, our recently awakened hero meets Wilma Deering, a terrified, persecuted twenty-fifth-century American. The "Yellow Peril" had triumphed and the United States had been conquered by the Mongols. A war of liberation had to come in which Americans must gain control of the invaders' advanced weaponry. Gravity repeller rays, rocket pistols, disintegrator beams, futuristic cities, and truth machines were worked into the stories and diagramed as if by an engineering draftsman. The interest of the local reader was increased by references to American cities. It was a shrewd idea to help sell the strip to local editors. The Pittsburgh papers bought "Alleghany Orgzone," and the Buffalo *Evening News* signed up when "Niagra" became the capital of the planet Earth. Also mentioned were San Francisco, Detroit, and New York. The strip was successful beyond all expectations and between 1929 and 1967, the year it ended, Buck Rogers had been translated into eighteen languages and had appeared in approximately four hundred and fifty newspapers.

A typical and devoted fanatic, Ray Bradbury, the excellent science-fiction writer, gives an on-the-spot report:

The most beautiful sound in my life, was the sound of a folded newspaper kiting through the summer air landing on my front porch.

Every afternoon from the time I was nine until I was fourteen that sound, and the thump it made hitting the side of the house, or the screen door, or a window, but never the porch planks themselves, that sound had an immediate effect upon one person inside the house.

The door burst wide. A boy, myself, leapt out, eyes blazing, mouth gasping for breath, hands seizing at the paper to grapple it wide so that the hungry soul of one of Waukegan, Illinois' finest small intellects could feed upon:

BUCK ROGERS IN THE 25TH CENTURY!

. . . Buck Rogers was his first, my first, huge mania.

. . . And I gave away my Buck Rogers collection.

My Buck Rogers collection! Which was like giving away my head, my heart, my soul, and half a lung. I walked wounded for a year after that. I grieved and cursed myself for having so dumbly tossed aside what was, in essence, the greatest love of my life.

And what a collection it could have been! No other comic character, with the exception of Mickey Mouse, provided such a vast variety of beautiful collectibles! In all of them there were the influences of Art Nouveau and Art Deco motifs mixed into the new world of the twenty-fifth century of space monsters and machines of fantasy. The toys were Nouveau-Deco industrial sculptures, as if one hand had designed them all, and the art of the comic page was primitive, simple, in a unique style.

The reasons for the swift commercial success enjoyed by Buck Rogers merchandise were that the comic strips and the radio programs preceded the introduction of the items and provided the nationwide publicity that in turn created a market. The first Buck Rogers broadcast was aired on November 7, 1932; the first strip appeared January 7, 1929; but the first Buck Rogers items did not appear in the marketplace before 1933, and the backlog of publicity and popularity was there to be commercially exploited. Much of the merchandise was worked into the radio programs and the strips. All was licensed by the John F. Dille Company, and the royalties produced a fortune during the worst years of the depression.

And during that depression it took great courage for a toymaker to decide to spend the start-up and promotional money for a new comic-strip character. One such man was Cass Hough, now president of the Daisy Manufacturing Company, who was directly responsible for much of the success of marketing Buck Rogers in many toy forms and should be considered the creative force behind the aesthetic and merchandising success of the finest single group of Buck Rogers collectibles: the seven different pistols. The first Buck Rogers Rocket Pistol was the XZ-31. It was made from heavy-gauge blued gun steel with nickel-plated trimmings, made a loud "zap" when fired, and was nine and a half inches in length. It was packaged in a handsomely designed, colorful carton with weird, long-legged creatures, space ships, and "Zap-Zap-Zap" shooting out of its muzzle. It was the same design as shown in the daily and Sunday comics and added *zap* and *to get zapped* to our language. It sold for 50¢ retail at Macy's and Gimbels and cost only 5¢ to make! It was the toy "hit" of 1934.

But 1935 was a tough year, and stockbrokers were still sleeping in Hooverville huts in Central Park, so the same pistol was reduced to seven and a half inches in length, packaged in a smaller carton, named the XZ-35, and retailed for 25¢! They were made as well as real guns, and therefore are easily restored to mint condition. In the comic strip it was much like an automatic, except that its magazine was much larger, and the propelling charge was in the small cartridge case that traveled with the highly explosive bullet instead of remaining in the pistol, giving a flatter trajectory and longer range. Some of these bullets had explosive power equal to artillery shells of the twentieth century. Imagine the fantasy of power the kid had who knew the strip and had that real rocket pistol in his hand!

In May 1935 the Buck Rogers Disintegrator Pistol was presented at the American Toy Show in New York City. It was called the XZ–38. It was made from copper, completely different from the rocket pistols, and packed a fantasy quite out of this world:

> It has an electronic compression viewplate in the top which lights up every time the gun is fired by a secret ray within. The process of disintegration of buildings, aircraft and people who get in Buck Rogers' way is accomplished by an electronic barrage created within the gun by means of an electronic compression chamber and a sub-atomic condenser discharged by an impulse generator controlled by a beam intensity selector and aimed by a disintegration beam director. Of course, as the electronic discharge leaves the gun, the barrel under normal circumstances would become very hot. Not in the Buck Rogers Disintegrator however, for the barrel is cooled by a tri-thermal convergence unit.

Besides being a pistol for a kid, it is a handsome, futuristic sculpture and a wild work of nineteen-thirties industrial design. With all these guns on the market, holsters had to be supplied. Daisy, always a quality manufacturer, provided them in real and thick leather; therefore, they are almost always found in excellent condition.

The Buck Rogers Helmet was also produced by Daisy and was an exact copy of Buck's own helmet as continuously shown in the daily and Sunday comics. It was made of leather and had nickel-plated radio antennae, earphones, and full-vision visor, and was model XZ-34. The box has superb artwork of outer space, with a large-face view of Buck wearing the helmet.

In 1936 Daisy brought forth the most attractive Buck Rogers pistol ever designed. It was the XZ-44 Buck Rogers 25th Century Liquid Helium Water Pistol, finished in brilliant yellow and red futuristic design and able to be shot fifteen times without reloading. A later model had a plain copper finish, and the box design is equally attractive. After World War II, the interest in atomic energy spawned two new pistols using the existing tools and dies from the 1936 Disintegrator Pistol. The U-235 Atomic Pistol was an immediate success in 1946, and Dick Calkins aided in the promotion, design, and packaging. And in 1948 the U-238 Atomic Pistol appeared, with a holster. It was the same gun but with another name.

What was it like to be there, to be the originator of all this circa 1934? For an eye-witness account here is Cass Hough, president of Daisy:

MEMORANDUM

THE DAISYBUCK ROGERS AFFAIR

Let me say at the start that after thirty five or forty years my memory isn't all it might be in some of the details, such as exact dates. It is entirely possible that some material that Mr. Lesser has will be more accurate in this respect than my memory. Needless to say, most of the Company records that would pinpoint dates have long since been destroyed.

I first met Dick Calkins in the late twenties in Chicago. I had been flying since 1921—that is, I soloed in October of 1921 and in those days anyone who had any relationship to an airplane belonged to a rather small and closely knit fraternity. Dick Calkins was a World War I pilot and was still very much interested in airplanes. Early in 1930 he got the idea of an Adventure Strip (erroneously referred to as a Comic Strip) dealing with five centuries from now. Whether the original idea was Dick Calkins' or Phil Nolan's I am not sure—as a matter of fact, talking to both of them at the same time I don't know that the matter ever came up. Pilot strips were drawn and the Calkins-Nolan team made a deal with National Newspapers Syndicate headed by John F. Dille to syndicate the Strip. It is my guess—but only a guess—that the first appearance of the Strip was sometime in 1930. In looking at some of the pilot strips, it occurred to me that here was a fertile field for some 25th Century "armament" to be sold to boys and girls who read the Strip. Many of the designs of 25th Century armament that were in the early strip were far too bizarre to make—that is, much too difficult to put into metal (and remember in those days we didn't have the widespread use of injection molding and die casting to come up with fancy shapes easily).

This required then that the hand guns and other items of that nature which Buck and his cronies used, should be a design that Daisy could duplicate in metal—pressed metal that is. And so, we worked very closely to make sure that such was the case. As a matter of fact, it was planned that none of the armament be brought out until after the Strips had been in circulation for quite some time and a real Buck Rogers following was developed. This gave us the opportunity, then, to change the shape of the gun in the Strips so that when we finally tooled for them the results would be actual "Spittin images" of what the youngsters saw in the Strip. And on top of this, we were making our weekly contributions in the nomenclature department, so that the whole project fitted like a glove when we were finally ready for the market with the original rocket pistol.

And if my memory is accurate, the first rocket pistol was shown at the American Toy Fair in February of 1934. At any rate, the fall before this, I had convinced my close friend Milton G. Brinkman who was then senior toy buyer for AMC and Manager of the toy department of the J. L. Hudson Company of Detroit that his Christmas theme might very well be a 25th Century one. He agreed and Hudson's designers came up with a whole set of Martian and other extraterrestrial figures and had a "real" rocket ship (which kids "rode" in) as the central theme of Hudson's toy department Christmas promotion.

Kids visited it and were treated to probably the first bit of real fantasy the public had ever seen (unless of course you count Red Riding Hood, Alice in Wonderland and some of the things that have been done before). The response to this was so overwhelming that it convinced me that we were on the right track to tool for a line of Buck Rogers merchandise. In the meantime I had worked out a contract with John Dille which gave Daisy exclusive rights to anything in the toy field, and in addition agreed to act as an Advisor to John Dille, (in respect of toys) in case people came to him with marketable ideas and in areas that we were not equipped to manufacture or sell. It was agreed that in a case like this we would relinquish our rights under the contract but would have first crack at any item submitted.

The biggest difficulty in designing the first rocket pistol was to come up with a noise that was close to the "zap" that was becoming standard vocabulary with youngsters. I had helped design a noise-making mechanism (back in the late twenties) which was applied to a pop gun, but wasn't terribly popular because the sound that came out of the gun was more a "zap" than a "boom" and the super-realist minds of the day insisted that a gun had to go "boom." Well, I thought about this mechanism and with a few minor adjustments on it, came out with a real loud "zap"—so the problem was solved.

For the Toy Fair 1934 when Buck Rogers was introduced, I had bought from J. L. Hudson Company, all of the "Martian" and other extra-terrestrial figures and used them as the center of our own Buck Rogers theme. We had only the one item, the rocket pistol (unfortunately). But I'm getting ahead of myself.

I was sales manager at the time and I must say that Uncle Charlie Bennett and my Dad were *at best* luke-warm to my ideas for the exploitation of Buck Rogers merchandise. It got down to a point where they finally threw up their hands, literally, and said they would humor me, but that the whole project would lay a real egg in their opinion. As evidence of this, a Chauncey Rauch, who was then head salesman for the company, came close to resigning because he was asked to go out and sell something like this. As a matter of fact he advised many customers that probably they ought to buy a few pieces to "humor the old man's son" but not to hold him responsible for the fact that it laid an egg. These same people, I might say, six months later were on the telephone demanding priorities on shipments simply because they had given a small token order to us early on. Anyway we brought it to the market (Toy Fair 1934) and I must say that the first customers that came in and saw our offering believed that Cass Hough had lost his marbles. They admitted that the gun was good value at fifty cents retail, that it made a pretty good noise, that it worked easily, but were sure at the same time it would have a limited sale *if any sale at all*. Most thought Buck Rogers was a cowboy! Some of them bought a few pieces just to humor me; but, in the middle of a depression they didn't turn loose many dollars for items that they felt were literally "out in orbit." At the end of the first week I was beginning to feel a little low. Late one

Friday afternoon of the first week, in walked Robert A. Wolfe, then head of the toy department of R. H. Macy and Company. I might say here that in my opinion Bob Wolfe was one of the most, if not the most imaginative of all toy buyers that I ever got to know. Not only could he recognize, quickly, a marketable idea, but what's more he had the guts to put Macy's money where his mind was. His ideas for the promotion of my project were almost bound to guarantee a success. He hadn't been in the room three or four minutes before I realized that here was the key to Buck Rogers so far as widespread sale was concerned. He took me to his home over the weekend and there we planned what turned out to be one of the most successful promotions ever to come into the toy business and certainly the most successful promotion ever up to that time. In exchange for the big promotion they were to give it, they were to have it exclusively in New York City for one week. And on top of that I agreed to loan him the weird extra-terrestrial figures that I had bought from the J. L. Hudson Company. As a matter of fact, these figures moved around the country for a year and a half and sparked displays of Buck Rogers merchandise in all the leading department stores around the country.

Macys did an excellent job of getting the public "ready for Buck Rogers," a week before the guns were put on sale. They did such a good job that, came Monday morning the guns went on sale, there were in the neighborhood of 2,000 people in line outside the door (according to the police) to buy this rocket pistol. And as the day went on the crowds grew so that by late afternoon when Macys were all but out of merchandise, we ran our own truck from Plymouth, Michigan (where we were then located) to New York, and kept trucks on the road all that week. In the meantime, of course, all the other department stores around the country—those that had literally laughed at the idea during the Toy Fair, wanted on the band wagon, and my Dad almost fired me because of all the heat being put on him at the plant, while, as he put it, I was "enjoying myself in New York City." As a matter of fact, it was fun to see the culmination of an idea in a successful merchandising event. Incidentally, Macys was selling the gun for forty-nine cents because it was always their policy to sell slightly under the suggested retail price—and still is I guess.

The week of exclusivity ended and true to my promise Gimbels got their shipment. This was at the beginning of the time when each said of the other "we will not be undersold" or words to that effect. So Gimbels priced their rocket pistols at forty-seven cents; Macys immediately priced theirs at forty-five, Gimbels at forty-three and so on down to the end of the first week of Gimbel's sale, they were selling for nineteen cents (some twelve cents under their cost). A low point in pricing was when Gimbels offered the rocket pistol for *two* for nineteen cents. The price in each of the stores changed almost every hour except when one or the other ran out of merchandise. The store that still had merchandise would then raise their price. In order to keep some semblance of order in this fight, I hired a group of women to go into Macys, buy the guns, bring them back to my suite of rooms at the McAlpin Hotel, take the Macy tags off, pack them and then take them over to Gimbels, and sell them to them. Then the same group of girls would go in and buy them from Gimbels at a lower price, take the tags off and take them over to Macys and sell them. This kept a relatively small amount of merchandise circulating pretty well between the two stores, supplemented, of course, by a daily truck shipment from Michigan to the two stores. I must say that at the end of any one particular day during those first two weeks the Gimbels and Macy's toy departments looked like a cyclone had struck, and people were still lining up to buy them.

By this time everybody in the United States wanted to sell Buck Rogers rocket pistols and Daisy was running nights and Saturdays to try to take care of the demand. Scheduling hadn't been very heavy at the Plant because, despite their promise to back me up on the Buck Rogers item (even though they knew it was going to lay an egg), the production schedules were pretty slim. We couldn't get steel overnight, nor could the box manufacturer keep up with the demand. I caught hell from everybody, the family for being away, my Dad and Uncle Charlie because of all the problems I created at the plant, the customers who couldn't get the guns and even from John

Dille who complained that we weren't making as many guns as we should make to take care of the demand because the stores were badgering him as well. But, I must say, to use a pretty trite old phrase, the same time all this was going on Daisy was "crying all the way to the bank"—and so were all the merchants who were selling it, except possibly Macy and Gimbel because of their price war.

It became evident that we should have other merchandise to go along with the rocket pistol for Christmas selling. So we developed the holster for the pistol, working with Sackman Brothers who at that time were probably the leading children's costume and play suit makers. They made a Buck Rogers outfit which used our helmet, holster and gun. These were very popular outfits during that particular Christmas and the next Christmas as well.

Obviously something that went as fast as the rocket pistol went was bound to taper off so we decided that to keep the momentum going we would have a new item the following year. The Disintegrator was next choice and this required a lot of tough work engineering-wise to be able to make a noise and at the same time show the "combustion" that took place when the disintegrator ray was produced inside the gun. Also we decided that we would make a smaller version of the rocket pistol to retail in the 25 cent range, which we did.

In the meantime I was acting as the "toy advisor" to John Dille. A number of other Buck Rogers items had come on the market, but my memory isn't very good in this respect. I know that a rocket ship was designed and built by Louis Marx and Company and we helped him in the promotion of this, giving up our rights under our contract with John Dille so that Louis Marx could deal direct with Dille. It was very successful too—it moved along the floor and sparks came out of the rear end. It was really one of the first exciting *action* toys that had ever been marketed.

The following year (1936) we brought out the Liquid Helium Pistol which wasn't a howling success *measured by rocket pistol standards*: but by any other standards it did pretty well. I don't remember how many we sold, but I'd guess that we probably sold two and a half to three million

rocket pistols the first year, probably close to the same number of Disintegrators and small rocket pistols the second year and perhaps a half million of the Liquid Helium pistols the third year, together, of course, with hundreds of thousands of holsters, helmets and so forth.

Promotion-wise we had an airplane going around the County Fairs, in the summer of 1935, I believe, flown by "Wilma." Wilma Deering who was the "companion" of Buck Rogers. In this series of County Fair and other similar promotions, the local dealers would have a group of youngsters at the airport to welcome the arrival of the Buck Rogers aircraft flown by Wilma Deering (then Alice Hirschman) and would then proceed to sell hundreds or thousands of Disintegrators, rocket pistols, and so forth at this particular point, many of the boxes autographed by "Wilma."

The bloom was off the rose at the end of the third year—actually lasting longer than I had thought it would. And while the Buck Rogers strip continued to be of great interest, the sale of merchandise dwindled—not because kids weren't interested, but because stores wanted something new—or something *not* Buck Rogers—because they had hung their merchandising plans for several years on the 25th Century theme. So we put the tools away, planning definitely to "revive" the craze when another generation of kids came along.

World War II intervened. Following that and particularly because of the dropping of the atomic bomb, the word atomic was on everyones lips so it occurred to me we ought to have an atomic pistol. Inasmuch as atomic meant fission, we had to *show* the fission. So the old Disintegrator pistol was dressed up and the name changed and the nomenclature changed. This then was late 1946 and raw materials such as steel were awfully hard to come by, so we purchased all the scrap metal we could get our hands on, plus steel rejected by the steel mills because of poor finish, in order to get enough steel to make this new "atomic pistol." The first version of it was blued steel—very much like the finish on our BB guns in those days. A little later on we were able to get our hands on some steel that had a copper flash coating, and we made a few hundred thousand from that. But most of the steel we were able to get was so poor that we could no longer blue the gun, so we had to take to painting them with a bronze/gold color which we continued right up to the time we stopped making the atomic pistol. We also marketed a holster along with it, but we did not market any other peripheral material, like helmets.

My guess is that we made and sold about three quarters of a million Buck Rogers Atomic Pistols and probably a quarter of a million guns and holsters in a combat set.

The very first atomic pistol was made on February 2nd 1946 just one week prior to the opening of the Annual American Toy Fair. My notes reveal that this gun retailed for 89 cents and *we* sold it for between 52 and 55 cents each.

The Buck Rogers strip was not running in a great number of papers. As a result, the interest in Buck Rogers was very much on the wane although his name had gotten to be a household word for describing anything futuristic. We actually wore out the tools on the last end of the run of this Atomic Pistol and decided that there was no need to build a new set of tools because neither the item or the Strip itself was popular enough then to spend a lot of time or money on.

Many people have asked why we haven't reintroduced Buck Rogers with all the interest in space and everything and I think the answer is a pretty simple one: when we first brought out our Buck Rogers merchandise, the Strip was new and fresh and it was pure fantasy. Man had not even launched an artificial satellite let alone think seriously about travels in space. So anything we put in the strip was "authentic" mainly because nobody could prove that it wasn't so. Today, however, with space travel getting almost routine, if measured by the public's near apathy about the last space flight—except for its near tragedy—and the high degree of sophistication about space on the part of youngsters today, I believe it would be nigh on to impossible to create the kind of interest we created then. After all space operations today are kind of ho-hum. To back up my contention is the fact that taken as a whole, space toys have laid more eggs lately than any other kind of toy.

The Buck Rogers strip and certainly the merchandise that was based on the Strip, opened up a whole new field of thinking for youngsters and adults as well. They were kind of swept up into an imaginative space ship, put into orbit, and started on their journey through space in their minds eye—and they got really excited about it. Its my opinion that that kind of excitement would be absolutely impossible to drum up today.

I think that the first presentation of Buck Rogers could have been even more successful than it was, although certainly it was highly successful, if John Dille himself had been a little more imaginative and had been willing to spend some promotional funds out of his receipts for the Strip which he syndicated and royalties from merchandise. But trying to get money out of John Dille for something like this was like trying to squeeze blood out of a stone. I could usually get what I wanted in the way of special art work and that sort of thing from Dick Calkins—by going around John Dille—but anything that came from John we paid for, believe me.

Todays interest in Buck Rogers is understandable because it was a phenomenon. And after all, it was a forerunner of things that are almost commonplace today. The guns themselves are collectors items, and rightly so, because, as I said earlier on in this monograph, the Buck Rogers phenomenon was the greatest thing that had ever hit the toy industry, and in terms of todays promotion, even Buck Rogers would come pretty close to leading the field.

RE: *Buck Rogers Rocket Pistol*

After a conference with McHenry and Cline of the Production Department and Lefever of the Experimental Department we believe that the dies for producing a pistol, similar to the one which you outlined to me, can be produced for approximately $5,500.00. This will include the necessary assembling jigs and fixtures. It is barely possible, however, that this cost will be increased somewhat, owing to the fact that we are, at present, considering the advisability of increasing the basic wage in our tool room, which, of course, would react directly upon the cost of the dies. If the quantities you indicated to me are to be taken as a basis of computation McHenry advised the making of two complete sets of dies rather than one, the cost of which would vary very little from the figure given you above, or approximately ten to eleven thousand dollars for the entire tooling up process.

As regards promotional costs—basing my judgment on amounts spent in the past for introducing new merchandise, and after conferring with you as regards space to be used in national advertising, I feel that an additional $15,000 would be spent in giving this new item the send-off that it should have in order to assure its success, to be consistent with our past advertising expenditure, and justify the quantity you anticipate we can sell (Promotional details on attached sheet).

It is evident, then, that at least $25,000 must be spent to insure immediate acceptance of this item and to manufacture it in quantities which would make it profitable for us to add to our line. On an estimated first run of 50,000 pistols this, as you can see, will amount to 5¢ per pistol, or $7.20 per gross, and which would represent 20% of our price to distributors.

I think you should reassure yourself as to quantity of this item that can be sold before you request such an appropriation for the make ready and promotional expenses, which are entirely "cash out of hand" items. If you still feel as you did, that one half million of this item can be sold, I feel sure that the directors will approve this expenditure.

F. J. Donovan, Auditor

The tremendous success of Daisy's Buck Rogers pistols gave other manufacturers the courage to enter the market. Louis Marx obtained the rights to produce his concept of a rocket ship based upon sketches submitted to the John Dille organization. It was an immediate success, and Sears, Roebuck included it in their catalog and advertised it heavily in local newspapers:

Buck Rogers 25th Century Rocket Ship! The toy sensation of 1934! Special 78¢ Wednesday only.

It flashes with a trail of sparks and a weird droning sound. Colorful lithography. Wing protected wheels. Powerful windup spring. Replaceable protected flint shoots the sparks. Heavy gauge metal; 12 inches long. Extra flint included.

There were cockpit windows on both sides: through one could be seen Buck Rogers and Dr. Huer, through the other Wilma Deering and Buck. Rocket tubes, turrets, wings, and fins completed the colorful fantasy of possible space travel.

The Buck Rogers toys of Hough and Marx were one-to-one transplants created from the characters and their exploits. They were not merely remaindered toys with Buck Rogers decals stuck on them to help sell dead stock. (That came later, after World War II.) Expensive tooling, new toy designs, point-of-sale displays, attractive cartoning, and advertising programs were required. In short, these collectibles of today were the result of a programed effort of toy designers, artists, tool makers, advertisers, precarious bank loans, and, truthfully, cheap depression wages, which all labored to bring forth unique, original, beautifully designed comic-character creations that many in the legitimate art world consider to be worthy of serious consideration as works of sculpture: industrial American comic art.

The increasing popularity of the daily and Sunday comics, combined with the now nationwide audience for the radio program, enlarged the consumer demand for new and imaginative Buck Rogers "things" that could be touched, played with, worn to school, and collected, even in those days. A flood followed: Marx designed a pair of roller skates that are pure museum material. Made from heavy-gauge, high-quality steel, they were shaped like rocket ships with red bicycle-style reflectors in the rocket tail.

Like Marx, Sackman Brothers of New York worked with Daisy to develop the Buck Rogers and Wilma Deering playsuits for boys and girls. The garments were realistically designed to be exact copies of the space suit as worn by Buck Rogers in the daily and Sunday comic strips. Special attention was directed to make the color scheme as attractive and bright as possible. A bright two-piece orange and black jersey shirt with a round leather medallion picture of Buck, rocket pistol in hand, riveted to the shirt, together with light tan suedine breeches and leggings comprised the suit. An official Daisy Buck Rogers pistol and leather holster and an official Buck Rogers suedine helmet came with each outfit. And it was marketed in sizes 4 to 14. It was packaged in a handsome large box with Buck in his suit shooting at strange space ships attacking a futuristic city. All of this for just $4.50 retail, Christmas 1934. It was sold in all leading department stores, clothing stores, and via the radio program for Cream of Wheat box tops.

In 1935, too late for the Buck Rogers gold rush of the 1934 Christmas, Rapaport Brothers of Chicago, hired a well-known sculptor to model heroes, villains, rocket ships, Teiko men, Tigermen, Mekkano men, Depth men, and Disintegrator machines into molds for the Buck Rogers 25th Century Casting Set. It came in three models: Electric, Midget, and Junior. Its popularity was amazing. In some of the big Chicago stores it was necessary to keep three people in the booth to handle the orders. The remarkable success was attributed to a dual sales appeal: first, the tremendous publicity behind the name of Buck Rogers; second, the substantial advertising campaign; and then the current fad of casting outfits. Even unsolicited orders poured into the Rapaport offices. The box itself had a brilliant lithographed and varnished label in four colors. All sets included equipment for coloring the figures as well as casting them and ranged in price from $1.50 to $3.50.

The stores found that a good part of the business was in extra molds. Purchasers of Buck Rogers Casting Sets often bought several extra molds to make additional figures not included in their set. There were eight extra molds available.

Why this popularity? The answer: a particular sales pitch keyed to the depression years:

YOU CAN MAKE MONEY WITH THESE POPULAR TOYS!

Get this great outfit! Make toy castings of Buck with his marvelous Disintegrator Pistol . . . Wilma Deering, his faithful Lieutenant . . . and Killer Kane, the arch criminal of the 25th Century. Paint your castings in bright, lifelike colors. Make all the toys you want. Sell them at a big profit! Millions of people are interested in Buck's adventures . . . and follow them daily in newspapers and radio. START YOUR OWN TOY BUSINESS WITH THIS COMPLETE OUTFIT. MAKE REAL MONEY!

And thousands of kids convinced their parents that it was a good investment, not just a toy, and proceeded to sell each other the painted comic figures of Buck's world. Today, there are collectors of these casting sets who still make side money by casting these figures, painting them, and selling them at flea markets, toy shows, and comic conventions!

As newspaper syndication of the strips spread, so did radio coverage. By the end of 1934 Boston, Buffalo, New York, Philadelphia, Pittsburgh, Albany, Baltimore, Cincinnati, Cleveland, Detroit, Syracuse, Washington, Charlotte, Columbus, Richmond, Rochester, Chicago, Indianapolis, Kansas City, Louisville, St. Louis, Minneapolis, New Orleans, San Antonio, Atlanta, and Dallas radio stations carried *Buck Rogers in the 25th Century* via the air waves to the millions. The R. B. Davis Company, makers of Cocomalt, a chocolate-flavored drink, sponsored the program, and a flood of radio premiums followed.

A catalog was made available. It was dubbed *Buck Rogers Solar Scouts . . . Secret Club of the Radio Friends of Buck and Wilma*, and it contained a vast number of premiums, some original to the radio show and some merely the commercial toys, such as the space suit and pistols.

Buck's sponsors were Kellogg, Cream of Wheat, Cocomalt, and later on, Popsicle and Post Toasties. Kellogg's-sponsored *Buck Rogers in the 25th Century* soft-cover book was one of the first premiums, and included the complete story of Buck, with handsome color pictures of the major characters, machines, and monsters. The cover has exceptional artwork and is signed by Dick Calkins.

One of the most coveted premiums among collectors is Cocomalt's Buck Rogers Map of the Solar System. It depicts the solar system, with Buck in his flying belt and the real Buck Rogers radio cast in outer space costumes, monsters, machines, rocket ships, meteors, and radio.

Three very handsome, very Art Deco badges were issued by Cocomalt: a Solar Scout Badge, with Buck, his two pistols drawn, seated in his rocket ship; and up one grade, the Chief Explorer Badge, in gold and red, with planets, stars, and a front view of Buck; last, the Space Commander Badge, with a secret whistle with Buck Rogers flanked by rocket ships and stars that is a piece of pure Art Deco jewelry. But the girl listeners were not left out. An extremely rare and beautiful radio premium was the Cream of Wheat Wilma Deering Medallion, gold plated with a sixteen-inch gold chain. On the face was a handsome profile view of Wilma in her space helmet and on the back: "To my pals in the Solar Scouts." And of course a radio ring, the Buck Rogers Secret Repeller Ray Ring. It had Buck Rogers seated in his open-air rocket sled molded into the top, with a green stone sunk into the side of the ship—the repeller. It was to be used as a seal ring on all secret club documents and correspondence. A later ring was the Buck Rogers Ring of Saturn, made from plastic, that glowed in the dark.

One of the most attractive and rare Buck Rogers premiums was the Buck Rogers Shoulder Patch. Three inches in diameter, it was made from a bright orange piece of felt, embroidered with a face view of Buck in front of a rocket ship, in blue, with space rays in red surging out in all directions, plus "Buck Rogers Solar Scouts" big and bold. It came with your membership card, a photo of the radio characters of Buck and Wilma, and a letter on Buck's own stationery signed by Buck Rogers and Wilma Deering, thanking you for drinking Cocomalt. What a package deal! Yes, there was also a knife, produced by Adolph Kastor and Brothers, shaped to simulate the form of a rocket ship, and Buck is pictured at the controls piloting it through space; retail, 25¢ or box tops.

Cream of Wheat tied in with Breyers Ice Cream and brought forth a Dixie Cup Lid portrait of Captain Buck in space gear clutching a CBS microphone (played on the air by Matthew Crowley). Other radio premiums included a flashlight, telescope, dog tag, movie projector, films, lunch box, model rocket-ship kits, cartoon books, sweat shirts, balloons, Big Little Books, watches, even chocolate bars and Buck Rogers' own health drinks!

What is the rarest Buck Rogers premium of all? I'd vote for the set of six Britains. These were molded-lead figures of Buck Rogers, Wilma Deering, Dr. Huer wielding a paralysis ray gun, Killer Kane, Ardala, and Mekkano Man with movable arms, two and one-quarter inches in height, finished in brilliant colors. Understand that there are literally thousands of Britains-collectors around the world; they collect mostly the soldiers, and no one has yet found a complete set. Perhaps they had a short production run, perhaps they were destroyed during the scrap-metal drive of World War II. The cost then? Three Cream of Wheat green triangles plus 50¢, for the set of six.

Past the rarest is the impossible. Impossible, because the Thornecraft Buck Rogers Strat-O-Sphere Balloon was made from rubber and has had to have shriveled into powder after forty years of aging. It included an "antigravity" gas made from two chemical ingredients in the package, a postcard with a 1¢ stamp already licked on (low postal rates in those thirties days), and a string to attach the card to the balloon. Up, up, and away, then down hopefully in some other city to be found by another Buck Rogers fan who would mail it back to you with his comments:

This card carries printed instructions for the finder to drop it in the nearest mailbox. A second card is retained for a "flight record." This item is intriguing because it carries the name of Buck Rogers . . . it's thrilling because of the fun and novelty of filling and launching the balloon.

It was handsomely packaged in a cardboard box, one dozen of which were packed in a beautifully decorated display carton.

The last known Buck Rogers premium was the most spectacular. There was a premium designer known to the trade as "Gold of Chicago" who, in the early nineteen fifties, designed for Sylvania Television a twenty-one-piece Buck Rogers Halolight Space Ranger's Kit. It consisted of bright, imaginative cardboard cutouts that folded into a Buck Rogers space helmet, a space ship that hummed as it flew, a supersonic-rocket launcher that actually shoots rockets, an atomic rocket, two Buck Rogers Interplanetary Space Phones that really work, a flying-saucer disintegrator that shoots, eight flying saucers, a space compass, a space ranger's mask, a pilot pendant, a space ranger's badge, a Martian Nodding Head Dynagator Target, and standing figures of Buck, Wilma, space rangers, and Martians. Assembled, it was a small Buck Rogers world, beautifully designed with action toys of play value.

Books. The Whitman Publishing Company, Racine, Wisconsin, was then and is now a fine publisher of children's books. As soon as they saw the early-thirties Sunday pages, they understood the potential and arranged with John Dille for a group of twelve Big Little Books. These books were dimensioned to fit into a kid's pocket and were only about four and one-half by three and one-half inches, but quite thick, and they cost a nickel. The front- and back-cover Buck Rogers outer-space art was superb, and there are thousands of Big Little Books collectors. Some, like the *Flash Gordon Dell Fast Action* book or the *Buck Rogers in the City of Floating Globes*, are rare and sell when found for as high as $75. The titles were fantastic inventions that promised wild outer-space adventures: *Buck Rogers in the City Below the Sea, Buck Rogers on the Moons of Saturn, Buck Rogers and the Depth Men of Jupiter, Buck Rogers and the Super Dwarf of Space*, and *Buck Rogers and the Overturned World*. They sold in such large quantities that even though forty years have intervened, they are not difficult to find in mint condition today.

Whitman also published the *Buck Rogers Paint Book*. Inside was black-and-white pure Calkins primitive art of the heroes, villains, monsters, and machines, which could be colored to fit the child's imagination. The full-color cover art pictured Buck Rogers complete with flying belt and radio helmet floating in a space filled with colored globes holding paint brushes!

Among collectors, Blue Ribbon Books, Inc., is generally considered the best publisher of pop-up books. They were selected in the mid-thirties by the Dille organization to produce the two Buck Rogers Pop-Up Books. The small one, *Buck Rogers in a Dangerous Mission*, opened up to unfold Buck and Wilma in the cockpit of an open-air rocket ship in a pitch-black sky filled with strange planets. *Buck Rogers in Strange Adventures in the Spider Ship* had three pop-ups that can be considered the most beautiful Blue Ribbon ever created: The first had Wilma, fallen in fright before a huge winged and clawed monster on a strange planet, being defended by Buck and his rocket pistol; the second, Buck and Wilma swimming below a strange sea; and the third, Buck and Wilma watching the coming battle between the Spider Ship and a sharp-beaked creature half monster, half machine. So marvelous and colorful are the pop-ups that they almost seem to come to life as the book is opened.

Watches. Ingraham obtained the license to produce the Buck Rogers Pocket Watch and Wristwatch. The pocket watch was produced in large quantities because it was adopted by Sears, Roebuck for their 1935 mail-order catalog. Buck and his upright rocket pistol protecting a terrified Wilma on the face with radio-flash-style copper hands comprising the face design, while the back had a hairy-legged, one-eyed monster with a large hypodermic needle obviously pursuing our team. The small box is the best of Buck Rogers art and makes no reference to the pocket watch inside. It is within the style of Tiffany Art Nouveau, and in 1971 the Huckleberry Time Company used the box as "pick-up art" to produce a pocket watch. It also had radio-flash hands and shaped the second hand into a thirties-style rocket ship, which gave it animation. It was designed to be used as a pocket watch, giant wristwatch, or, with a small case, a table clock. But it had a short production run and has already become a collector's item.

The 1935 Ingraham Buck Rogers Wristwatch? Records prove that Ingraham produced it, but there must have been a very small production run because to this date not one has been found. Gray-haired jewelers have described it as a large wristwatch with bright colors and a wide metal band having rocket ships and planets cast into it. Good hunting! The U.S. Rubber Company produced a pair of sneakers, but not even a picture of them has been found. And the Gropper Company produced a chemistry set, again not even one picture exists.

The most expensive item made during the depression years sold for the astronomical sum of $13 retail, often a whole week's salary to an average worker! It was designed by Stephen Slesinger, Inc., and produced by the Porter Chemical Company of Hagerstown, Maryland. The Buck Rogers 25th Century Scientific Laboratory combined chemistry, microscopy, and astronomy in a gigantic, super science set. It was packaged in a large box and, with all of the equipment, weighed a heavy twelve pounds: It included: chemistry—a complete set of chemicals, apparatus, and instructions for more than 300 scientific experiments; microscopy—a complete set of accessories, apparatus, and instructions for preparing, mounting, and studying microscopic objects; also a powerful, tested microscope and a big instruction book explaining 120 different things to observe; astronomy—a complete astronomical set for star study any time and any place, including star maps, constellation charts, book of instruction, and a powerful long-distance Buck Rogers telescope. Perhaps not very many were sold at that $13 high depression price, and that could be the reason that not one, not even a piece, has been found by any of the many Buck Rogers collectors to this date. Only the advertisement records its existence.

One of the most popular fads during the nineteen thirties was the rubber-stamp set. With a big ink pad, crayons, and rubber stamps of your favorite comic characters, you could stamp the characters on the newly painted kitchen walls, your father's white silk summer suit, your younger sister's arms, legs, and face, and other convenient objects. The Buck Rogers Printing Set was produced by the Superior Type Company, and in comparison to other stamp sets of the period it was superior. It consisted of fourteen stampers, twenty-five blank strips, and six crayons and, as was typical with all Buck Rogers merchandise, was packaged in a brightly colored box. One of the advantages to a current collector is that you can stamp your letters with these decorations. They look like this:

Buck	Wilma	Dr. Huer	Killer Kane	Buddy
Rocket Ship	Ardala	Zap!	Robot	Black Barney

Related school supplies included the Buck Rogers tablet covers and composition books manufactured by the White and Wyckoff Company, introducing a new feature with its continued story on the back cover. One found that he had to buy the whole series of six in order to get Buck safely through the story! The Solar Scout School Kit to hold your school books was made of heavy, weather-resisting duck, with big pictures of Buck and Wilma stamped in blue and white on the front, and had a heavy black-leather carrying strap. A large variety of the Buck Rogers Pencil Boxes were made by the American Lead Pencil Company with typical Twenty-fifth-century scenes stamped on the outside. They had a built-in secret drawer for safe-keeping of outer-space maps and private Solar Scouts secret documents. And educational games abounded. Perhaps the best was produced by the Warren Paper Products Company in which a Rocket Ship Control Base (very much like today's Houston Space Center) could be constructed with cardboard characters and rocket ships and two Force Ray guns that

> Get their men with deadly accuracy at ten feet away! You'll be surprised how easily you can pick off Killer Kane! Of course he's only temporarily paralyzed and soon is on his feet again to make more trouble for Buck!

Even something for the handicapped child: Dictagraph Products Company in 1937 produced a hearing aid for deaf children called the Accousticon. Their sales pitch:

Thousands of kids are shy about wearing visible earphones and thus handicap themselves terribly. The Buck Rogers Accousticon makes it a game and they don't mind wearing the small plug-style earphones . . . indeed not, they insist on having them!

Outside of school during recess, on the street corner was the ice-cream man selling Tarzan Ice Cream. Twelve Tarzan cup lids collected and sent to the company would get you *The Buck Rogers Story,* a small premium book filled with pictures.

And, of course, you could skate home after school on your Buck Rogers rocket-shaped roller skates, then off to the playground with your Buck Rogers Football! It had a beautifully silvered fabric cover, genuine needle valve bladder, four red fins, yellow lacing, and red lettering. It was called the Buck Rogers Rocket and was delivered to the store already inflated, packed in an attractive box by the Edward K. Tryon Company.

And on the Fourth of July, the other kids on the block had the ordinary firecrackers, Roman candles, and cherry bombs. You could buy from the National Fireworks Company in Boston "The Sun Gun of Saturn," which would shoot fiery balls into the air, or the "Battle Fleet of Rocket Ships," with launching pad and quite similar to today's Cape Kennedy method. These rocket ships could be directed in flight! Even more spectacular was "The Battle of Mars," with targets to hit of the Tigermen of Mars. The most intriguing would have been "The Chase of Killer Kane," in which Buck's rocket ship is in a deadly circular dog-fight with the Killer's ship.

Great fun could be had from the Buck Rogers Rocket Ship. The recoil rocket projector was operated by complicated spring pressure. Igniting the fuse automatically sent the ship into high flight. It could be recovered, reloaded, and sent up again. Rocket projector, rocket ship, and release fuses were contained in a metal can for safety purposes. All of these fireworks kits were packaged in attractive, full-color packages, with scenes depicting the rockets, battles, and guns operating on strange planets. Needless to say, none of the fireworks or even the empty boxes have as yet been found.

For Halloween 1933 the Einson-Freeman Company made paper masks of Buck and Wilma. They are pure Art Deco and among Buck Rogers collectors are considered the most beautiful of all the paper items and very suitable for framing.

Christmas 1934 witnessed the greatest of all Buck Rogers promotions. In Macy's, a full human-size Martian city was created in the center of which was a huge Buck Rogers rocket ship identical in design to the Marx wind-up sold in the store. In the background were the weird-looking buildings of Mars and the flashing lights of that strange planet. A futuristic train with real cars transported forty children at a time from a big platform in the center of the city, around sharp curves, and into a tunnel. Inside the tunnel were four lighted scenes showing mechanical figures of men from Mars, Atlantis, and Gigantica. One scene showed Buck Rogers flying through space with his rocket pistol tightly grasped in his hand. Finally, the train emerged from the tunnel and came to a stop in front of the huge rocket ship. The little terrified passengers were led back to safety by adults dressed as Buck and Wilma who gave a surprise package to each child. There was an admission cost of 39¢, but that didn't seem to stop the depression child, because all during the holiday season long lines of children eagerly awaited their turn to visit with Buck and Wilma and ride on the train. A measure of its popularity is that tens of thousands of tickets were sold, and the store counters, loaded with Buck Rogers pistols, space suits, games, and toys were stripped bare as if a plague of locusts had descended—from outer space, of course!

The John Dille Company supplied a large and varied amount of display store material, from complete booths to window displays, and during the 1933 Chicago World's Fair created a magnificent Buck Rogers show with loads of kids dressed as Buck Rogers and Wilma Deering. Unfortunately, all of the point-of-sale materials were thrown away, and only a few photographs remain.

For those kids who couldn't afford the 39¢ to get into the Macy's show, 1¢ was enough to start a Buck Rogers collection. For just 1¢ you could buy a square of Big Thrill Chewing Gum manufactured by the Goudey Gum Company of Boston. In each 1¢ package was a two-inch-by-three-inch, four-page booklet beautifully illustrating Buck's adventures. They carried such titles as *Buck Rogers Thwarting Ancient Demons*, *Collecting Human Specimens*, *The Fight Beneath the Sea*, and *A Handful of Trouble*.

For any gum company willing to pay the royalties to the Dille Company there was a set of twenty-four strip cards available without any commercial message on them. They were divided into three subsets, each having a leading portrait card of Buck, Wilma, and Dr. Huer, and carried scenes of space ships, floods, and other mishaps of outer-space adventures.

A magnificently designed and printed full-color card game, similar to Old Maid, was manufactured by the Richardson Company in the early nineteen thirties. The cards are valuable to collectors because they depict all of the major characters, monsters, and machines and were designed by Dick Calkins, the originator of the strip. It was undoubtedly some of his best work.

The Buck Rogers Cut-Out Adventure Book was a Cocomalt premium. The cut-outs created a theatre of the twenty-fifth century, with all of the individual players and theatrical background of the future cities, wars, rockets, guns, and weird machines. But it was tough to get:

Now you can have all the famous Buck Rogers characters right in front of you!

Here are the 4 easy things you must do—

1. Drink Cocomalt regularly—at least once a day for 30 days.

2. Note your weight and general improvement on chart on back page.

3. Have your mother, father or guardian sign the chart.

4. Send the chart with about two inches of the strip of tin that comes off the can of Cocomalt, when you open it, to R. B. Davis Co. Hoboken N.J.

And we will send you the famous Buck Rogers Cut-Out Adventure Book.

No wonder it's so hard to find one today!

The earliest cut-outs were the six Bucktoys. They were made from thick cardboard, with space people and machines in black and white so that they could be hand colored. They could be cut, folded back to stand upright, and moved into battle. The most interesting was the Bucktoy Number 5, the Gyrex Bullet Space Racer, which had the primitive-art quality of the early comic drawing. In the same package was a handsome, helmet-to-boots-size Buck Rogers in a uniform resembling a World War I biplane pilot, signed by Dick Calkins, the artist.

With all of this came the 1933 *Woofian Dictionary*. A Woof was an amazing wolflike animal found living on the plateaus of the planet Jupiter. Buck had learned that these highly intelligent animals had a means of communication by sounds. The dictionary presented the words as Buck had learned them:

A

Akh..............one
Akh-akh..........two
Akh-akh-akh......three [and so on]

B

Byakh............make
Bfubv............home

***

G

Grrrr............Anger, "I defy you!"
Gwoof............man, human being

***

W

Woof............woof (wolf-like animal of Jupiter)

The Woofs appeared in the Sunday comics and intrigued the young readers so much that they wrote letters to the newspapers asking what the words meant. The *Woofian Dictionary* allowed them to translate.

The last cut-out toy was the Buck Rogers Rubber Band Gun produced in 1940, made by Onward School Supplies, which utilized Buck Rogers art in the early style. The handsome gun folded into shape and shot rubber bands at three targets: the sea monster, the space ship, and a horrible, sharp-toothed Chinaman wearing sunglasses, wide ears, and a bald head, called Wing Bat Wu. It looks great displayed in a picture frame.

In the same year Eastern Publishing brought to the newsstands and candy stores of America the first six comic books of *Buck Rogers in the 25th Century*. The cover of the number-one issue had artwork by Dick Calkins, the others did not. These six books are avidly sought by the at least 100,000 comic-book collectors, not just by Buck Rogers collectors.

Another "crossover" is the set of Buck Rogers Tootsietoy Rocket Ships. There are vast numbers out there in the world of grown men who just collect Tootsietoys, and they all seem to be millionaires, at least to Buck Rogers collectors competing with them. The Dowst Manufacturing Company, in 1937, produced a group of three Tootsietoy rocket ships named the Flash-Blast Attack Ship, Venus Duo-Destroyer, Buck Rogers Battle Cruiser, and just to fill up the large box it included a dirigible, the U.S.N. Los Angeles, plus lead figures of Buck and Wilma. The ships had pulleys at the top so that by tying a cord to the living-room chandelier and the other end to the window ledge, down would fly the heavy die-cast rocket ship, smashing its way out through the glass pane, creating the sound of explosion!

Buck Rogers bicycles, tricycles, wagons, and scooters were tried but were never produced in large quantities, simply because they were expensive "high ticket" items beyond the reach of most depression families.

But the very essence of the art of Buck Rogers in the 25th Century is the comic page: the Sundays and the dailies from 1929 to 1940. Yet these are the most difficult to find because they were "just paper," either gathered and destroyed during the patriotic scrap-paper drive of World War II or merely thrown away as old newspapers. Worse, if not properly stored, the paper crumbles into dust from old age after a passage of twenty years.

The artists who drew them decided at the beginning to keep the Sunday and daily episodes as separate story lines and to number each strip consecutively, which makes it quite easy to collect them in their proper sequence. Dick Calkins, Russell Keaton, and Rick Yager were the artists during the strip's golden age, and the style and content vary from a 1929 child's primitive concept of outer space to the super-slick science fiction of 1940. Phil Nowlan wrote the stories from the beginning in 1929 to his death in 1940, after which Dick Calkins controlled both art and story line. Russell Keaton drew the first 183 Sunday pages, although Calkins signed them, and it is this group that should be the center of any collection. The most rare and most prized would be the Number One page, untrimmed, four color, in good printed registration and in mint condition. At this point in time there are only five known to be in existence. To preserve Sunday pages, they should be kept in clear acetate folders so that they can be viewed without being touched, and the rare ones should be professionally framed.

Even more suitable for framing are the proof pages, prepared by the printer for the artist's approval of printing registration and color for the Sundays. They were printed on glossy stock and the colors were always brighter than the actual newspaper pages, but these are very rare.

But the rarest of the rare is Buck Rogers original art from 1929 to 1940. The artist starts with a large sheet of white cardboard and with black ink and pen draws the strip. There were thousands of dailies and Sundays prepared in this manner, but late one afternoon fifteen years ago (the criminal shall be nameless) an artist associated with the strip took all of the original art into his backyard, poured gasoline over it, lit a match, and burned it up. All that remains are four dailies, two Sundays, a few proof pages, and a magnificent 1936 portrait of Buck Rogers as a giant Gulliver standing over the U.S.A., one foot in New York, the other in Los Angeles, in full uniform, with his rocket pistol pointing east, guarding us all from the "Yellow Peril." Typical of this changing marketplace, what was considered worthless fifteen years ago if found today would be worth thousands of dollars from museums and millionaires.

Also nonexistent are the recordings from the radio programs previous to World War II. The programs were recorded on discs, and none have been found. But a brisk market continues for the existing programs that are postwar, and tapes are available at inexpensive prices. The original radio program featured Matthew Crowley as Buck, Adele Ronson as Wilma Deering, and Edgar Stehli as Dr. Huer. Columbia Broadcasting Studios used twenty-five different motors to imitate the various mechanical devices of Dr. Huer, and the sound of the Psychic Restriction Ray was made by one of the first Schick electric razors!

In 1939 Universal Pictures released the long-awaited film version, starring Larry "Buster" Crabbe as Buck, Constance Moore as Wilma, Jackie Moran as Buddy, and C. Montague Shaw as Dr. Huer, with story and screenplay by Norman Hall and Ray Trampe. This futuristic filmplay unreeled in twelve wild chapters, and the eighth chapter, "Revolt of the Zuggs," is almost a Marxist-oriented workers' revolution, but with rocket ships! Later, Goodwill Pictures made it full length and called them *Planet Outlaws*. Original lobby cards, movie posters, press books, and, of course, the film prints of the twelve chapters are the collectibles, but demand from the thousands of movie buffs has started a minor reproduction industry, and it is difficult to tell these reproductions from the originals.

The point of it all is this: The advantage of selecting a Buck Rogers in the 25th Century to collect is that you can collect a collection. There were literally dozens of items manufactured in large production quantities. The Buck Rogers fantasy so captured the world's imagination that it led to a great surge in the production of Buck Rogers merchandise. Therefore, continuous hunting can lead to the discovery of collectibles previously unknown and unrecorded, whereas in selecting a Flash Gordon or a Tarzan only a small collection is possible because so few items were manufactured.

The sculptor Nogouchi views all sculpture as flying off into space and summarizes his art as a flight from gravity. In a similar sense Buck Rogers in the 25th Century was a flight from gravity: a chance for the imagination of the young to enter a future free from all the gravities, simple good freed from evil, the possible freed from the impossible, the dreams of science freed from the limitations of nuts-and-bolts technology, and the natural optimism of American children freed from the harsh reality of parental despair during the depression years. A strange and beautiful art emerged, worked into paper and sculpted into metal, an American comic industrial art form—Buck Rogers in the 25th Century—a fabulous fantasy.

	Manufacturer	*Date*
Buck Rogers Rocket Pistol, XZ-31	Daisy Manufacturing Co.	1934
Buck Rogers Rocket Pistol, XZ-35 (smaller version)	Daisy	1935
Buck Rogers Disintegrator Pistol, XZ-38	Daisy	1936
Buck Rogers Helmet, XZ-38 and XZ-42	Daisy	1934
Buck Rogers Liquid Helium Water Pistol, XZ-44	Daisy	1936
Buck Rogers Atomic Pistol, U-235	Daisy	1946
Buck Rogers Atomic Pistol, U-238, with Holster	Daisy	1948
Buck Rogers Rocket Ship	Louis Marx	1934
Buck Rogers Police Patrol	Louis Marx	1939
Buck Rogers Rocket Skates	Louis Marx	1935
Buck Rogers Strat-O-Sphere Balloon	Thornecraft	1935
Buck Rogers Space Suit	Sackman Bros.	1934
Buck Rogers Printing Set*	Superior Type Co.	1934
Buck Rogers Knife	Adolph Kastor & Bros. Co.	1934
Buck Rogers Casting Sets (Midget, Junior, Electric casters, and eight extra molds)	Rapaport Bros.	1934
Buck Rogers 25th Century Scientific Laboratory	Porter Chemical Co.	1937
Buck Rogers Chemistry Set	Gropper Co.	1937
Buck Rogers Sneakers	U.S. Rubber Co.	1937
Buck Rogers Pencil Boxes	American Lead Pencil Co.	1934
Buck Rogers Pop-Up Books:	Blue Ribbon Books, Inc.	1935

   1. *In a Dangerous Mission*
   2. *Strange Adventures in the Spider Ship*

Buck Rogers Pocket Watch	E. Ingraham Co.	1935
Buck Rogers Wristwatch	Ingraham	1935
Buck Rogers Pocket Watch, Pendant Watch, Wristwatch, and Clock	Huckleberry Time Co.	1971
Buck Rogers Tootsietoy Rocket Ships	Dowst Manufacturing Co.	1937

   1. Flash-Blast Attack Ship
   2. Venus Duo-Destroyer
   3. Buck Rogers Battle Cruiser
   4. U.S.N. Los Angeles
   5. Cast figures of Buck and Wilma

Buck Rogers Big Little Books	Whitman Publishing Co.	1934

   1. *Buck Rogers 25th Century A.D.* (hard cover)
   2. *Buck Rogers 25th Century A.D.* (soft cover, Cocomalt premium)
   3. *Buck Rogers in the City Below the Sea*
   4. *Buck Rogers on the Moons of Saturn* (soft cover, first edition)
   5. *Buck Rogers and the Depth Men of Jupiter*
   6. *Buck Rogers and the Doom Comet*
   7. *Buck Rogers in the War With the Planet Venus*
   8. *Buck Rogers and the Planetoid Plot*
   9. *Buck Rogers and the Overturned World*
  10. *Buck Rogers and the Super Dwarf of Space*
  11. *Buck Rogers vs. The Fiend of Space*
  12. *Buck Rogers in the City of Floating Globes* (soft cover, Cocomalt premium)

* Smaller set had fourteen stamps; larger set had twelve stamps.

	Manufacturer	Date
Buck Rogers Paint Book	Whitman	1935
Buck Rogers Balloons, Rubber Balls, Paddle Ball	Lee-Tex Products	1935
Buck Rogers Hearing Aid "Accousticon"	Dictagraph Products Co.	1937
Buck Rogers Rocket Football	Edward K. Tryon Co.	1935
Buck Rogers Construction Kits for Space Ships	Buck Rogers Co.	1934
1. Buck Rogers Battle Cruiser		
2. Buck Rogers Martian Police Ship		
3. Buck Rogers Flash-Blast Attack Ship		
4. Buck Rogers Super Dreadnaught		
5. Buck Rogers Venus Fighting Destroyer		
6. Buck Rogers Pursuit Ship (fighting fleet poster)		
Buck Rogers Sweat Shirt		1935
Buck Rogers Sweat Shirt	Varsity House, Inc.	1974
Buck Rogers Fireworks	National Fireworks Co., Inc.	1937
1. "Chase of Killer Kane"		
2. "The Sun Gun of Saturn"		
3. "The Battle of Mars"		
4. "Battle Fleet of Rocket Ships"		
Buck Rogers in the 25th Century Comic Books (Nos. 1–6)	Eastern Publishing	1940
Buck Rogers Solar Scout School Kit	Cream of Wheat premium	1934
Buck Rogers Sweater Emblem Shoulder Patch	Cream of Wheat premium	1934
Buck Rogers Interplanetary Games	Cream of Wheat premium	1934
Buck Rogers Movie Projector and Films	Cream of Wheat premium	1934
Buck Rogers Lite-Blaster Flashlight	Cream of Wheat premium	1934
Buck Rogers Badges	Cream of Wheat premium	1934
1. Space Commander		
2. Chief Explorer		
3. Solar Scout		
Wilma Deering Medallion and Chain	Cream of Wheat premium	1934
Buck Rogers Secret Repeller Ray Ring	Cream of Wheat premium	1934
Buck Rogers Ring of Saturn	Post Toasties premium	1936
Buck Rogers in the 25th Century storybook	Kellogg's premium	1933
Buck Rogers Map of the Solar System	Cocomalt premium	1933
Buck Rogers Dog Tag		1942
Buck Rogers Solar Scout Handbook and Manual	Cocomalt premium	1934
Buck Rogers Set of Britains figures		1934
1. Buck Rogers		
2. Wilma Deering		
3. Killer Kane		
4. Ardala Valmar		
5. Dr. Huer		
6. Robot		
Buck Rogers Telescope	Popsicle premium	1939
Buck Rogers Flying Space Ship Construction Kit	Cocomalt premium	1934
The Buck Rogers Story	Tarzan Ice Cream premium	1935
Buck Rogers Ice Cream Cup Lid (picture of Matthew Crowley)	Breyers Ice Cream radio premium	1935
Buck Rogers Space Ranger's Halolight Kit	Sylvania TV premium	1953
Photograph of Buck and Wilma and Letter on Buck Rogers Stationery	Cocomalt premium	1934

	Manufacturer	Date
Bucktoys (cardboard figures)	newspaper premium	1933
1. Buck Rogers		
2. Killer Kane		
3. Ardala Valmar		
4. Wilma Deering		
5. Gyrex-Bullet Space Racer		
6. Dr. Huer		
Halloween Masks of Buck and Wilma	Einson-Freeman Co.	1933
Buck Rogers Big Big Book	Whitman	1934
Buck Rogers Cut-Out Adventure Book	Cocomalt premium	1934
Buck Rogers Rubber Band Gun	Onward School Supplies	1940
Buck Rogers All-Fair Card Game	Richardson Co.	1936
"Buck Rogers in the 25th Century" strip cards (complete set of 24 cards numbered from #425 to #448)	John F. Dille Co.	1936
Buck Rogers Big Thrill Chewing Gum Booklets	Goudey Gum Company	1934
1. *Thwarting Ancient Demons*		
2. *Collecting Human Specimens*		
3. *The Fight Beneath the Sea*		
4. *A One Man Army*		
5. *An Aerial Derelict*		
6. *A Handful of Trouble*		
Woofian Dictionary	newspaper premium	1933
Buck Rogers Buttons:		
1. "I Saw Buck Rogers"	Chicago World's Fair	1934
2. "Buck Rogers"	Saturday Chicago *American*	1934
3. "Buck Rogers"	Pittsburgh *Post Gazette*	1934
4. "Buck Rogers Rocket Rangers"		1936
5. "Buck Rogers in the 25th Century"		1935
6. "Buck Rogers Club Member"		1937
7. "Buck Rogers and Dr. Huer"		1936
8. "Buck Rogers Satellite Pioneers"		1946
9. "Member Buck Rogers Rocket Rangers"		1946
Buck Rogers Cardboard Helmet and Noisemaker Rocket Pistol	Einson-Freeman Co.	1933
The Buck Rogers Idea (poster depicting the inventions of Buck Rogers in the 25th Century with Noisemaker Rocket Pistol)	S. D. Warren Co.	1969
"Armageddon—2419 A.D." (first Buck Rogers story)	*Amazing Stories*	August 1928
"Armageddon—2419 A.D." (reprint: first Buck Rogers story)	*Amazing Stories*	April 1961
"The Airlords of Han" (second Buck Rogers story)	*Amazing Stories*	March 1929
Great Classic Newspaper Comic Strips		
Buck Rogers in the 25th Century. Reprints of the strips. Books 1–6 and 1931–1932 Collectors Edition. Edited and published by Edwin Aprill, Jr.		
"Buck Rogers" Sunday newspaper pages, proof pages, and original art, particularly Nos. 1–183*	Artist: Russell Keaton	1929–1932
"Buck Rogers" daily newspaper strips, proof pages, and original art	Artist: Dick Calkins	1929–1940
Recordings of the *Buck Rogers* radio broadcasts	Columbia Broadcasting Co.	1932–1940
Prints, lobby cards, posters, and stills of the *Buck Rogers* motion picture serial (12 chapters)	Universal Pictures	1939

* Keaton did the artwork for the first 3½ years of the strip.

The first Buck Rogers Rocket Pistol—XZ-31. 1934.

Daisy Manufacturing Co. advertisement for pistols, holsters, and helmet.

Display of early rocket pistols, holsters, and ads.

Advertisement for Disintegrator Pistol, helmet, and combat sets.

Advertisement for the Buck Rogers Liquid Helium 15-Shot Repeater Water Pistol, a beautiful sculptured design.

Buck Rogers combat game with launching platform for rocket ships programmed for Mars, Saturn, and Jupiter. Inside, Dr. Huer's laboratory plus rubber-band guns to shoot them all down! Warren Paper Products Inc., 1937

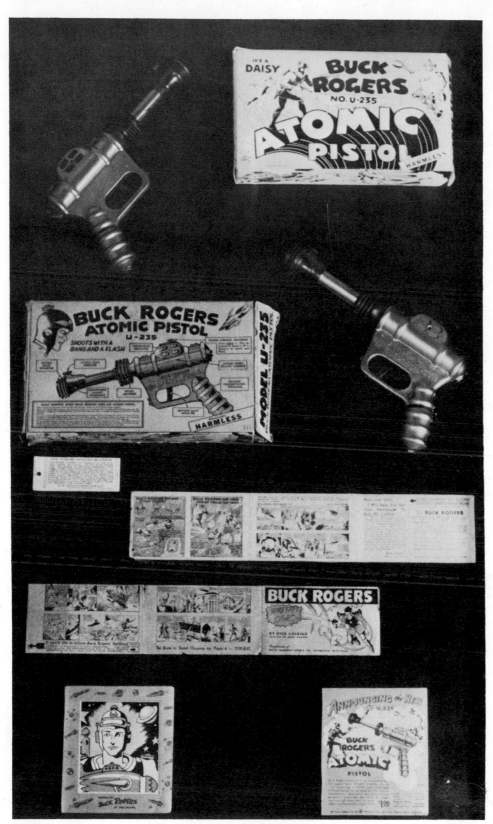

Display of the U-235 Atomic Pistol.
Adapted from the prewar
Disintegrator Pistol. 1946.

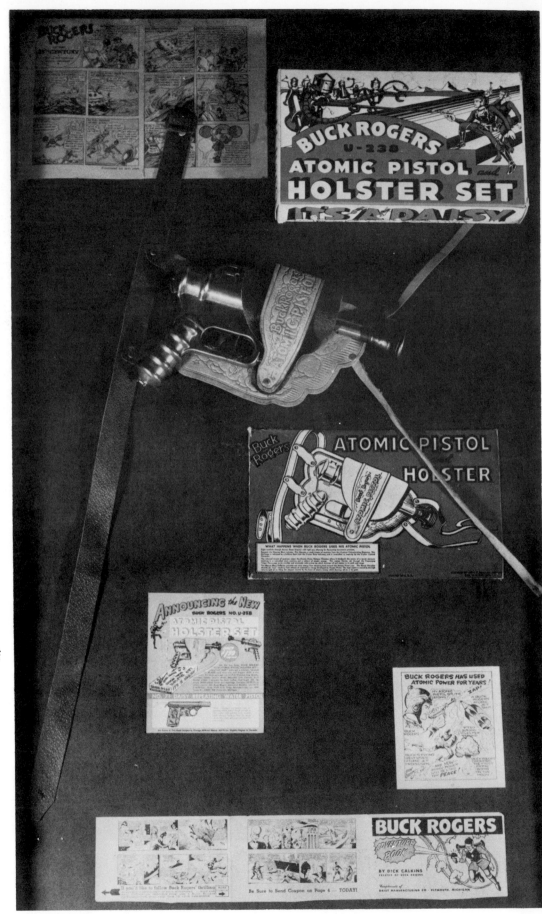

Display of the U-238 Atomic
Pistol with holster, the last of
the Buck Rogers guns. 1948.

The Buck Rogers Cardboard Helmet and "Zap" Noisemaker Rocket Pistol by Einson-Freeman. 1933.

Handsome cover art for Daisy Manufacturing Co. catalog.

The catalog picturing all the varieties of guns, holsters, helmets, and combat sets.

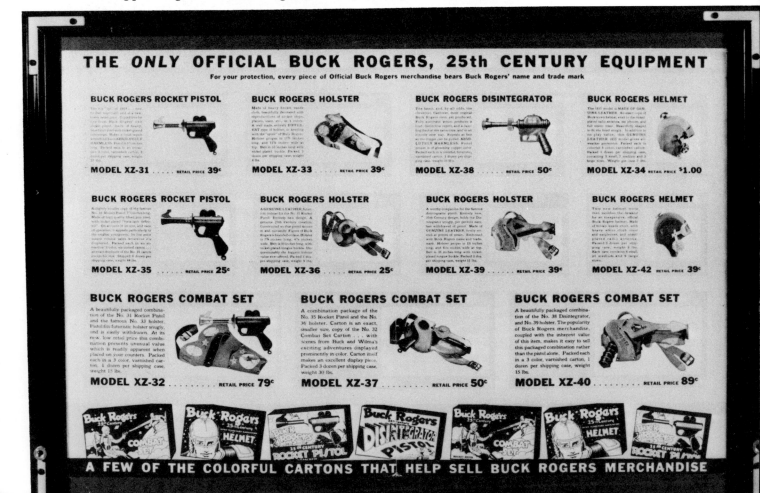

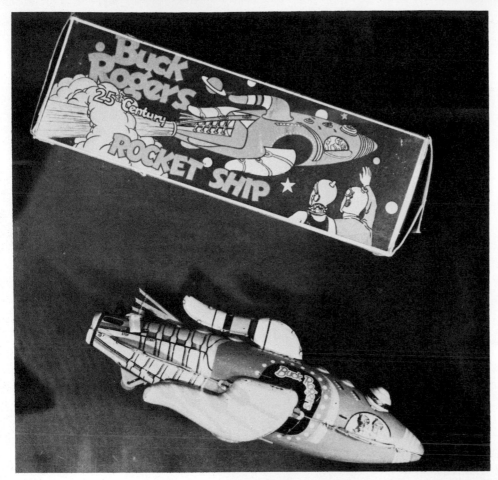

The Buck Rogers 25th Century Rocket Ship—shoots sparks from its rocket exhaust, with bright colors and pictures of Buck and Wilma, and Buck and Dr. Huer at the controls. Designed by Louis Marx, 1934.

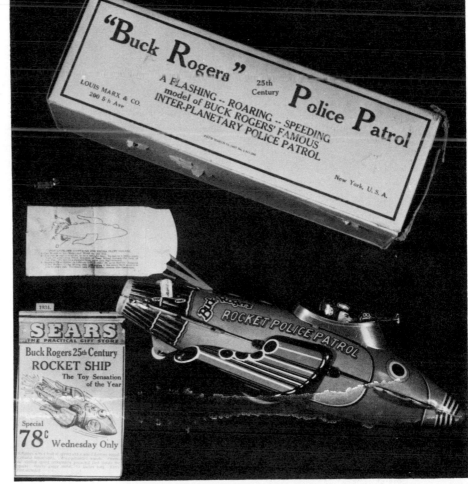

Buck Rogers Police Patrol, a flashing, roaring, speeding, model of Buck Rogers' famous Interplanetary Police Patrol. Designed by Louis Marx, 1939.

Construction kit with paint, balsa wood, sandpaper, and construction print. The very handsome box was designed by Dick Calkins, 1934.

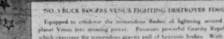

The Buck Rogers Space Suit.

Cover art from the Buck Rogers Space Suit box, designed by Dick Calkins.

Advertisement for the Buck Rogers Space Suit.

The Buck Rogers Rocket Skates. The rocket ship is made from heavy steel.

The Buck Rogers Electric Casting Set for making the comic-strip characters in lead, painting them, and selling to friends.

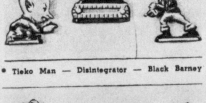

Advertisement for the sets and the extra molds.

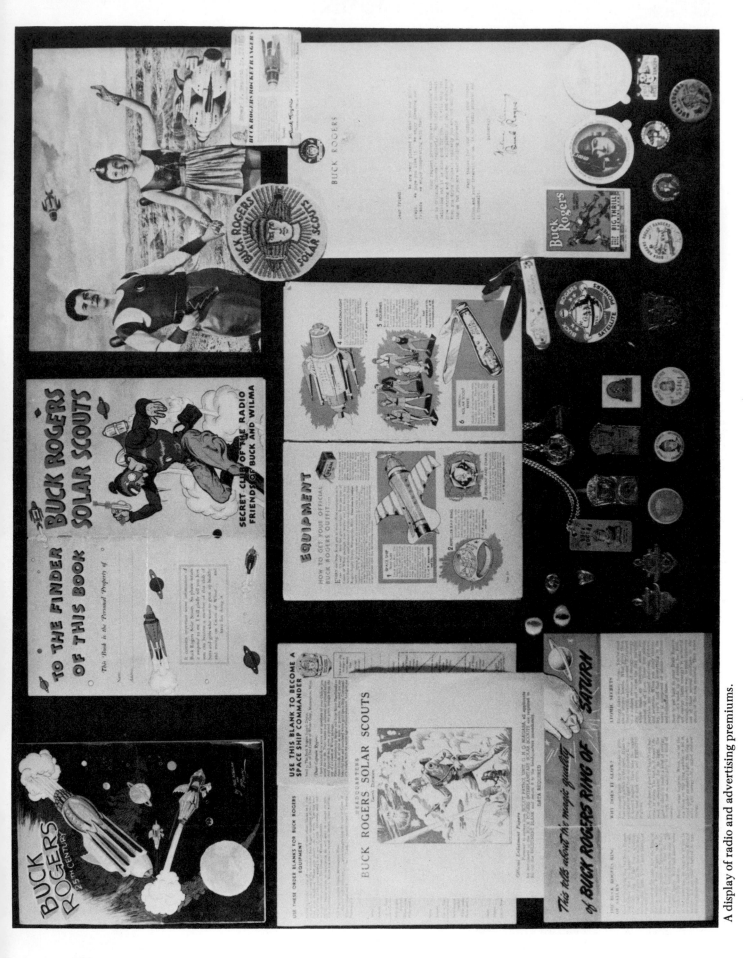

A display of radio and advertising premiums.

Space Commander, Chief Explorer, and Solar Scout Membership Badges; and the Secret Repeller Ray Ring.

The rarest of all the radio premiums—obtainable for 50¢ and three Cream of Wheat green triangles—a complete set of Buck Rogers Britains:Killer Kane, Ardala, Buck, Wilma, Dr. Huer with his paralysis ray, and Robot.

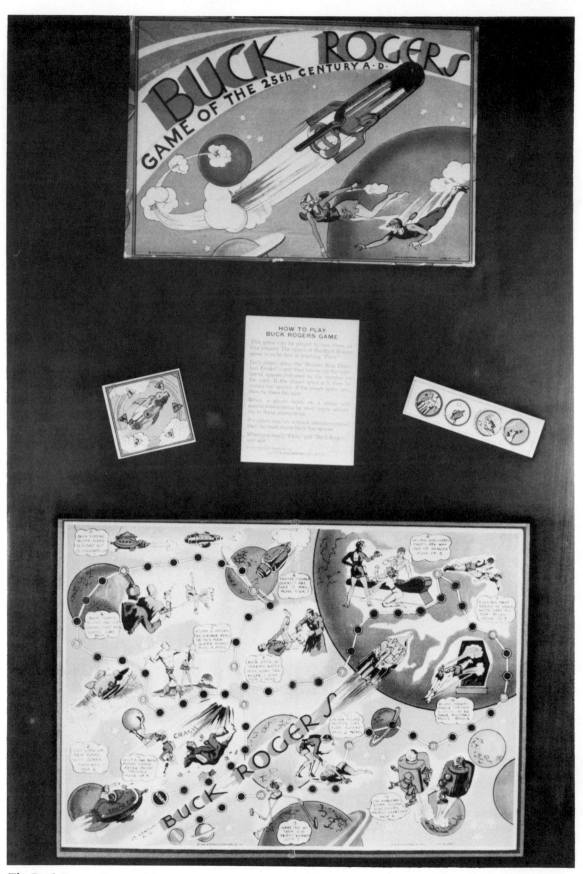

The Buck Rogers Game. (Wilma is barefoot. She's flying through outer space without any shoes on!)

The Strat-O-Sphere Balloon, with
"anti-gravity" gas and postcard.

Buck Rogers Space Ranger's Halolight Kit.
Sylvania TV premium.

The complete set of twelve Buck Rogers Big Little Books. The rarest is the *Buck Rogers in the City of Floating Globes,* a Cocomalt premium.

Buck Rogers Paint Book. All of the interior art was drawn by Dick Calkins for Whitman Publishing.

The Buck Rogers Watch and the superbly designed Art Nouveau-style box. The back of the watch should be debossed to be an original. Only 98¢ at Sears in 1935!

Recent Buck Rogers wrist/pocket/pendant watch with orbiting rocket ship. Notice that the face design was "picked up" from the 1935 original box.

The rarest and most expensive of all! The Buck Rogers 25th Century Scientific Laboratory. Sold for $13 at the bottom of the Depression. None have been found, only this advertisement records it!

Buck Rogers Printing Set. Very rare.

Send in twelve **Tarzan** Ice Cream Cup Lids and you would get any one of these booklets.

Advertisement brochure for Buck Rogers Fireworks.

Christmas Feature
Creates Business

Buck Rogers Attracts Thousands of His Little Admirers to the Macy Christmas Toy Department

THE Christmas season at Macy's, in New York City, got off to a flying start when on Saturday, November 17th, the official opening of the toy department was celebrated. In response to the numerous advertisements appearing in the local papers thousands of customers visited the department on the opening day. In fact so great were the crowds that it looked more like a scene from the closing days of the season rather than just the beginning.

Christmas Feature Appeals to the Children

Toy Buyer R. A. Wolfe made a wise move when he decided to feature Buck Rogers as the main attraction. The mere fact that this enterprising young man is in the Macy toy department has already proved effective in making it one of the most popular departments in the metro-politan area. The followers of Buck Rogers are legion and it is only natural that the children living in and around New York City should express a desire to be taken to Macy's in order that they may meet this 25th Century man in person.

The feature, which is situated in the rear of the department, appeals highly to the child's imagination. A Martian city has been constructed, in the center of which is the Buck Rogers' Rocket Ship. In the background and at the sides of the ship are weird looking building and gadgets painted in a myriad of colors. A train ride in a miniature train, with cars that will hold forty children, has also been included to make the feature even more appealing. The train starts from a big platform in the center of the city, rounds a curve and disappears into a tunnel. Inside the tunnel are four lighted scenes showing mechanical figures of men from Mars, Atlantis and Gigantica. One scene shows Buck Rogers flying through space

Macy's Buck Rogers City. 1934.

The Buck Rogers Rocket Ship and Train Ride, the Holiday Feature at Macy's

A display of the Buck Rogers Big Thrill Gum Booklets.

An important list for Buck Rogers collectors: the Buck
Rogers Licensees and what they produced.

The very rare and very beautiful Buck Rogers All-Fair Card Game with original box.

A complete set of the "Buck Rogers in the 25th Century" strip cards.

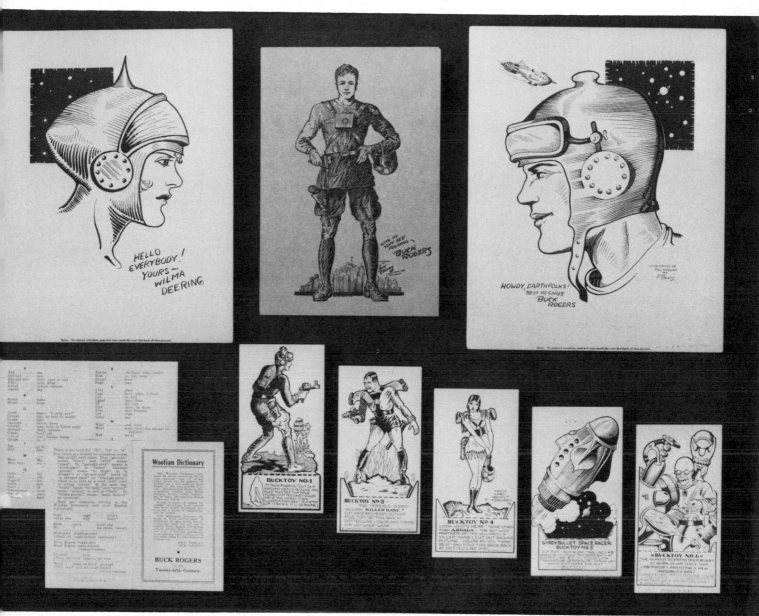

Very early radio and comic-strip premiums.

A display of the figures from the *Buck Rogers Cut-Out Adventure Book,* a rare Cocomalt premium.

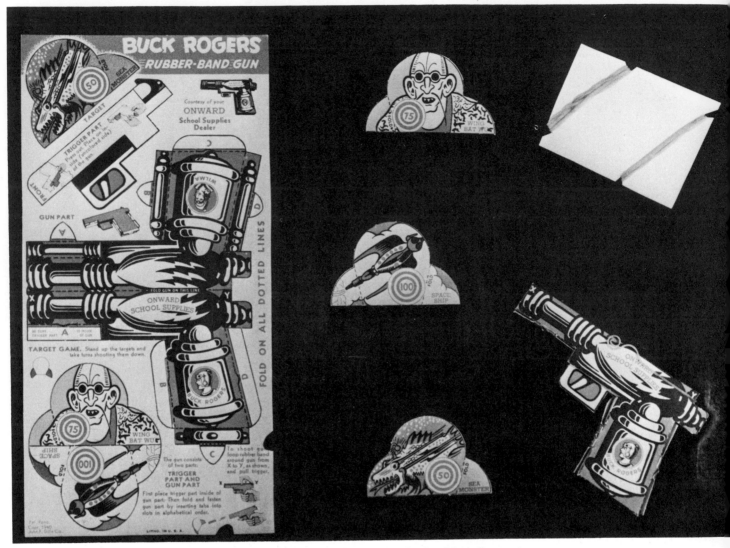

The Buck Rogers Rubber Band Gun with targets. Designed by Onward School Supplies, quite late—1940, but handsomely produced.

Buck Rogers in the 25th Century Comic Book, No. 4, with the original cover art.

A display of the ships in flight.

Buck Rogers Tootsietoy Rocket Ships in the original box, including: Flash-Blast Attack Ship, Venus Duo-Destroyer, Buck Rogers Battle Cruiser, U.S.N. Los Angeles, and cast figures of Buck and Wilma. 1937.

Advertisement for the Tootsietoy Battle Fleet.

The first Sunday comic page of "Buck Rogers"—in four color.

A color proof for the Sunday page, May 30, 1937.

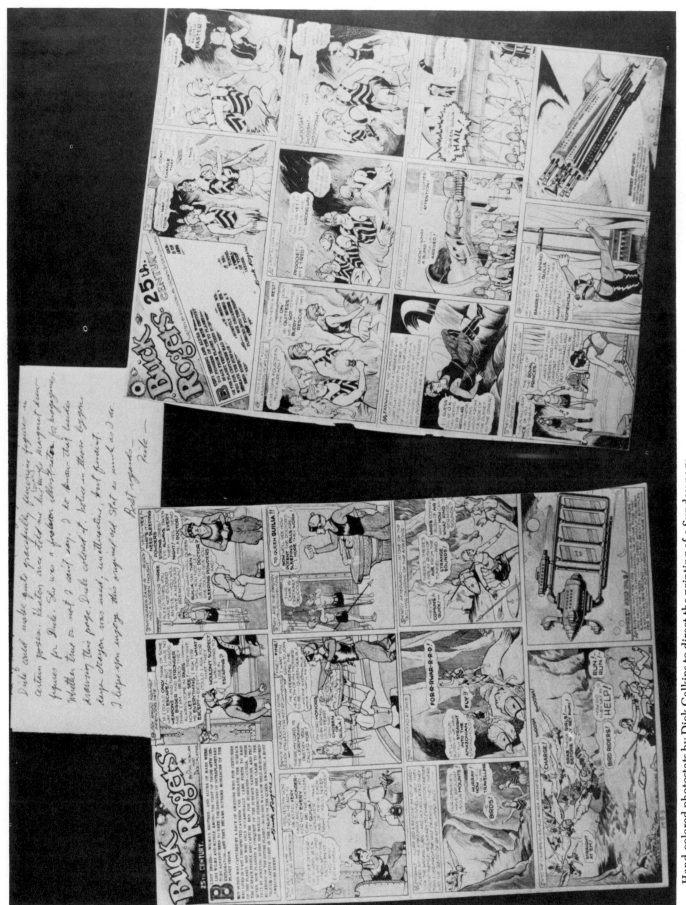

Hand-colored photostats by Dick Calkins to direct the printing of a Sunday page.

The end of the fad: an advertisement trying to interest new licensees. It is important because it lists many of the last products. 1937.

Lobby card for Universal's *Buck Rogers* serial, starring Buster Crabbe.

Planet Outlaws was the full-length feature made from the serials.

Another lobby card, showing the bad guys leading a "worker's revolt!"

Buck Rogers Movie for Stores

Buck Rogers, Dr. Huer and Wilma Deering, Portrayed by Actors, Seen in a "Still" from the Movie — Battle Scene from the Picture, Showing Buck Rogers Fleet of Rocket Ships Speeding to Battle — King Grallo, the Tiger Man of Mars, Killer Kane and Ardala Plot Some Devilment for the Hero

A SPECIAL movie short for department store promotions featuring Buck Rogers in the 25th Century has recently been produced. The picture presents a series of exciting scenes and is complete with sound effects. Characters include Buck, Wilma, Dr. Huer, Killer Kane, Ardala, King Grallo and mechanical robots. The picture is available for department store promotions in any juvenile department such as the boys' clothing section, and, of course, is particularly suited for toy departments.

A special cast was employed to produce the picture which was filmed in the studios of the Action Film Company, Chicago, under the personal direction and supervision of Dr. Harlan Tarbell.

Stores have found that Buck Rogers' two-fisted exploits combined with Killer Kane's deviltry and Dr. Huer's amazing inventive genius have a powerful appeal to the imaginations of modern youth and rank as high favorites among the current "characters." The Buck Rogers idea of characters living 500 years from now amid advanced mechanical developments—and their ability to communicate and travel among the various planets of the Solar system is a story which cannot be beaten for youth appeal, particularly as it is backed up by such tremendous publicity forces as the nationwide Buck Rogers radio chain,

and a daily and Sunday newspaper readership of over 32,000,000.

In addition to its ability for drawing crowds, department store buyers and publicity departments have lauded this film because it is definitely tied up with Buck Rogers merchandise right in their stores. This gives the film a double-barrelled value because it is more than just a good "crowd-getter"—it is also a "seller-of-merchandise."

●

Praises our Import Stand

To the Editor:

The information and value I derived from the first copy of TOYS AND NOVELTIES, sent to me in April, is so great that I am prompted to enclose herewith $1 to cover subscription for a year. I shall not miss any number hereafter.

The policy of preserving the American toy industry by not allowing any foreign competition creeping into your advertising space should be an example for others to follow. I want to praise you for such a strong stand.

YEW CHAR,
Honolulu, T. H.

A special movie for department-store promotions.

Buck Rogers Pencil Boxes.

BUCK ROGERS

Public Fascinator No. 1

One of the outstanding merchandising trends of recent years has been the hook-up with cartoon and comic characters. Since Daisy Mfg. Co. first offered its Buck Rogers gun several years ago, the Buck Rogers standard has been a popular one in the toy field. The gigantic publicity tie-up around Buck Rogers name is outlined in this article—the tremendous force that keeps youngsters on the *qui vive* waiting for the next Buck Rogers adventure.

The lead characters in a recent Buck Rogers amateur dramatic skit

THAT remarkable chap, Buck Rogers, keeps looming up! Just recently *Saturday Evening Post* and *New Yorker*, mentioned Buck editorially. *Colliers, Judge, Ballyhoo* have just run Buck Rogers cartoons. New Pocket size *Coronet* opens a recent issue with an article on inventions. Buck's and Dr. Huer's inventions are the theme song. New 1,000,000 circu-

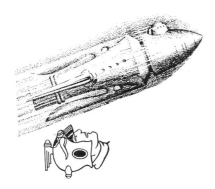

lation *Life* shows a photo of arc-welder in his protective helmet, so the editor makes a crack about Buck Rogers. Picture book *Look* has another. With over 6,000,000 circulation these magazines represent about 24,000,000 readers.

On the air we find none other than Fred Allen, Stoopnagle and Bud, and Ken McMurray using Buck Rogers as

important material in their programs. Another 20,000,000 listeners!

What is this permanent fascination which Mr Buck holds for an ordinarily fickle public? Our dashing Rocketeer has been in the rip-roaring rocket-busting business for several years but his fans scan the papers, listen to his programs, buy his toys more enthusiastically than ever. And each new crop of youngsters goes for Buck Rogers 100%. Now everybody knows that our old friends, Mickey Mouse and Popeye, keep their customers in line by keeping them laughing. But this fellow, Buck, seems to have a different technique . . . he's simply Public Fascinator No. 1!

Key to Popularity

There must be some answer. All we can guess is: Ever since Buck awoke once A. M. and found himself 500 years older but still 20, physically, he started a line of thought which is just too fascinating for the normal mind to let go of! Kids, with highgeared imaginations that are normal to their age, find in Buck more food for thought than in a barrel of story books. Adults enjoy speculating on "what's it going to be like in 2437 A. D.?"—and of course adults enjoy kidding Buck at every opportunity in humor magazines, etc. But while they're laughing, they're fascinated by Buck too. He's in the public eye!

Buck Rogers Toys

Toy makers will see Buck frequently this year. Besides his regular line of pistols, books, suits, mechanical toys,

rubber novelties, film and other items which have lined the pockets of several manufacturers and filled the coffers of the Buck Rogers Company with royalties, Buck appears this year in eight new toy roles. Metal Rocket Ships (Dowst Mfg. Co.) that land, take-off, and fly (on a string of course), with considerable speed and realism through a new mechanical stunt; Buck Rogers Safety Fireworks (National Fireworks Co.), a splendid group of items by a manufacturer who is doing an effective designing job to reduce accidents. His rocket ship pursuit game with two real fire-powered rocket ships chasing each other in a circle, is the most exciting and realistic toy we've seen in some time, yet it's absolutely harmless. Buck Rogers Combat Game (Warren Paper Products Co.), provides fun by the hour in constructing and playing with a Rocket Ship Control Base together with cardboard characters and rocket ships and two Force Ray guns that "get their men with deadly accuracy" (at eight or ten feet). They shoot ruh-

her hands and you'd be surprised how easily you can pick off Killer Kane at ten feet! Of course he's only temporarily paralyzed and soon on his feet again to make more trouble for Buck.

Buck Rogers Chemistry

There's an interesting new Buck Rogers Chemistry Set (Gropper Mfg. Co.), with Dr. Huer strutting his stuff; handsome new Leather Belts (Reliable Belt Co.), destined to hold up millions of pairs of small pants, with exciting action pictures all the way around their circumference. Buck Rogers Tablet Covers and Composition Books (White & Wyckoff Mfg. Co.), introduce a new feature with a continued story on the back of the covers. Little Johnny finds he just has to buy the whole series of six in order to get Buck safely through the story! The new Buck Rogers Acousticon (Dictograph Products), is a hearing aid for deaf kids, which removes the embarrassment of wearing

a phone! A new Buck Rogers Interplanetary Telescope is now in the making and should be out soon.

Unchallenged Position

Buck's position as Public Fascinator No. 1 has proved immensely profitable for his trainers and his manufacturers. Although Mickey Mouse holds the palm for sponsored merchandise, Buck is a close second and when it comes to sales volume in individual items, Buck is said to reign supreme. Sales in the several millions are nothing to Buck and we wish him many more years of spell-binding, fascinating fun with the usual per cent paid for his services.

TOYS and BICYCLES—April, 1937

The Annual Dinner and Dance of the Toy Wholesalers Association will be held at the Hotel Pennsylvania, Wednesday, April 14.

117

Buck and Dr. Heuer rescue Wilma from the Tiger men in the nick of time!

TOYS and BICYCLES—April, 1937

116

6

Comic Insert Cards

From the turn of the century to the present day millions of children have bought candy, gum, and other products in order to collect the card inserts that depicted their favorite sports hero or comic character. The cards were numbered, and it was the passionate goal of each young collector to become the proud possessor of a complete set. For the manufacturers and the printers this meant a continuous stream of pennies and nickels and a never-ending search for new subjects to ensure the financial loyalty and enthusiasm of their young customers. Talented artists were employed to paint the scenes, in oils and watercolors, and skilled writers wrote tales of action that carried over from card to card, assuring their employers of participation rights in next week's allowance.

Invented in 1933, bubble gum, square and flat, was packaged in a wax gum wrapper with a thick picture card that prevented the gum from breaking into pieces. The golden age of comic-character insert cards was from 1933 to 1942, and almost every bubble-gum manufacturer used them to spur his sales. World War II declared them nonessential, and the postwar spiral of inflation and the beginning popularity of television combined to end the production of these sometimes exquisite and imaginative comic-art miniatures.

The names of the artists and writers are lost, and most of the companies have disappeared into that re-

cent past without a trace. But the art remains. It remains because many of the children who collected them remembered the struggle to complete a set, loved the pictures, and saved them. Most of the cards were two and a half by three inches and did not require much space for storage. Often the gum and candy makers would provide albums for easy mounting and preservation. Nevertheless, most were thrown away, so that insert cards have become quite scarce and are seldom offered. It is almost impossible to find complete sets in mint condition.

Comic-insert-card collecting is a recent addition to the vastness and diversity of card collecting; postcards, playing cards, greeting cards, paper dolls, stereoscope cards, baseball cards, football cards, boxing cards, trade advertising cards, match folders, pin buttons, silks, leathers, and other groups comprise the millions of items that have been gathered into the great card collections that exist throughout the world. The greatest collection can be found in the Metropolitan Museum of Art: the J. R. Burdick Collection of Paper Americana. In it one will find everything ranging from the Frank Buck Bring 'Em Back Alive gum cards and wrappers and Mickey Mouse Bubble Gum cards to a complete set of the beautiful Horrors of War cards. All counted, there are 306,353 items in this collection, including 60 original gum wrappers. The richness and variety of this collection is unequaled. There are albums filled with comic cards, postcards, cigar bands, posters, banners, vaudeville flyers, linen labels, liquor labels, playing cards, greeting cards, and tens of thousands of trade cards that had been inserted into tobacco, gum, cereals, and other products.

This collection was the passion and life's work of Jefferson R. Burdick, a pain-racked arthritic who poured his money, time, and life into amassing his collection of ephemera. The Metropolitan gave him a desk in the print department to catalog the collection. He spent three painful years mounting, marking, and cataloging. On January 10, 1963, at 5:00 P.M. he stood up and announced that he had mounted his last card. "I shan't be back," he said quietly as he twisted his arms into his coat. He entered University Hospital the next day and died there two months later at the age of sixty-three. This is an example of the intensity of the passion that card collecting engenders.

The lust for picture cards began with the invention of the woodcut. It is the oldest known method of reproducing pictures in large quantities at inexpensive costs. It first appeared in ancient China, spread to India where it was used to print pictures on cloth, and then to all the countries of Europe. In the sixteenth century it reached its peak of development with the works of Hans Holbein and the supreme master, Albrecht Dürer. The woodcut pictures were inexpensive and were collected by people of average means, because it enabled them to learn to read. This method of printing persisted, and woodcuts became most popular during the period of 1860 to 1900 for use as greeting cards, playing cards, and trade cards.

The invention of lithographic printing by Senefelder in 1798 added an alternative method; engraved-plate printing permitted the talent of the artist to be duplicated in mass production. An example is Currier of Currier and Ives fame, who was called "The Printmaker of America." Prior to the Civil War, photography and steam-driven printing presses combined to permit the picture printing of cards that businessmen could give away to promote their products. But it was at the American Centennial Exposition of 1876 that the trade or advertising card achieved widespread popularity, and it was there that the insert card, the forerunner of Mickey Mouse bubble gum or Horrors of War cards, was invented.

These insert cards were packed with a product and could only be obtained by buying that product, such as candy, gum, tobacco, or coffee, hence, the cards gradually became known as gum cards, candy cards, or cigarette cards. They were made with the collector in mind, with the hope that once he was bitten by the card-collecting bug, continuous, repeat sales would be automatic. Today most insert-card collecting means baseball. The baseball-card collectors are the most avid, and recently one rare card, the A. Honus Wagner card, was sold for $1,500, and now is reputedly worth $2,500! Why? Because Wagner was a hard-shell Southern Baptist who woke up one morning to find his picture on a cigarette card; enraged, he had the printing stopped, and only seven of those cards exist, but there are thousands of baseball-card collectors—supply and demand again! In fact, because the supply of early sports cards has plunged to zero in recent years, this group is rapidly becoming the prime collectors of comic-character cards, and the prices are beginning to zoom. Value is also based upon condition. The goal is always a complete set in mint condition, and worn corners, creases, stains, tack holes, and poor registration of the printing decreases the value considerably.

In general, all cards were numbered, and the higher the number, the more valuable the card. Why? In order to collect a complete set of Horrors of War, the trapped 1938 bubble-gum freak had to pay for and chew 288 sticks of gum. By the time he had accomplished this feat, his teeth had worn down to his gums, he was flat broke, and probably had learned to hate the taste of bubble gum as much as spinach. The kids simply gave up before completing a set.

Much of the art is superb. But during the period in which it was created most commercial art was considered worthless; therefore, the names of those talented artists have disappeared into limbo, and the original watercolors and oil paintings have been destroyed. Yet those cards that have found a safe haven in private collections are visual evidence of the artistic excellence and originality of this genre of American comic miniatures.

One of the most desired sets is the Mickey Mouse Bubble Gum cards. There were ninety-six cards in this set and they were produced by the Mickey Mouse Bubble Gum Company in Philadelphia during the early nineteen thirties. The graphics are early Mickey: pie-cut eyes, pot belly, long rat tail, and the general rodent look that is so much preferred by Mickey Mouse collectors. Each card is designed around a pun, such as the Number 1 card that has Mickey holding a hoop, pointing his finger at Pluto, and saying, "Let's make hoop-ee!" On the back was a commercial gimmick that inspired the young collector to buy the Number 2 card.

Can You Answer This Question?

Mickey was standing on a soap box. He was making a speech. Around him were lots of cats and lots of dogs. They listened to him eagerly. Suddenly it started to rain. Mickey looked up and said something.

What Did Mickey Say?

For the answer to this question see [buy] Card No. 2.

Save all your cards to paste in your Mickey Mouse Picture Card Album to get a complete set of questions and answers.

After you bought the Number 2 card and found that the answer was "It's raining cats and dogs," the back of that card had another question, and on and on and on up to Number 96: The poor kid was hooked.

For five wrappers and 5¢ the store where you bought your Mickey Mouse Bubble Gum would give you a Mickey Mouse Picture Card Album that had a beautifully illustrated cover with all the questions printed in it along with places to mount the picture cards. The first album was for series 1 to 48 and the second for 49 to 96. Two of the cards of extreme interest are those that depict a youthful, thin Walt Disney at his drawing board. Number 21 has a red-sweatered, open-shirted Uncle Walt drawing Mickey Mouse, while Horace Horsecollar is looking over his shoulder punning, "He's sure a handy man around the mouse!" Number 92 has Mickey and Minnie heckling Walt while he is trying to concentrate on a drawing.

The commercial success of these cards led to another related venture: a set of twenty-four cards entitled Mickey Mouse With the Movie Stars, combining a large caricature of the Hollywood star, with Mickey acting his role. Edward G. Robinson, Wallace Beery, Eddie Cantor, Constance Bennett, Joe E. Brown, Ed Wynn, Greta Garbo, and others were used in their most characteristic poses, while Mickey Mouse punned and pummeled their fame.

These cards were numbered 97 to 120 and are very rare. Typical is card 104 showing Mickey Mouse masked, with a six-gun pointed at Edward G.

Robinson, hands up. The star of Little Caesar looks scared and puns at Mickey: "The Little Seizer." Wait, the worst is yet to come! On the back:

MICKEY MOUSE WITH THE MOVIE STARS

Mickey was watching a famous movie star doing a gangster picture. Suddenly Mickey picked up a toy gun and pointing it at the star said, "Hand it over, I'm a-ROBBIN, SON!" The famous star then said something to make Mickey laugh.

Who Was The Star?

For a clue to the answer, see other side

MICKEY MOUSE BUBBLE GUM—The best BUBBLE GUM in the world—Makes the BIGGEST BUBBLES.

But among the "Mouse junkies," it is the set of the Mickey Mouse bread cards from the early thirties that is considered the most desirable because of the beautiful action graphics. Any bread manufacturer could subscribe to the advertising program and his name would be printed on the back of the card, which contained a recipe that used bread as its major ingredient. Mom had to buy that brand of bread because packaged inside was the Mickey Mouse bread card Junior was saving. A handsome Mickey Mouse Recipe Scrap Book Album was given away free for mounting the pictures and to push Junior into becoming a bread salesman with one active account: his mother.

Certainly one of the most stunning sets of cards is the Dick Tracy Caramels cards produced for the Walter H. Johnson Candy Company in the early nineteen thirties. There were 144 cards in a complete set, and the somewhat two-dimensional, flat comic-art draftsmanship combined with bright colors is handsome proof of comic art as legitimate art. On the back was a complete spine-tingling gangster adventure story that made you chew up those caramels faster in nervous excitement:

EPISODE NO. 1
DICK TRACY'S NARROW ESCAPE

Big Boy and Ribs Mocco had laid a clever trap to "erase" Dick Tracy, ace detective of the Elton force. Mocco was to have Tracy trail him in a taxi-cab, while not far away, other members of the gang waited with machine guns. They had instructions to drill the occupant of the second cab. But the driver of Mocco's cab became excited and turned the wrong corner. This made Tracy suspicious and he refused to let Mocco's cab pass him again. The gunner's high powered sedan fell in behind the second cab, which they thought carried Tracy, but when the hot lead poured from their guns, Ribs Mocco, their own pal was the target and Tracy made good his escape!

DICK TRACY CARAMELS
Walter H. Johnson Candy Company, Chicago, Illinois.

Each card had a similar short-short story on the back with a bright-color action scene on the face to depict it. Kids of the thirties flipped "heads or tails" with each other to complete a set, and the competition to become the first kid on the block to have a complete set was fierce. Another set of Dick Tracy cards was printed in 1937 by the Whitman Publishing Company to help sell their Big Little Books. These cards, numbered 33 to 64, are quite rare but do not compare in beauty with the Caramels cards. The earliest set was published by the Chicago *Tribune* in 1935 and was numbered 101 to 108, but these were only strip cards, without any story on the back.

American youth were fascinated by the fantasy of good policemen versus bad gangsters, and a variety of card sets followed similar to the Dick Tracy set. American G-Men series pitted the government men against hijackers, counterfeiters, fences, river thieves, lunatics, dope peddlers, diamond smugglers, tramps, Chinatown Charlie, and even pants thieves! In a circle in the upper left-hand corner of each card was a clue, such as a dagger, an old hat, or footprints, and on the back was the complete, exciting short-short story of the crime and the capture.

In 1936 Gum Inc. distributed G-Men and Heroes of the Law in a set of 168 cards that was probably the best of all the crime sets. Each depicted a square-framed portrait of the criminal, an action scene of his crime, and on the back the "True Official Story" of the case. Card Number 10 was devoted to a criminal still strong in the memory of America: John Dillinger.

G-Men Get Their Man!
Trailed for countless crimes, sneering at capture, blasting his way from every jail that held him, ruthless and calculating . . . John Dillinger, whose life seemed charmed against the bullets of the law!

His face had been completely changed by surgery, his hair dyed black, cruel lips concealed by a moustache, yellow snakelike eyes hidden by smoked glasses. A perfect disguise . . . to all but G-Men!

On a July night in 1934, mysterious cars stopped before a Chicago theatre. The world's most relentless man hunt was coming to an end!

A young man in the crowd leaving the theatre glanced about and lighted a cigar. A hand in one of the cars was raised as a signal.

Fingers darted swiftly to the young man's hip. An automatic leaped from its concealment!

Crash! Crash! . . . Crash! . . . Crash! echoed four shots, as the waiting G-Men opened their deadly fire. The outlaw staggered, cleared the sidewalk with a bound, turned into an alley a hundred feet away, as a .45 caliber bullet ripped through his breast. Another tore through his neck and brain, coming out over the right eye!

John Dillinger had met his match at last, the end that all killers sooner or later find before the unswerving aim of G-Men who take their trail and track them down.

Similar cards were created for Pretty Boy Floyd, Machine Gun Kelly, and Baby Face Nelson, and other well-known baddies.

The quality of the art varies from set to set, but certainly the most professional are the action pictures shown on the Lone Ranger Chewing Gum cards produced by Gum Inc. in 1940. The set is comprised of forty-eight cards. Perspective, color harmony, accurate detailing, and fine registration suggest a careful and talented artist. It is unfortunate that his name is not known and that his original art (which was probably large-size oil paintings) has never been found. They are beautiful examples of Western scenes in the genre of representational art, not merely slapdash sketches created for commercial purposes.

Possibly the same artist in the same year for the same company created the handsome set of seventy-two Superman Gum cards. They were created in the same style but without the fine background details. Nevertheless, they are excellent examples of miniature comic art. In each card Superman is in motion demonstrating his Krypton-acquired strength and his fight against evil: holding a poisonous snake by the throat, lifting a gangster's car, stopping an airplane, rescuing a sexy girl from a blazing fire, punching a shark in the mouth, with stories on the back of each card describing the action in gory detail.

One of the most successful salesmen operating in the early thirties, selling gum, candy, breakfast cereals, and a host of children-oriented products was the famous Tom Mix. He was the first of the Hollywood-created multimillionaires, and young girls and fast cars were his off-screen hobbies. In 1934 the National Chicle Company published forty-eight gum booklets, each with a picture of Tom Mix on the cover in action. They told a complete story in eight pages involving our hero, his horse Tony, the Bar Diamond ranch, and a bunch of baddies. They were shirt-pocket size, two and three-eighths by two and three-quarters inches and were extremely popular with preteen collectors.

So popular in fact that the Goudey Gum Company had to meet this competition in order to maintain its market position. Buck Rogers, Dick Tracy, Tailspin Tommy, and Buck Jones each had six gum booklets devoted to their adventures, and the front covers were professionally designed and printed in bright four-color process. The center page also included a full-color action scene, and appropriately, the gum was named Big Thrill Chewing Gum. The gum wrapper and booklet sold for the huge sum of 1¢. "Start NOW!—Collect all the books in every set and complete your BIG THRILL library" was the company's investment advice, and good advice it was considering that the capital appreciation today could be measured in many thousands of percentage points.

Then the printer himself decided to go into the same business and provided booklets without any manufacturer's name, so that they could be sold, quite simply, to any manufacturer for any product. He avoided expensive royalty payments by using hardly known comic characters, such as Hal Hunter Among the Savages, Crafty Keen the Detective, Mirtho the Clown, Yip Roper the Young Cowboy, Operator 7 of the Secret Service, and, the best of the lot, Reckless Steele Soldier of Fortune. The stories were exciting; the booklets are very rare and are the only evidence of their comic's existence.

The job of the advance man working for the circus was to paste up posters for the show in the town before the circus arrived; in short, to presell the product. During the nineteen thirties the Whitman Publishing Company of Racine, Wisconsin, did the same thing for their Big Little Book series. Instead of posters they used comic cards to introduce their books to potential purchasers. The style of the art was the same as the typical Sunday newspaper comic page: flat, colorful, and two-dimensional. The series included sets for Dick Tracy, Popeye, Tom Mix, Buck Jones, Dan Dunn, G-Man, and, best of all, the only set of Flash Gordon cards with obvious Alex Raymond art. Each card was numbered and on the back was the story plus an obvious commercial message:

SAVE THESE CARDS—Nos. 1 to 32 are about
FLASH GORDON
No. 1 The Tournament opens.

Ming the Merciless, Emperor of Mongo, seeking to destroy Flash Gordon, the Earthman, readily consented to Vultan's demand for a Tournament of Death. Vultan, ruler of the Hawkmen, was Flash's staunch friend. In calling for this contest of mighty battles and terrific tests, Vultan was giving Flash an opportunity to fight for his freedom. This, Flash heartily agreed, was far better than a calm subjection to Ming's torturers. But Dale Arden, the Earthgirl and Flash's sweetheart, begged her hero not to enter the horrible tournament. However, on the day appointed Flash was ready. Strange and fearsome creatures from the four corners of the planet Mongo filled the mammoth arena. Suddenly a blast of many bugles heralded the arrival of the Emperor Ming. The Tournament of Death was about to open!

READ THE BIG LITTLE BOOK ABOUT
FLASH GORDON!

This story format ensured a continuous payout from small pockets to publisher.

The difficulty in being or becoming a Tarzan of the Apes collector is that other than the books by Edgar Rice Burroughs there is very little to collect. As in the case of Flash Gordon, the collector is defeated before he begins, since almost no toys, few premiums, and related collectibles were ever made. But there are thousands of Tarzan collectors around the world, and the competition is fierce. One of the most sought-after Tarzan items is a complete set of candy cards produced by the Schutter-Johnson Candy Corporation in the mid-nineteen thirties: Tarzan and the Crystal

Vault of Isis. The complete set consists of fifty cards and tells the story of the quest for the largest diamond in the world. It is an exciting story, and the action art depicting various scenes from the story is excellent. The first card is a fantastic Tarzan as Lord Greystoke in a tuxedo!

TARZAN AND THE CRYSTAL VAULT OF ISIS
1. The Urge of the Blood!

TARZAN stood looking at the mighty steel skeleton of the huge skyscraper which was rising to the east of his mansion in the fashionable suburb of London. As he watched the crimson sun's last rays reaching their red fingers through the black network, he felt again the old unrest. He remembered the sunsets and dawns in the forests of his first home. Often in the cold light of dawn he had swung his way through the skyscraper-like treetops of his native forests, searching for food.

Then off to the jungle and off went the tuxedo and off went Tarzan in search of the largest diamond in the world:

TARZAN AND THE CRYSTAL VAULT OF ISIS
48. Priceless: The Diamond Trillion!

The next of their thrilling discoveries made TARZAN and his allies gasp! Golden steps three in number, led upwards to another chamber. A shining black door opened without a sound as they stepped on the release, and there before them, towering in air, was a diamond as large as a small house! How Maj. Falsburg had hauled it there, inch by inch, and how he had cut it so that its gleaming surface cast rainbow lights all around them, were secrets buried with the Major, as the secrets of pyramids had been lost centuries before. A trillion in wealth!

TARZAN was speechless!

The only other set of Tarzan cards known were strip cards with no stories on the back and were produced by Stephen Slesinger, Inc. in 1936 and were numbered 409 to 416. In these Tarzan fought crocodiles, bull apes, lions, and Monkey Men, and this set is equally rare. In the same series were similar sets for Tailspin Tommy and Broncho Bill.

The mysteries and adventures lurking in the jungles, filled with wild animals, continued to capture the imagination and pennies of the young, and in 1938 Gumakers of America, Inc., issued a set of beautiful Frank Buck cards. Frank Buck was famous for always bringing jungle animals back alive. Each card showed our fearless hero wrestling with a ferocious beast, and on the back was a description of the struggle and an autograph of Frank Buck attesting to the truthfulness of the story:

4. CRUSHING COILS!

. . . Suddenly my upper arm was seized in an excruciating grip. I felt a score of triangular teeth bite deep into quivering flesh, and one horrified glance told me I was held by a giant Python! These great serpents kill by crushing in their powerful coils. The pain was intense!

"Ali!" I called to my Number One Boy, "quick Ali!" With a movement incredibly swift a horribly muscular coil encircled my shoulders. Ali crashed through the bushes and raised his rifle. "Don't shoot!" I yelled, "You'll hit me!" With his keen knife Ali hacked frantically at the tough hide with little result. Another coil and more agonizing pressure—a third might snuff out my life as one blows out a candle!

I could reach my belt holster. Twisting my revolver muzzle upward, and carefully avoiding shooting my own arm, I crashed three leaden slugs into the ghastly head. The coils relaxed and the great python slipped to the ground—twenty seven feet of terrible death. It's immense jaws had left twenty-two triangular teeth in as many wounds, which were sore and aching for a week —but I had escaped!

This time he had brought himself back alive!

Others followed, and the Planters Nut and Chocolate Company issued a set of twenty-five cards of hunted jungle animals that were primarily educational and described the animals, though on the fronts many were depicted as excitingly ferocious. A larger and more colorful set was issued by Jungle Chewing Gum's World Wide Gum Company and had as its motto: "START A ZOO AS YOU CHEW!" They merely depicted the animal in its native habitat and on the back described its size, coloring, and habits. In 1933 the Sweets Company of America issued a set of twenty-five cards that depicted animals much less wild, those of the circus, plus circus scenes that were quite colorful and advertised a candy long since gone: the coconut tootsie roll.

Back from the jungle and up into the outer space of 1936. The John F. Dille Company controlled all rights to "Buck Rogers in the 25th Century" and issued a set of strip cards that could be used to spur the sales of any commercial product since there were no stories or advertising on the backs. They were numbered from 425 to 448, and each group of eight had a portrait card as its first, of either Buck, Wilma, or the great scientist Dr. Huer.

A huge set of photographic cards was issued during World War II based upon the patriotic adventures of Smilin' Jack taken from the stills of the motion-picture serial by Universal Pictures and based on the adventure comic strip by Zack Mosley. Its patriotic message included in bold print a plea to buy War Bonds and Stamps for victory, plus certification of the Chinese as good guys, while the Nazis and Japs looked like beasts and acted like demons. In order to intensify the image of the awful Jap, some of the cards were drawn comic-art style, with the Japs drawn like half-human rats with large, sharp front teeth and high cheekbones; and a special card was even issued: an official-looking hunting license that entitled the bearer to hunt down and kill Jap-Rats.

But the beginning of a nationwide paranoia is well documented in the set of Thrilling True Spy Stories cards issued in 1939 by Gumakers of America. The first card bears the title "Spy Web Over Washington" and shows in bright colors the Capitol dome covered with a spider web and surrounded by black, yellow, and female spies. The story on the back is a picture of some Americans' minds at that point in time:

SPY WEB OVER WASHINGTON

This is a TRUE SPY STORY. The names of some of the characters have been changed in order not to embarrass the government.

In the shadow of the Capitol in Washington, a great number of foreign spies threaten the safety of our Nation. More than 120,000 of these Agents, in the pay of Foreign Powers, are operating in every corner of America. They have wormed their way in factories, munition plants and Government departments to carry on their underhanded work.

Who are these spies? What information are they seeking? They wish to obtain important mili-

tary and State secrets; all the facts about our newest airplanes, our guns and our fortifications. Millions of dollars are spent by them to buy our secret formulas which might aid an enemy in an attack on our country.

No crime is too foul for these Spies in securing plans of Army, Navy and Air Defenses. They use every means known to modern science to uncover and send this information to their headquarters in foreign capitals throughout the world.

But the eyes of our Counter-Espionage Service constantly watch their work. In the files of this Department of the Federal Government are records of thousands of these treacherous enemies. When the evidence against them is complete, our Government will destroy this menace to our National Safety!

Other cards tell similar stories, and some way back in 1939 suggest the holocaust of Pearl Harbor and the "Red Menace."

If one set of insert cards can be submitted as proof that comic art is a legitimate American art form worthy of acclaim and acceptance, the composition, draftsmanship, and originality of the Horrors of War cards drawn by George Maull in 1938 is the single witness. They were so effective that the Japanese government protested to the U.S. State Department and requested their suppression. Because of the terror and violence shown, mothers ordered their children not to buy the gum, a boycott was organized, and many a kid's collection was burned or thrown into the garbage. It reached such a fever pitch that *Life* Magazine published an article about these gum cards in 1938:

... THIS IS BUBBLE GUM'S WAR IN CHINA

The course of the war in China may be very confusing to adult Americans but it is becoming very clear and familiar to a myriad of American youngsters who are bubble gum chewers. The reasons appear in the illustrations on these pages. These drawings, printed in vivid color, are given away by Gum Inc. of Philadelphia with every slab of its "Blony" bubble gum. The buyer collects or swaps the cards. He blows the gum out of his mouth into huge balloon-like bubbles.

Giving war-picture cards away is old candy-trade practice but cards have usually related old-hat history like the massacre of Custer's men. Gum Inc. gets its wars hot off the battlefield, is satisfied with nothing older than a slaughter in Nanking. These cards are executed by Gum Inc.'s advertising counsel, George Maull, a Sunday-school teacher who lends a peaceful tone to the otherwise martial cards by printing on each the motto: "To know the HORRORS OF WAR is to want PEACE." It is no fault of Mr. Maull's that children ask for the product as "WarGum."

On the back of each card are detailed captions, which are very specific about destruction and are anti-Japanese because Mr. Maull feels America is anti-Japanese. But some future historian may trace a cause for a U.S.-Japanese war to the fact that the generation which was pre-adolescent in America in 1938 had received severe anti-Japanese prejudices through its curious liking for blowing bubbles with Blony Gum.

Great minds throughout history have speculated on the causes of war—but bubble gum?

As the cards progressed from 1 to 288, Franco, Mussolini, Chiang Kai-shek, and even Adolf Hitler, and Neville Chamberlain shaking hands with the Fuehrer were depicted. The higher the card number the more rare and expensive in today's collecting world, since most of the kids gave up early rather than wear their teeth 288 times down to the gums. The most wanted card in this set is Number 283, which is a portrait of Adolf Hitler in a green uniform making a speech to a bunch of *Sieg-Heil*ing buddies surrounded by red swastika flags. Since Maull was for peace at any price, and in 1938 Hitler was selling peace at a low asking price, Maull was slightly pro-Hitler.

The most horrifying card in this set is Number 99. Parents were enraged. By 1938 the war-ravaged region of the great delta between Shanghai and Nanking had become a region of utter desolation and ruin. In most of these hopeless, terrifying ruins the only signs of life were great carrion birds attracted by the presence of death and packs of ghoulish dogs whose only sustenance came from the rotting corpses dotting the war wreckage. The face of the card shows the dogs eating the bloody flesh from the dead and one large white dog with a human hand and wrist dripping with blood in his mouth. In the background are the large, evil birds waiting for the dogs to leave so that they can come in and finish the meal of human flesh.

The Horrors of War set was so commercially successful that in the same year the International Chewing Gum Company issued a set of twenty-four gum inserts entitled Don't Let It Happen Over Here. These depicted equally horrendous scenes of war:

BRUTAL NAZI LASH

When Hitler, German Dictator, made his notorious entry into Austria, March 1938, immediate attack was made upon the Jews. Vienna was the home of many famous Jews. All Jews, regardless of position, were insulted and abused. In fear they barricaded themselves in their shops and homes. But the Nazi Storm Troopers dragged out the merchants, looted their stores and smashed windows and doors. The Storm Troopers also amused themselves by flogging the screaming Jews to their knees with horse whips. With their bodies cut and bleeding, the Jews begged for death, but the cruel lash kept descending.

Our forefathers fought and bled to make this a free land. Let us keep it that way.

DON'T LET IT HAPPEN OVER HERE

Do your bit—get all the cards and show them to everyone.

On the face of the card Nazis are beating Jews, and the store signs are in Hebrew.

But the rarest, most beautiful cards ever produced were printed in Spain for "Charlot," better known as Charlie Chaplin. There people were poor and children even poorer, too poor to afford a movie, so as a substitute candy cards were printed to depict scenes from the movies. *Charlot en El Circo* is a set of forty-two cards, each of which creates a comic scene from *The Circus*. The art is inspired, the colors super bright, and the printing is perfect. Here, movie art has been transformed into comic-strip art with originality and great success. Another set was issued for *Modern Times* that consisted of black-and-white stills from the movie. But the rarest and most intriguing set was a series of cards that showed scenes from Charlie Chaplin's silent movies. Each card had a secret section. When placed in proper sequence these sections formed a large, full-sized figure of the beloved Charlie. It was distributed as an insert card for the Amatter-Barcelona Chocolate Company of Barcelona, Spain. Only one complete set is known to be in existence.

The earliest series of comic insert gum cards was produced in 1896 for The Yellow Kid to spur the sales of the Adams Gum Company's Yellow Kid Chewing

Gum, and it may be assumed that this was the beginning of this particular phase of comic commercial art. The comic-character insert card was a highly successful merchandising aid, so successful that between 1896 and the present, millions of them have been inserted with candy, gum, breakfast cereals, and cigarettes in all of the languages of the world in all of the countries of the world. Collecting them is a fascinating passion because often the quality of the art is superb and complete sets can be picture-framed to make an effective display of American comic art.

COMIC INSERT CARDS:

SUGGESTED LIST OF COLLECTIBLES

	Distributor	*Date*
Mickey Mouse Bubble Gum cards (1–96) (two albums issued)	Mickey Mouse Bubble Gum Co.	1933–1935
Mickey Mouse With the Movie Stars cards (97–120)		
Mickey Mouse bread cards (96—not numbered) (scrapbook album issued)	Mickey Mouse Bubble Gum Co.	1934–1935
Felix the Cat El Domino cards (Spanish) (75—not numbered)	Evaristo Juncosa Hijo Chocolates	
Dick Tracy Caramels cards (1–144)	Walter H. Johnson Candy Co.	
Dick Tracy Big Little Book cards (33–64)	Whitman Publishing Co.	1937
"Dick Tracy" strip cards (101–108)	Chicago *Tribune*	1935
American G-Men cards, First Series (101–148), Second Series (701–748)		
G-Men and Heroes of the Law cards (1–168)	Gum Inc.	1936
G-Man Big Little Book cards (129–161)	Whitman	1937
Dan Dunn Big Little Book cards (193–224)	Whitman	1937
Popeye Big Little Book cards (65–96)	Whitman	1937
Tom Mix Big Little Book cards (97–128)	Whitman	1937
Buck Jones Big Little Book cards (162–193)	Whitman	1937
Flash Gordon Big Little Book cards (1–32)	Whitman	1937
"Little Orphan Annie" strip cards (109–116)	Chicago *Tribune*	1935
"Moon Mullins" strip cards (125–135)	Chicago *Tribune*	1935
"Joe Palooka" strip cards (133–140)	Chicago *Tribune*	1935
"Harold Teen" strip cards (117–124)	Chicago *Tribune*	1935
"Terry and the Pirates" strip cards (141–148)	Chicago *Tribune*	1935
Lone Ranger Chewing Gum cards (1–48)	Gum Inc.	1940
Tom Mix gum booklets (1–48)	National Chicle Co.	1934
Buck Jones gum booklets (1–6)	The Goudey Gum Co.	1934
Buck Rogers gum booklets (1–6)	Goudey	1934
Tailspin Tommy gum booklets (1–6)	Goudey	1934
Dick Tracy gum booklets (1–6)	Goudey	1934
Superman Gum cards (1–72)	Gum Inc.	1940
"Buck Rogers in the 25th Century" strip cards (425–448)	John F. Dille Co.	1936
Tarzan and the Crystal Vault of Isis cards (1–50)	Schutter-Johnson Candy Corp.	1936
"Tarzan of the Apes" strip cards (409–416)	Stephen Slesinger, Inc.	1936
"Broncho Bill" strip cards (417–424)	Stephen Slesinger, Inc.	1936
"Tailspin Tommy" strip cards (401–408)	Stephen Slesinger, Inc.	1936
Frank Buck Bring 'Em Back Alive gum cards (1–48)	Gumakers of America, Inc.	1938
The Adventures of Smilin' Jack cards (1–128)	Samuel Eppy Co.	1942
Welch comic-character cards (1–50)	James O. Welch Co.	1946
Henry cards (not numbered)	Tareyton Cigarettes, J. Wix & Sons, Ltd.	1936
Alice in Wonderland cards (1–48)	Carreras Ltd.	1925
Skippy "Wheaties" cards (1–12)	Wheaties	1933

	Distributor	Date
Yellow Kid Chewing Gum cards (1–25)	Adams Gum Co.	1896
Jungle Gum cards (1–192)	World Wide Gum Co.	1934
Hunted Animals cards (1–25)	Planters Nut and Chocolate Co.	1933
Tootsie Circus cards (1–25)	The Sweets Company of America	1933
Government Agents vs. Public Enemies cards (A201–A224)	M. Pressner and Co.	1934
Thrilling True Spy Stories cards (1–24)	Gumakers of America	1939
Indian Gum cards (1–216)	Goudey	1934 approx.
Indians, Cowboys, Western Scenes cards (1–48)	(No Company Name)	1934 approx.
Boy Scout cards (1–48)	Goudey, Some Boy Gum	1933 approx.
Believe It Or Not Ripley cards (1–48)	Believe It Or Not, Inc.	1937
Pirate's Pictures (1–72)	Pirate's Picture Bubble Gum Co.	1933
Sea Raider Gum cards (1–24)	World Wide	1933
Skybirds cards (1–108)	Goudey Gum Co.	1934
Horrors of War cards (1–288)	Gum Inc.	1938
Don't Let It Happen Here cards (1–24)	International Chewing Gum Co.	1938
Defending America cards (201–248)	W. S. Co.	1941
The Second World War cards (140–172)	W. S. Co.	1939
Army, Navy and Air Corps cards (601–648)	W. S. Co.	1942
Generals and Their Flags cards (425–448)	W. S. Co.	1939
Heroes of the Sea cards (449–472)	W. S. Co.	1939
The Foreign Legion cards (325–372)	W. S. Co.	1939
Strange True Stories cards (1–24)	Wolverine Gum, Inc.	1936
Dare Devils cards (1–24)	National Chicle	1936
Film Funnies cards (1–24)	Gum Inc.	1936
Hollywood Picture Stars cards (1–40)	Hamilton Chewing Gum, Ltd.	1935 approx.
Charlot en El Circo cards (Charlie Chaplin in The Circus) (1–42)	Boferull	1937 approx.
Charlie Chaplin cards (1–18)	Amatter-Barcelona Chocolate Co.	1920 approx.

Mickey Mouse Bubble Gum Card Album.

Mickey Mouse With the Movie Stars cards and Mickey Mouse Bubble Gum cards. 1933–1935.

Mickey Mouse bread cards. 1933.

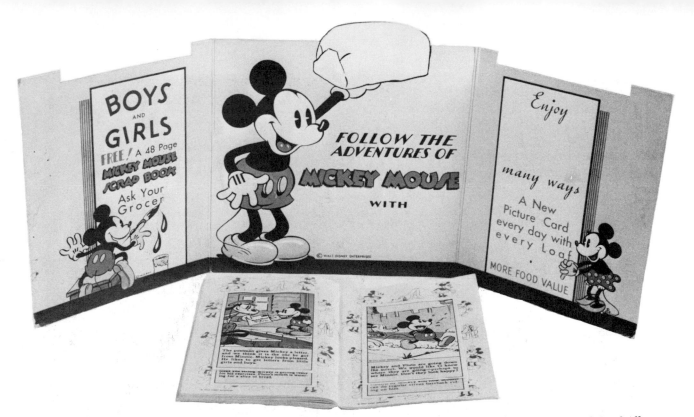

Mickey Mouse Bread Card Album
and advertising display.

Mickey Mouse Jig Saw Puzzle.

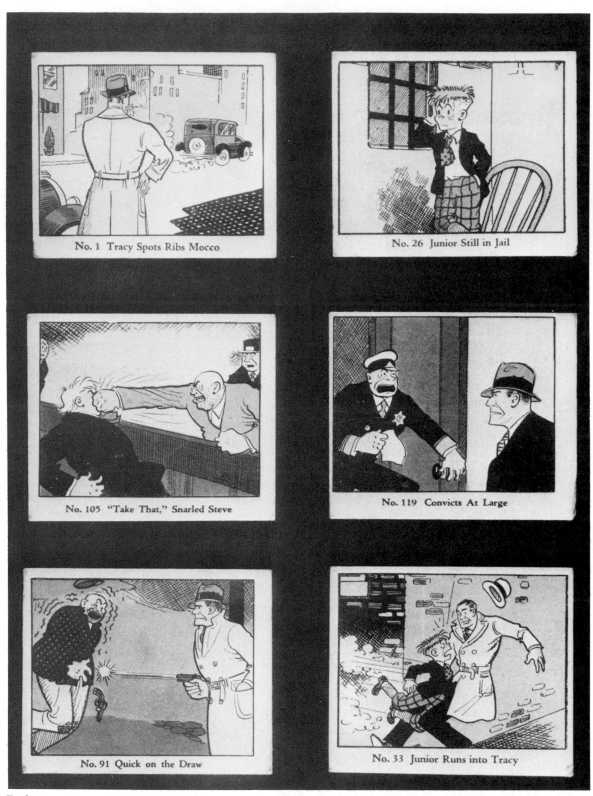

Dick Tracy Caramels cards.

G-Men and Heroes of the Law cards. 1936.

Superman Gum cards. 1940.

Lone Ranger Chewing Gum cards.

Tom Mix gum booklets. 1934.

Flash Gordon Big Little Book cards.
1937.

Popeye Big Little Book cards. 1937.

Tarzan and the Crystal Vault of Isis cards. 1936.

"Tarzan of the Apes" strip cards. 1936.

"Buck Rogers in the 25th Century" strip cards. 1936.

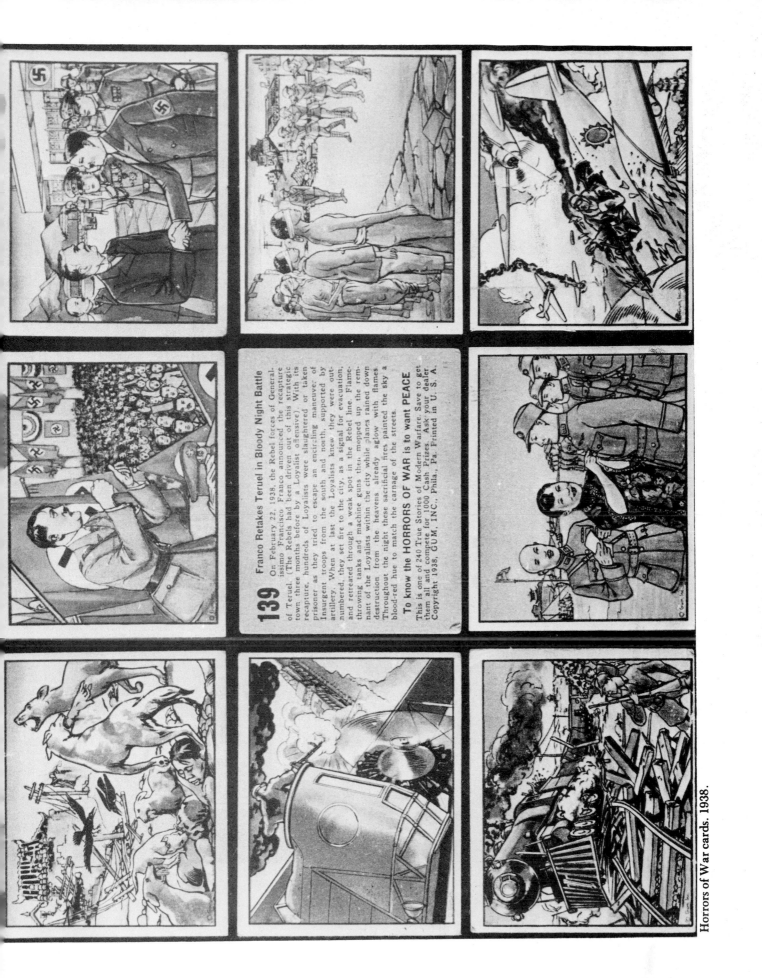

139 Franco Retakes Teruel in Bloody Night Battle

On February 22, 1938, the Rebel forces of General-issimo Francisco Franco announced the recapture of Teruel. (The Rebels had been driven out of this strategic town three months before by a Loyalist offensive). With its recapture, hundreds of Loyalists were slaughtered or taken prisoner as they tried to escape an encircling maneuver of Insurgent troops from the south and north, supported by artillery. When at last the Loyalists knew they were out-numbered, they set fire to the city, as a signal for evacuation, and retreated through a weak spot in the Rebel line. Flame-throwing tanks and machine guns then mopped up the rem-nant of the Loyalists within the city while planes rained down destruction from the heavens already aglow with flames Throughout the night these sacrificial fires painted the sky a blood-red hue to match the carnage of the streets.

To know the **HORRORS OF WAR** is to want **PEACE**

This is one of 240 True Stories of Modern Warfare. Save to get them all and compete for 1000 Cash Prizes. Ask your dealer. Copyright 1938, GUM, INC., Phila., Pa. Printed in U. S. A.

Horrors of War cards. 1938.

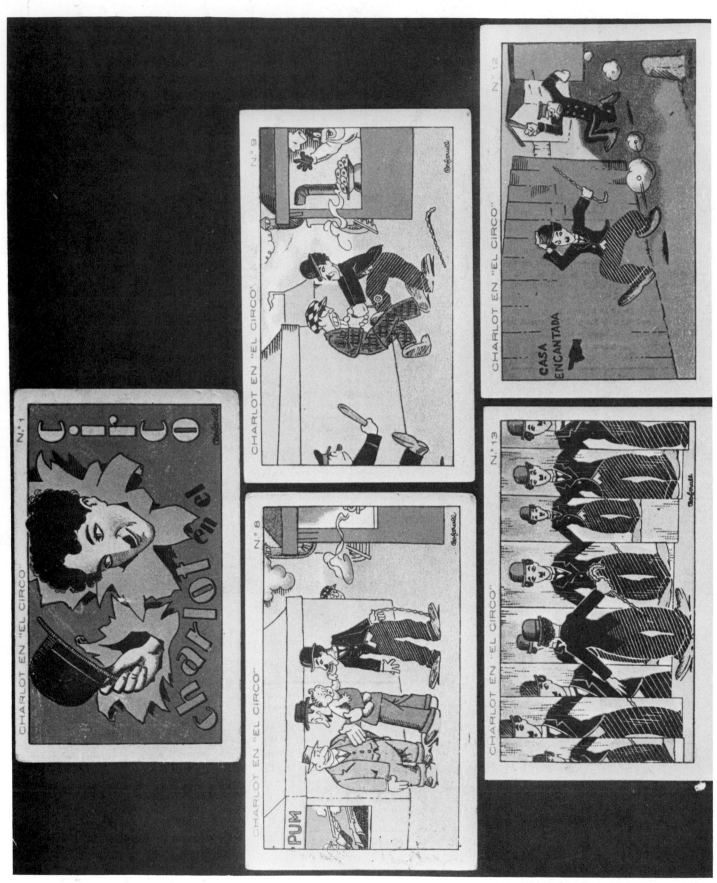

Charlot en El Circo cards (Charlie Chaplin in *The Circus*).

Charlie Chaplin. 1920. Amatter-Barcelona Chocolate Co.

The Yellow Kid Chewing Gum cards, the first comic-character insert cards. 1896.

Chicago *Tribune* comic-strip cards.

Welch comic-character cards. 1946.

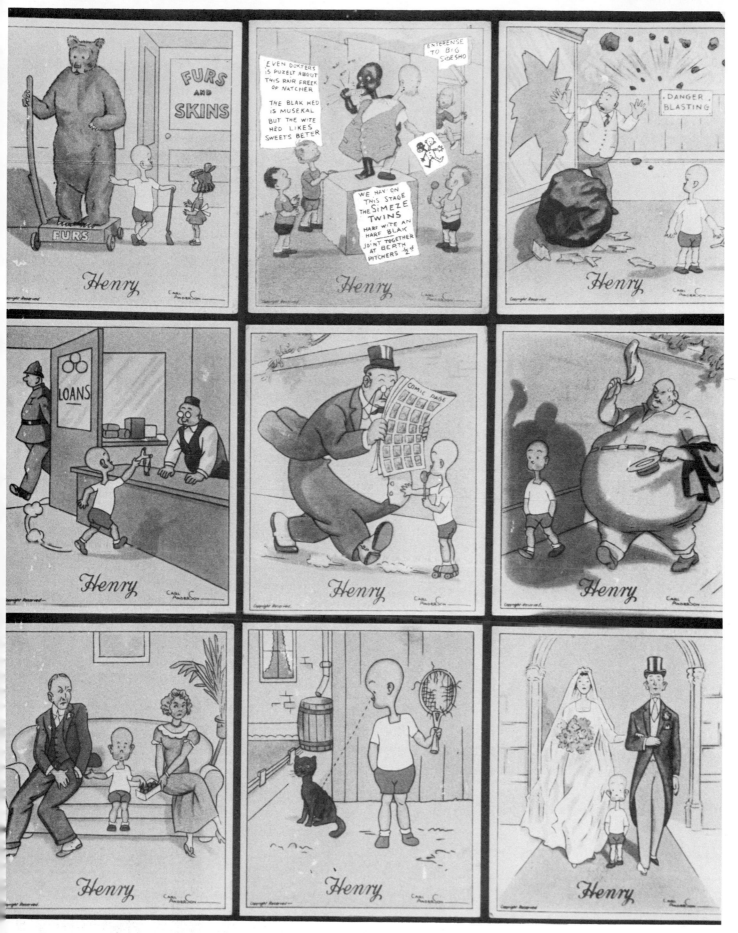

Henry cards. Tareyton Cigarettes, England, 1936.

Skippy "Wheaties" cards. 1933.

Comic-character postcards from the early years of this century. The rare mechanical postcard goes into action when thumb is pressed against forefinger, whereupon the "Captain" gets clubbed by the angry native chasing him.

7

The Decoders and Their Manuals

During the age of radio, Tom Mix, Orphan Annie, Captain Midnight, and others sent secret signals to boys and girls all over America that could not be decoded by their parents. During the nineteen thirties and forties, millions of kids sat by their radios waiting with their intricate metal decoders and decoding manuals for the cryptic signals that could be deciphered into the secret message of that afternoon.

Most radio premiums offered for a few box tops simply had to be awful in design, because they had to be cheap to manufacture. But the handsome graphic art of the manuals and the sculptured designs of the metal decoders with their high quality of workmanship seemed to have escaped this law of economics. The low wage and materials costs of the thirties, combined with the large-volume production of the decoders, provided an economic base for these excellent examples of American industrial comic art. And it is specifically that large volume that makes becoming a decoder collector an easy and inexpensive pursuit. These small machines are simple to understand and operate but they do require the manuals that explain them. The manuals are more difficult to acquire than the decoders and more expensive, but they are a must.

The decoders became a nationwide craze during the nineteen thirties, perhaps because they appealed to the delight and joy of mystery—mystery pure and simple in which kids could participate, combined with

young imagination and innocent fun during the great age of radio. Kids love a secret, and the basic, built-in appeal for the entire craze was a tone of secrecy best described in the Tom Mix Secret Manual:

KEEP THIS BOOK IN A SECRET PLACE!
Show this book only to friends whom you want to become Straight Shooters. But do not show anybody except your family the sections marked "CONFIDENTIAL"!

And additional messages of warning were created that almost resemble current U.S. Washington–Government–Modern:

IMPORTANT
The information contained on these pages is very confidential. You must never reveal the SECRETS of the STRAIGHT SHOOTERS to anyone, either by telling anybody about them or by showing these pages of your Manual. Remember to keep your Manual in a secret place!

Then followed descriptions of the Secret Salute, the Secret Grip, the Secret Password, the Secret Knock, the Secret Whistle, and the Secret Flashlight Signal.

But it was the Tom Mix Ralston Straight Shooters of America Official Decoder Membership Badge that was the super prize. It was made from a high-quality brass and had embossed on its surface a handsome Tom Mix logo, the legend "Ralston Straight Shooters of America," and the code symbols, such as a skull, heart, dagger, horseshoe, anchor, star, and key. Each badge had a serialized number and a rotating six-gun. It was quite simple to operate:

HOW TO DECODE A SECRET MESSAGE

Each symbol on the badge stands for a secret word. HEART stands for TOMORROW—Gun means WATCH FOR—DAGGER stands for CLUE. To find the secret word just point the gun on the badge at the symbol. The Arrow on the back of the badge will then point out the secret word.

When a secret radio message is read over the air LISTEN for TWO things—(1.) THE NAME OF THE PERSON and (2.) A SECRET CODE SYMBOL—DISREGARD EVERYTHING ELSE! For Example: Secret Message: JOHN wears an ANCHOR on his watch chain. Decoded means: JOHN GUILTY

If the NAME OF THE PERSON DOES NOT APPEAR in a secret message then pay attention ONLY TO THE CODE SYMBOL. For example: Secret Message: I saw a STAR tonight. Decoded means: DANGER AHEAD.

REMEMBER: LISTEN ONLY FOR SECRET SYMBOLS AND NAMES OF PERSONS. PAY NO ATTENTION TO ANYTHING ELSE. With a little practice you can use this secret code in talking with other STRAIGHT SHOOTERS and NO ONE WILL KNOW WHAT YOU'RE SAYING!

This radio-premium program was so successful that it measurably increased the sales of Ralston Whole Wheat Cereal and Shredded Ralston. Decoder buttons were issued, each with a picture of the secondary characters on the radio show: Mike Shaw, Jane, Wash, Curley Bradley, and of course Tom Mix's horse Tony. Don Gordon, the Tom Mix announcer, would say: "To find out whether Mr. Zero is the murderer look behind the button with the picture of Tony on it." You turn over the Tony button and you find the word "Guilty." Millions of these button-type decoders were produced, but you had to convince your mother to buy the cereal because the button was inside the box.

One of the most popular radio programs of the nineteen thirties was *Radio Orphan Annie.* From 1935 to 1940 it offered a huge diversity of wild premiums. But the catch was that you had to buy and drink Ovaltine. I can personally attest to the fact that it was the worst god-awful-tasting children's health drink ever invented. I am certain that thousands of other kids had the same vomiting spells from it, but those that survived were rewarded with some of the most handsome metal decoders ever designed.

The first effort, in 1935, had modest results and produced a manual entitled *Radio Orphan Annie's Secret Society.* The usual secret signs and signals were explained, with a secret code for radio messages. It offered a wonderful Lucky-Piece Wishing Coin about the size of a half-dollar. On the front side was a beautifully embossed portrait of the popular orphan with a lucky wishbone and equally lucky four-leaf clovers. On the back it had the words—"Good Luck" in seven different languages to make it seven times lucky: German, French, Italian, Greek, Swedish, Spanish, and even Chinese!

Absolutely free?

HERE'S WHAT YOU DO

All you have to do to get your Orphan Annie Lucky-Piece absolutely free is to keep track of the days you have Ovaltine 3 times a day and mark it down on the handy chart below. Just make a little cross in each square to show that you had OVALTINE at breakfast, lunch and dinner or between meals, a total of *three times* that day!

Then when you've done this for 15 days and have a cross in each one of the 15 squares—sign your name on the line at the bottom of the chart.

THEN—take the pink slip that comes with this book and write your name and address in the top half that's marked —"USE THIS HALF TO GET LUCKY-PIECE FREE!"—then sign your name. And have your mother and Dad cosign it underneath too. . . . Mail the top half to Radio Orphan Annie's Secret Society, 180 North Michigan Avenue, Chicago, Illinois—together with one thin aluminum seal from the inside of the top of a can of OVALTINE to show that you have really earned your Lucky-Piece!

Free? . . . Aw c'mon! Certainly there must be a fraternity of forty- and fifty-year-olds at this date, who, when they are in need of a good throw-up, use neither the tickling feather nor fingers-in-the-throat method but merely shout "Ovaltine!" and rush off to toilet bowl or sink.

The first Radio Orphan Annie decoder was produced in 1935 but was not well designed or very interesting in operation. But the 1936 decoder was a great improvement. It had a beautiful Art Deco jewelry design and could be used today as a handsome high-camp brooch. The year "1936" is deeply embossed on the top of the brass face. It served three purposes: it was a badge that could be pinned to your sweater to prove to all the other kids on the block that you were an R.O.A. member, it decoded Annie's secret radio messages automatically, and it had a secret mystery compartment in the back for carrying code messages and money. Yes, it is a beautiful piece of Deco, but even with the manual instructions it would take a CIA cryptographer to operate it. On the face there is an inner circle of numbers from one to twenty-six. Outside of that there is an outer circle made up of all the letters of the alphabet stamped into the metal (not in their regular order) that can be seen through a series of small square slots. Turn the disc and the numbers and letters lined up with each other in a certain relationship. The messages over the radio were given in numbers, not letters, and only after the radio program was over and you had heard all of the commercials for Ovaltine would the announcer tell you where to set the decoder. After giving the code key he would read the string of numbers to be translated into letters that comprised the message. The code would be changed periodically so that outsiders could not figure out the secret messages, and typical radio instructions went like this:

> Listen closely. Tonight's secret message is given in the A-15 code. I repeat A-15. This means that when you start to figure out your message after the broadcast is over, you must set your dial on your decoder so that the A comes opposite the 15.

The 1937 R.O.A. decoder was similar in operation but even more handsome in design. It is pure jewelry design, a fine-lined sunburst in the best tradition of Art Moderne. A rotating decoder disc with small round holes was used to decode the messages and enhanced the appearance.

By 1938 *Radio Orphan Annie* had achieved nationwide popularity. Annie was president of the Secret Society, Joe Corntassel was vice president (played as a boy by Mel Torme, the now famous singer), and Sandy was the official mascot. The decoder for this year was the largest of all, a full two inches in diameter, star shaped, with a big "1938" at the top, with five stars to signify that this was the fifth-anniversary year of Radio Orphan Annie's Secret Society, plus the Mysterious Crossed Keys of the club to show that it was the "key" to her secret code. But the biggest difference was that the decoding mechanism was completely hidden. It could be worn on the front of your coat or dress and no outsider would ever suspect that it was a secret-code decoder! It had the special "Telematic" feature, which consisted of two small openings on the face that revealed the code number and letter.

The Mysterious Crossed Keys on the decoder became the 1938 Secret Salute. To greet another member you would cross your arms, hold them against your chest, and clench your fists, with fingers turned toward you. Just in case you don't remember, the 1938 Secret Password was "War-Tassel." It was taken from the first syllable of the orphan's last name—Warbucks—and the last two syllables of Joe's last name—Corntassel. The Secret Handshake included pressing your thumb gently against the other suspected member's hand exactly five times (because Annie's Secret Society was in its fifth year). But you had to make certain the other person pressed your hand exactly five times in return: "Otherwise you can be pretty sure he's an outsider and doesn't really understand what you are doing at all!"

Much used and very popular were the Secret Wig-Wag Signs, a "deaf and dumb" language that members could use to talk to each other without opening their mouths or speaking a word:

1. When you touch your ears with the first fingers of each hand—it means: "BEWARE! OUTSIDERS ARE LISTENING, TRYING TO FIND OUT OUR ORPHAN ANNIE SECRETS!"

2. When you hold your two hands in front of you with the tips of your first fingers and thumbs touching so that they form a letter "A"—it means: "HURRY HOME. IT'S ALMOST ORPHAN ANNIE TIME ON THE RADIO!"

3. When you clasp your right wrist with your left hand and wiggle the outstretched fingers of your right hand, it means: "LET'S GET AWAY WHERE WE CAN TALK OVER OUR PLANS IN PRIVATE!"

Other "free" gifts were offered that year, including the Radio Orphan Annie Silver Star Ring, with a removable secret compartment on top for carrying secret messages; and again, vast amounts of Ovaltine had to be consumed to acquire these radio premiums.

A much less complicated and easier to operate decoder was issued in 1939. It consisted of two simple discs that rotated to decode the messages, and it lacks the sculptured appearance of the more spectacular ones.

By 1940 patriotism was on the rise, and the last of the Radio Orphan Annie gadgets bore the name "The 1940 Speedomatic Double-Track Decoding Machine." The manual's description was: "Note the beautiful patriotic design on the front, showing our military shield and the American Eagle, with our flag waving in the background. Note also the letters U.S.A. that show you live in the United States and love your country!" Then a commercial message followed linking chocolate-flavored Ovaltine, drunk at least three times a day, to becoming a good American: product married patriotism. But it was a beautiful design and well made. The simplified decoding mechanism and ease of operation were the result of continuous research and mechanical progress.

And if you drank even more Ovaltine and became their block salesman by getting three of your friends to sign a pledge to bathe their stomachs in the brown sludge regularly, you could prove it by sending in three metal-foil seals from under the lids and 10 ¢ with each one, plus cosignatures from the six mothers and fathers involved, and you would be sent soon and "Absolutely Free!" an official Code Captain Belt. The shiny Victory Metal Buckle was patterned after the regular U.S. Army garrison buckle, and the red-white-and-blue cloth belt was self-adjustable to fit even the smallest waist. Special code messages were broadcast for Code Captains only, and the key to the secret code was a series of numbers stamped into the back of the buckle. This was the seventh anniversary of Radio Orphan Annie and the last. Perhaps the war was turning the imagination of young America away from the simple good-and-evil innocence of Orphan Annie and toward an at least fantasy-level involvement in the coming war through which they could share and try to understand the real involvement of their fathers and older brothers.

Having discovered profits through patriotism via their 1940 *Radio Orphan Annie* campaign, and having clearly in focus the fact that young girls don't

fight wars, Ovaltine switched. And it was very successful. From 1940 to 1949 Ovaltine sponsored the *Captain Midnight's Secret Squadron* radio program. The popularity of the metal decoders rose straight up, because real grown-up Jap and Nazi spies were everywhere and were probably sending secret messages on decoders just like Captain Midnight's!

The first was the Captain Midnight 1941 Code-O-Graph, shaped much like a radio dial and quite simple to operate. Its two patriotic emblems were the American Eagle and the military shield. Again, the code numbers would be broadcast and the decoder would translate them into letters. The tone of the program was always one of excitement:

THE SECRET SQUADRON MEETS TONIGHT!

The very air throbs to the roar of the plane in a thundering power dive! It's the signal for red-blooded boys and girls throughout the nation to gather 'round radios for another thrilling adventure with CAPTAIN MIDNIGHT! Every week day except Saturday Captain Midnight is on the air. And he expects every loyal member of his Secret Squadron to be listening in at every "meeting."

THERE WILL BE MANY IMPORTANT MESSAGES broadcast in the Secret Squadron's own secret code! Besides, every member wants to keep right up-to-date on the exciting adventures of Chuck and Joyce in helping Captain Midnight oppose the traitorous plots of IVAN SHARK! Never miss a program! Tune in every night for more adventures with CAPTAIN MIDNIGHT AND THE SECRET SQUADRON!

And tune in they did and drink Ovaltine they did—by the ton. Juvenile patriotism was pushed to its fever-limit, and the Captain Midnight Radio Bulletin set the tone:

You should be very proud of your membership in Captain Midnight's great organization of patriotic young Americans! For we are banded together for a real purpose. We are helping to guard the future of America! We are opposed to everything that is dishonest, disloyal and Un-American! We are pledged to honor the flag and all that it represents!

The program was so popular that even the United States Government took an interest and allocated very scarce brass sheet metal for the production of the 1942 Photo-Matic Code-O-Graph Decoder Badge. It had a beautiful design, perhaps the most handsome of all the metal decoders. At the top were flowing-in-the-wind flag banners with our hero's name. The spinning decoder disc was an embossed old-fashioned six-cylinder Curtis-Wright air-cooled airplane engine with a propellor that was a throwback to the Spads of World War I. But at the very top, pasted into a one-half-inch-square picture-frame opening was a photograph of Captain Midnight himself! Wearing flight goggles and open-cockpit leather helmet, serious-faced, our hero could be seen at last! It looked like a very small television screen.

Materials became very scarce into the middle of the fighting years. In 1944 a very handsome embroidered service-insignia shoulder patch was issued, with yellow wings outlined in red. In the center was a blue clockface with yellow-dot numbers, and both clock hands pointed to midnight!

By 1945 some brass and plastic were available again and the large Magni-Magic Code-O-Graph Decoder was issued to loyal Ovaltine-drinking members.

In 1946 the Captain Midnight Mirro-Flash Code-O-Graph Decoder was produced. At the top was the Winged Star, the new symbol of the Secret Squadron, and around the edge was the inscription "Captain Midnight's 1946 Secret Squadron," and it was in bright gold, with a raised decoder dial in the center. The dial looked like glass but was a reducing mirror that showed a much bigger area than would an ordinary mirror of the same size. You could keep an eye on what your enemy was doing behind you or even watch a whole roomful of people without anyone knowing you were doing it. It was also a flasher; you could send messages by reflecting light either directly at a person or by flashing them at a wall, ceiling, or school desk. By this time the code mechanism had become almost professional. The stationary circle had the twenty-six letters of the alphabet embossed. The moving, circular disc had numbers 1 to 26. Therefore, you could send and receive Secret Squadron messages in 26 codes with a total of 676 code combinations!

Mr. Unknown Nameless, who designed these decoders, was going wild with new ideas! In 1947 he designed the Whistling Code-O-Graph, which could be used to send secret signals by sound. Basically, it was a whistle, made of durable, handsome blue and red plastic. On one side was the famous winged Captain Midnight insignia with the letters *SS1947*. On the other side, in red plastic, was the code dial itself, with letters that matched the twenty-six numbers. The master-code key for the day was given to members via the radio broadcast, and the special message could be deciphered. But signaling by sound was done with the simple Morse code that could be found in the manual. It was also to be used as a distance meter:

USE YOUR WHISTLE AS A "DISTANCE METER"

Learn to judge distances. Have a friend blow a sharp blast, and wave a handkerchief at the same time. Count the seconds from the instant of the wave until you hear the sound of the whistle. Every second means 1000 feet. If it takes five seconds, the other fellow's 5000 feet—or almost a mile away from you!

The 1949 Key-O-Matic Code-O-Graph Decoder was certainly the most amazing instrument Captain Midnight ever issued. The story has it that Ovaltine received a request from the FBI for samples, it was that advanced. Inside the shiny brass case was a carefully calibrated set of plastic gears, with the usual set of twenty-six numbers and letters cast into each surface. There were two small openings in the case to reveal one letter and one number. Both letters and numbers would change as you turned the red gear wheel at the bottom with your thumb:

HOW TO SET YOUR CAPTAIN MIDNIGHT CODE-O-GRAPH FOR KEY CODES

Keep turning until you see the number you want. For example let's imagine you want 6, for Key Code B-6.

Keep your Code-O-Graph set with number 6 showing. Now put your key in the two small openings near the top of your Code-O-Graph—beneath the letters S.S. Push down on the key and hold it down. You will then find that you can turn the red wheel WITHOUT CHANGING THE NUMBER—only the letters change. Now turn the red wheel until the letter you want shows in the opening—in this case letter B. Then take out the key. You now have set your Code-O-Graph for Key Code B-6 and are ready to start decoding any message in Key Code B-6 automatically.

Do not lose the very important little key. Tie a string to your key so that it won't get lost easily.

Perhaps somewhere in the secret files of the CIA there is a file on Captain Midnight. It might prove interesting to read because it is a fact that this was the last decoder produced, and Mr. Unknown Nameless, the designer, disappeared.

During the beginning years of television Peter Pan Peanut Butter sponsored the still popular radio show *The Adventures of Sky King*, and one of the premiums was the Sky King Spy Detecto Writer Decoder. Certainly it must have been engineered by our friend the decoder designer, Mr. U.N. It had an even more complicated gear train, with the red wheel at the bottom, but with the amazing feature of an inside ink pad and a print wheel at the other end that would actually print the decoded messages! It is very rare and must have cost a fortune to produce.

Literally dozens of different radio rings were issued, sometimes with the decoders, and are shown in the manuals. Most were cheap, badly designed brass stampings, but some were quite intriguing. Perhaps the rarest and most sought-after ring is the Captain Midnight Secret Squadron Mystic Sun God Ring. It was created to celebrate the Secret Squadron's successful adventures in Mexico, ancient home of the Aztecs, and on the side of the ring was pictured their sun god, Tonatiuh. Besides the Aztec designs it contained an ingenious secret compartment hidden beneath the red stone, for carrying secret messages. It is quite a handsome piece of radio jewelry, but unfortunately it is usually found without the stone because the metal grooves at the side held the sliding stone too loosely.

Equally rare and desirable is the Shadow Blue Coal Ring that glows in the dark. It was made from irradiated plastic and had a simulated chunk of blue coal as a stone. It was sponsored as a premium by the Blue Coal Company, and the radio program was exciting and popular, but anthracite coal was doomed as an American industry. The program stopped, and the great voice of Orson Welles as the Shadow was heard no more.

"Dad," Brit Reid said to his father, Dan, "I know personally that the Green Hornet is no criminal. In his own way he fights for law and order. Can you believe that?"

Old Dan Reid nodded his gray head slowly. "I think I know what you are trying to tell me."

The young publisher met the eyes of the man who had built the Daily Sentinel into one of America's greatest newspapers. "Dad, I am the Green Hornet!"

"I suspected as much," the elder Reid said.

"How could you? The world thinks I am nothing but an idle playboy, dabbling in the newspaper business."

"Son, you've seen the painting on this wall many times. I gave it to you years ago."

"Why yes, Dad—the picture of the Masked Man on the great white horse."

"Everyone knows who he was. But the world does not know that the Masked Man is your ancestor. Brit—my uncle and your great-uncle."

The Green Hornet certainly was a real relative of The Lone Ranger, and during the middle thirties it was the intention of George Trendle, who had created both popular fighters for law and order, to put the Masked Rider of the Plains into a more modern format. Like his great uncle, the Hornet wore a mask, took on a colorful name, and instead of the great white horse Silver had a super-powered car, the Black Beauty.

The radio program issued one of the most complicated and attractive rings, the Green Hornet Ring. It glowed in the dark, and the round front was an embossed brass seal that could be used with hot wax to seal envelopes containing secret messages. It swung up on a hinge to reveal a secret compartment, and it is certainly one of the most beautiful radio rings ever designed.

Portrait rings were also popular and were distributed for Orphan Annie, Frank Buck, Gene Autry, and Hopalong Cassidy, but one of the most handsome was the ring for Dick Tracy showing his bent-nose profile and a green-enameled wide-brimmed fedora hat. The Lone Ranger Six-Shooter Ring mounted a large replica of the gun that won the West. A small cigarette-lighter flint was inserted so it could spark like a real gun! The detailing resulted in a very accurate miniature reproduction of the real gun. The Buck Rogers Repeller Ray Ring, issued as a radio premium during the mid-thirties, was made from "simulated gold" and had our hero molded into the face riding a space sled with a green stone embedded in the side: the Repeller Ray.

During the age of radio those many rings, badges, decoders, buttons, telescopes, periscopes, games, guns, parachutes, airplanes, shirts, ties, sneakers, and movie cameras, anything and everything a premium designer could imagine, went via the post office into millions of homes. The decoders and the rings were the best of all in terms of imaginative design, workmanship, and originality and are prime examples of excellent American comic industrial art.

THE DECODERS AND THEIR MANUALS:
SUGGESTED LIST OF COLLECTIBLES

	Distributor	*Date*
Tom Mix Straight Shooters Decoder (with manual)	Ralston	mid-1930s
Tom Mix Decoder Buttons (5) (with manual)	Ralston	mid-1930s
Radio Orphan Annie Lucky Coin	Ovaltine	1935
Radio Orphan Annie Decoder (with manual)	Ovaltine	1935
Radio Orphan Annie Decoder (with manual)	Ovaltine	1936
Radio Orphan Annie Decoder (with manual)	Ovaltine	1937
Radio Orphan Annie Telematic Decoder (with manual)	Ovaltine	1938
Radio Orphan Annie Decoder (with manual)	Ovaltine	1939
Radio Orphan Annie Speedomatic Double-Track Decoding Machine (with manual)	Ovaltine	1940
Radio Orphan Annie Code Captain Belt	Ovaltine	1940
Captain Midnight Code-O-Graph Decoder (with manual)	Ovaltine	1941
Captain Midnight Photo-Matic Code-O-Graph Decoder (with manual)	Ovaltine	1942
Captain Midnight Magni-Magic Code-O-Graph Decoder (with manual)	Ovaltine	1945
Captain Midnight Mirro-Flash Code-O-Graph Decoder (with manual)	Ovaltine	1946
Captain Midnight Whistling Code-O-Graph Decoder (with manual)	Ovaltine	1947
Captain Midnight Mirro-Magic Code-O-Graph Decoder (mirror on the back) (with manual)	Ovaltine	1948
Captain Midnight Key-O-Matic Code-O-Graph Decoder (with manual and key)	Ovaltine	1949
Sky King Spy Detecto Writer Decoder (with manual)	Peter Pan Peanut Butter	1940s
Captain Midnight Secret Squadron Mystic Sun God Ring (with manual)	Ovaltine	1946
Captain Midnight Flight Commander Ring (with manual)	Ovaltine	1941
Captain Midnight Mystic Eye Detector Ring (with manual)	Ovaltine	1942
Shadow Blue Coal Ring	Blue Coal Company	mid-1930s
Green Hornet Ring	General Mills	mid-1930s
Buck Rogers Repeller Ray Ring (with manual)	Cream of Wheat	1934
Buck Rogers Ring of Saturn (with manual)	Post Toasties	1946
Lone Ranger Six-Shooter Ring (with manual)	Cheerios	mid-1940s
Lone Ranger Film Strip Ring (with manual)	Cheerios	mid-1940s
Lone Ranger Atom Bomb Ring (with manual)	Cheerios	mid-1940s
Lone Ranger Flashlight Ring (with manual)	Cheerios	mid-1940s
Terry and the Pirates Gold Ore Detector Ring (with manual)	Quaker Oats	mid-1940s

	Distributor	Date
Tom Mix:	Ralston	1930s and 1940s
Signet Ring		
Horseshoe Tail Ring		
Look Around Ring		
Initial Ring		
Siren Ring		
Magnet Ring		
Whistle Ring		
Signature Ring		
Magic Tiger Eye Ring		
Elephant's Hair Ring		
Sky King:	Peter Pan Peanut Butter	1940s
Magni-Glow Ring		
Signal Ring		
Aztec Indian Ring		
Teleblinker Ring		
Portrait Rings:		
Orphan Annie	Ovaltine	
Dick Tracy	Quaker Puffed Wheat & Rice	
Frank Buck	Ralston	
Gene Autry	Ralston	
Hopalong Cassidy	Ralston	
Radio Orphan Annie Birthstone Ring (with manual)	Ovaltine	1935
Radio Orphan Annie Signet Ring (with manual)	Ovaltine	1937
Radio Orphan Annie Silver Star Ring (with manual)	Ovaltine	1938
Radio Orphan Annie Mystic Eye Ring (with manual)	Ovaltine	1939

During the metal shortage of World War II, decoders were
made from available cardboard. They are very rare and
very collectible:

	Distributor
Dick Tracy Junior Detective Kit	Sweets Company of America
(Consists of Secret Symbol Decoder, decoder manual, membership card, Sabotour Suspect Card, 18″ rule to measure saboteurs, wall chart, and Dick Tracy Official Junior Detective Badge)	
The Junior Justice Society	All-Star Comics
(Consists of Secret Code of Junior Justice Society of America Decoder, silk shoulder patch for Junior Justice Society, and printed wartime patriotic material)	
Captain Marvel Decoder	Fawcett
Orphan Annie Slid-O-Matic Decoder	Ovaltine

Tom Mix Manual and Tom Mix Decoder Buttons.

How to Use Your Tom Mix Decoder Buttons

Notice that each of your decoder buttons has a secret code word on the back. With these buttons you can decode important messages that will be read from time to time over the Tom Mix radio program and solve many of the Tom Mix radio mysteries long before your family and friends know the answers.

For example, suppose Don Gordon, the Tom Mix announcer, says: "To find out whether Mr. Zero is the murderer look behind the button with the picture of Tony on it." You look under the Tony button and you find the word "Guilty."

Or suppose Don Gordon says: "When will Tom Mix capture the criminal? Look at the Jane decoder button." You look at the Jane decoder button and it gives the answer "Tomorrow."

How to Send and Receive Messages With Other Straight Shooters

By arranging with other Straight Shooter pals you can exchange secret messages by wearing on your shirt or dress the decoder button with the message you wish to send. For example, if you want to warn another Straight Shooter pal there is danger ahead, wear the button with Wash's picture on it. Or to flash the message you are going to have a Straight Shooter meeting tomorrow, wear the button with the picture of Jane on it. You can work out all sorts of secret signals with these buttons and have lots of fun!

IMPORTANT: Don't let anyone except another Straight Shooter look at the secret decoder words on the back of your buttons!

How to use your Tom Mix Decoder.

How to Use Your Official Decoder MEMBERSHIP BADGE

With your official membership decoder badge it's easy to decode secret radio messages INSTANTLY. You need not write anything down. There's nothing to remember.

Each symbol on the badge stands for a secret word. For example, the word HEART stands for TOMORROW—GUN means WATCH FOR—DAGGER stands for CLUE, etc. To find the secret word just point the gun on the badge at the symbol. The arrow on the back of the badge will then point to the secret word.

How to Decode a Secret Message

When a secret radio message is read over the air LISTEN for TWO things:—
(1). THE NAME OF A PERSON and (2). A SECRET CODE SYMBOL.—
DISREGARD EVERYTHING ELSE. For example:

Secret message: *JOHN* WEARS AN *ANCHOR* ON HIS WATCH CHAIN
Decoded means: JOHN   GUILTY
Secret message: *JOHN* HAS A *KEY* TO THE RANCH HOUSE
Decoded means: JOHN   INNOCENT

If the NAME OF A PERSON DOES NOT APPEAR in a secret message, then pay attention ONLY TO THE CODE SYMBOL. For example:
Secret message: I SAW A *STAR* TONIGHT
Decoded means: DANGER AHEAD
Secret message: THERE'S *LIGHTNING* IN THE SKY
Decoded means: YES

When TWO SYMBOLS appear in the message, use both. For example:
Secret message: A COWBOY WEARS A *GUN* NOT A *DAGGER*
Decoded means: WATCH FOR   CLUE

REMEMBER: LISTEN *ONLY* FOR SECRET SYMBOLS AND NAMES OF PERSONS. PAY NO ATTENTION TO ANYTHING ELSE. With a little practice you can use this secret code in talking with other Straight Shooters and no one will know what you're saying.

A typical radio premium: Tom Mix Blow Gun with darts and target, advertising Ralston and the radio program.

Radio Orphan Annie Decoders, 1935–1940.

Radio Orphan Annie's Secret Society 1936 Manual, front cover.

How to use your 1936 Radio Orphan Annie Decoder.

Radio Orphan Annie's Secret Society 1935 Manual, back cover.

How to use your 1938 Orphan Annie Decoder.

● Your new 1938 membership pin is the most important secret symbol of Radio Orphan Annie's Secret Society! Always wear your pin on your left side (over your heart)—and guard it as one of your most valuable possessions, because it does these 3 things:—

First—It proves you're a 1938 member in good standing. *Second*—It decodes Annie's secret radio messages automatically. *Third*—Its brand-new Telematic Feature fools outsiders—makes decoding quicker—and easier for you.

If you were a member last year and compare your *old* 1937 pin with this *new* 1938 pin, you can see right away how completely changed and different it is! Note its beautiful star shape—and the big "1938" at the top. And notice, there's a small star in each of the 5 points—5 small stars in all—signifying that this is the 5th Anniversary Year of Radio Orphan Annie's Secret Society!

This pin also has the Mysterious Crossed Keys of the Club on it—to show it's the "key" to Orphan Annie's secret code.

But here's the biggest difference of all! Its decoding mechanism is completely *hidden!* You can wear it right out on front of your coat or dress—and outsiders will never suspect for a minute that it is *actually a Secret Decoding Pin!* Because even if an outsider looks at the front of your pin closely—all he'll see are two small openings—which he probably will think are unimportant! But *you* know they're *very* important! They're the secret *Telematic Openings* that tell you at a glance exactly what each one of Orphan Annie's secret messages mean when she broadcasts them on the radio!

Turn to the next page—and read how to decode messages with your new Telematic Decoder Pin!

[7]

Radio Orphan Annie's Secret Society 1940 Manual, front cover.

Radio Orphan Annie's Secret Society 1940 Manual, back cover.

Captain Midnight's Secret Squadron 1946 Manual, front cover.

Captain Midnight decoders and shoulder patch.

Your Official Secret Squadron MIRRO-FLASH

IT IS ALSO THE IDENTIFICATION BADGE OF THE GREATER 1946 SECRET SQUADRON!

Agents of the CID (Criminal Investigation Department of the U.S. Army), FBI and other crime detection organizations are issued official badges. Your Mirro-Flash Code-O-Graph Badge is the official badge of the 1946 Secret Squadron.

DIRECTIONS FOR RECEIVING AND DECODING SIGNAL

TODAY'S MASTER CODE COMBINATION IS G-1

G-1

25 · 6 · 7

1. Be sure to have pencil and paper handy when listening to Captain Midnight, so you'll always be ready to take down Secret Code Messages. This is very important.

2. As soon as you hear the Master Code Combination, write it down at the top of the page, and put a circle around it so you will know it is the Code for this particular message.

3. Suppose the announcer says, "Today's message is in Master Code G-1"—then you will know the Master Code Combination for that day is G-1. Write "G-1" at the top of the page.

4. When the announcer says "FIRST WORD", write down the numbers just as he gives them to you. Put a dash after each number to keep them separate, and write them in neat rows.

How to use your Captain Midnight Mirro-flash Code-O-Graph Decoder.

Captain Midnight's Secret Squadron 1947 and 1949 manuals, front covers.

How to use your Captain Midnight 1947 and 1949 Decoders.

Captain Midnight Secret Squadron Mystic Sun God Ring.

Captain Midnight and Orphan Annie Ovaltine mugs.

Tom Mix, Captain Video, and Sky King decoders.

Rings: Shadow Blue Coal, Captain Midnight Secret Squadron Mystic Sun God, Green Hornet, Terry and the Pirates Gold Ore Detector, Dick Tracy Portrait, Lone Ranger Six-Shooter Ring.

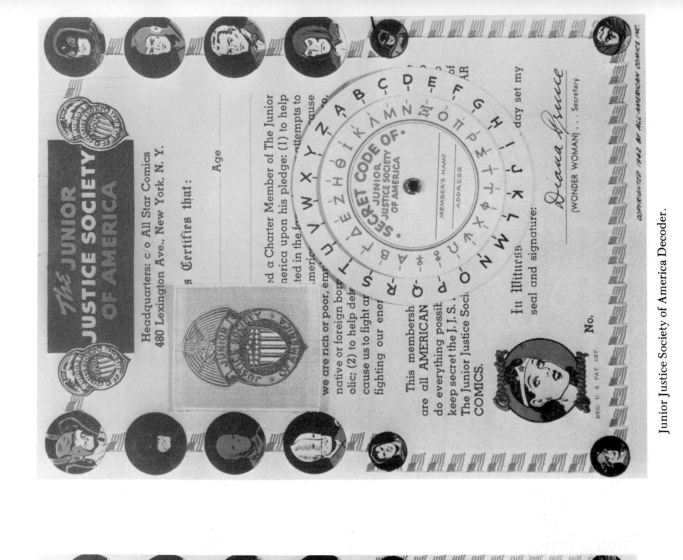

Junior Justice Society of America Decoder.

Junior Justice Society of America Pledge.

SHADOWING SUSPECTS

Good detectives can follow a suspect without being seen by the man they are trailing. Dick Tracy does, and he's one of the best "shadows" in the business.

1... Act naturally—don't let your man know you're wise to him.

2... Take cover in crowds, bushes, doorways and dark areas. If your quarry turns around, he won't see you.

3... Be casual—pretend you are on an errand that takes you in same direction he is going. Don't follow too close behind him.

4... Jot down a description of your man, what he does and where he goes. Be specific, get all information correct. Turn this information over to the police with your name and address.

5... BE CAREFUL — EXERCISE CAUTION — TAKE NO UNNECESSARY CHANCES.

How to use DICK TRACY DECODER

With this decoder you can send secret messages and also decipher the ones that are sent to you.

HOW TO USE THE CODE SYSTEM

Tracy's movable hand points to the letters of the secret code. The letters of the regular alphabet appear in the red circle next to Junior.

Encoding: To put a message into code, first write the message into code, first write the message down in the regular way, using regular alphabet. Then move the lever until the first letter of your written message appears in the red circle next to Junior. The code symbol for that letter will be the one which Dick Tracy points to with his movable hand. Write this code letter under the regular letter of your message. Continue until you have thus rewritten the entire message. The rewritten message is the one you send.

Decoding: To put a code message you have received into the regular alphabet so you can read it, move the lever until Tracy's movable hand points to the first letter (symbol) in the message you have received. Then look at the "letter" appearing in red circle next to Junior. The letter appearing there is the regular alphabet letter. Write this letter down over the first letter of the received message. Continue until you have thus rewritten the entire message. You will then be able to read the message.

4

OFFICIAL DICK TRACY'S

JUNIOR DETECTIVE MANUAL

★ TRACY TELLS ABOUT...

PAGE		PAGE
❶ HOW TO ACT IN EMERGENCIES	❺	HOW TO SLAM A SABOTEUR
❷ DICK'S "FIND-THE-CLUE" QUIZ	❻	HOW MARINES HANDLE 'EM
❸ SHADOWING SUSPECTS	❼	TYING UP SABOTEURS
❹ USING SECRET CODE	❽	PLAYING "SABOTEUR SHOW-UP"

How to use your Dick Tracy Junior Secret Symbol Decoder.

A group of comic-character buttons.

Index

Ace Comics, 54
Ace magazines, 55–56
Action Comics, 46–47, 51, 53, 54
   origin of Superman, 48, 49, 59
Adams, Neil, 10
Adams Gum Co., 237
Adventure Comics, 49, 54
Adventure magazine, 13
Advertising memorabilia, 5, 10–11
   Buster Brown pocket watch, 121
   commercial preparatory art, 5, 10–11
   Disney character merchandise, 100
   point-of-sale, 120
   Yellow Kid Cigars, 17
"Aesthetic Civil Right," 1–2
Aggie, Reg'lar Fellers Girl, 83, 114
Alice in Wonderland
   cards, 236
   timepieces, 126, 132
All American Comics, 54, 63
All Flash, 54
All-Select Comics, 54
All Star Comics, 54, 267
All Winners, 54
"Alley Oop" (original art), 13
Allied Manufacturing Co., 126, 132
Amatter-Barcelona Chocolate Co., 237
Amazing Mystery Funnies, 54
Amazing Stories, 13, 170, 187
American Centennial Exposition (1876), 229
American Lead Pencil Co., 181, 185

American Merchandising Co., 129
American Toy Fair, 173
   Buck Rogers promotions, 172–174, 176
America's Greatest Comics, 54, 63
Amos 'n' Andy toys, 78–79
   "Check and Double Check," 79
   Fresh Air Taxicab, 70, 78–79, 82
   sparklers, 81
   Walking Figures, 69, 79, 82
Anderson, Carl, 78
Andy Gump in the 348 Car, 81, 82, 116
Animated cartoon films, 5
   sketches and cels, 6, 11, 41, 42
   studio art, 11–12
   technical process, 11
Annie Oakley, "Six-Shooter" wristwatch, 129, 133
Ansonia Clock Co., 119, 121, 133
Ardala (Buck Rogers), 170
Argosy magazine, 11, 13
Army, Navy and Air Corps cards, 237
Art. *See* Comic art
Art Deco designs, 73, 79, 171
Art Nouveau designs, 52, 171
Associated Editors Syndicate, 7
Auction houses, manipulative practices, 75–76

Badges
   Buck Rogers, 178, 186, 203
   Orphan Annie, 262

Balls and balloons, 186
Banks
   Bugs Bunny cast-iron banks, 114
   Buster Brown, 4
Barks, Carl, 13
Barnacle Bill
   toys, 74, 101
   walking figure, 83, 101
"Barney Baxter," 37
Barney Google and Sparkplug toys, 82, 117
Baseball cards, 228, 229
Batman, 3, 54
   character merchandise, 50
   collecting, 46
   comic books, 46
   enemies, 50
   original art, 45
   origin in *Detective*, No. 27, 49–50, 59
   other characters, 50
   television series, 50
   timepieces, 129, 133, 134, 166
Bayard Co., France, 125–126, 132
   comic-character timepieces, 147
Beatles
   timepieces, 131, 134, 166
   Yellow Submarine, 12, 131
Beck, Charles Clarence, 10, 50–51, 129
Believe It or Not Ripley, insert cards, 237
Bennett, Charles, 173–174
Bergen, Edgar, 80

Berndt, Walter, 70, 78
Better Publications, 56
Betty Boop, 14, 74
    animation instruction chart, 41
    button, 280
    character merchandise, 127
    dolls, 83
    films, 6
    "Nodder" wind-up doll, 83, 113
    original art, 6, 11, 41
    pocket watches, 127, 133, 165
    radios, 83
    "The Story of Betty Boop," 11
    studio art, 14
Big All-American, 54
*Big Bad Wolf and Three Little Pigs,
    The* (1934), 125
    watches, 125, 132, 142
Big Little Books, 53
    Buck Rogers, 179-180, 185, 206
    insert cards, 236
Big Shot, 54
Big Thrill Chewing Gum, 182, 232
Bilbo and Lang, 55
Billy Boop studio art, 14
Bimbo studio art, 14
Bixby's Best Shoe Polish animated
    clock, 118-119, 131, 135
Black and White, 16, 20, 54
Black Barney, 170
Black Book Detective, 13
Black Mask, 11, 13
Blacksmith Clock, 119, 131
"Blondie" (Chic Young), 80
Blue Beetle, 54
Blue Bolt, 54
Blue Coal Company
    Shadow Blue Coal Ring, 265, 266,
        277
Blue Ribbon Books, Inc., 53, 185
    Buck Rogers pop-up books, 180
Bond drives, toys to stimulate, 80
Borgfeldt, George and Company, 77,
    81, 89
    Felix the Cat toys, 111
    Mickey Mouse toys, 100
Boring, Wayne, 49
Boxing cards, 228
Boy Commandos, 54
Boy Scout cards, 237
Boy Scout watches, 122
Bradbury, Ray, 171
Bradley Time Co., 124-125, 127, 130,
    131, 133, 134
Branner, Martin, 34
Brawn, John, 4-5
Breyers Ice Cream radio premiums,
    186
Brick Bradford wristwatch, 133

Bringing Up Father (McManus), 5, 13,
    77
    original art, 28
    toys, 77
Brinkman, Milton G., 173
Britain Figures, Buck Rogers set, 179,
    186, 203
"Broncho Bill" strip cards, 236
Brookwood Publications, 56
Brown Shoe Company, 120-121, 133
    Buster Brown Shoes, 120-121
Bubble gum cards, 2, 228-236
    gum booklets, 232, 236
    See also Card inserts
Buck Jones
    Big Little Book cards, 236
    gum booklets, 232, 236
Buck Rogers comic books, 54, 183,
    186, 217
Buck Rogers Big Big Book, 187
Buck Rogers Cut-Out Adventure Book,
    182, 187, 215
"Buck Rogers in the 25th Century," 3,
    13, 21, 38, 70, 168-227
    art work by Dick Calkins, 6, 10, 13,
        38, 39, 70, 170, 172, 176, 178,
        180, 182, 183, 187, 196, 199,
        207, 222
    atomic pistols, 172, 175-176, 185,
        191, 192
    badges, 178, 186, 203
    balloons, rubber balls, paddle ball,
        186
    Big Little Books, 179-180, 185, 206
    Big Thrill Chewing Gum Booklets,
        182, 187, 211
    books, 179-180, 185, 206
    Bucktoys, 182, 187
    buttons, 187, 280
    cardboard Helmet and Noisemaker
        Rocket Pistol, 187, 193
    cast figures of Buck Rogers and
        Wilma Deering, 82
    casting sets, 178, 185, 200, 201
    character merchandise, 86
    chemistry sets, 180, 185
    collectibles, 171, 184
        list of, 185-187
    comic books, 54, 183, 186, 217
    comic strips (1929-67), 38, 170-171,
        172, 177-178, 183
        artists, 183
        original art destroyed, 183-184,
            187
        Sunday pages, 38, 183-184, 187,
            220, 221, 222
    commercial preparatory art, 10, 39
    construction kits for space ships,
        186, 196, 197

"crossovers," 183
cut-out books, 182-183, 187, 215
disintegrator pistols, 170, 172, 175,
    185, 190
educational games, 181
fireworks, 10, 181, 186, 210
games, 181, 182, 186, 187, 204, 213
"Gulliver Buck Rogers," 10, 39
gum booklets, 232, 236
halloween masks, 181, 187
hearing aid "Accousticon," 181, 186
helmets, 70, 172, 177, 185, 188
ice cream cup lids, 179, 186, 209
Interplanetary Games, 186, 204
introduction to, 168-170
knife, 185
liquid helium water pistols, 172,
    175, 185, 190
list of licensees and products, 171,
    173, 211, 222, 223
Lite-Blaster Flashlight, 186
Map of the Solar System, 178, 186
motion pictures, 184
    Buster Crabbe in role, 184
    lobby cards, posters, 184, 187
    Planet Outlaws, 225
movie projector and films, 186
original art, 6, 10, 38, 39, 183-184,
    187
paint books, 180, 186, 207
pencil boxes, 181, 185
pistols, 170, 172, 175, 185, 190
police patrol toy, 185, 195
pop-up books, 53, 180, 185
popularity of, 177, 184, 223
premiums, 178-179, 181, 202-203,
    215
    Cocomalt, 178-179, 182, 186
    Cream of Wheat, 177, 179, 186
    Tarzan Ice Cream, 181
printing set, 180, 185, 208
promotions, 171, 173-176
    American Toy Fair, 173, 176
    department stores, 181-182, 210,
        226
radio programs, 171, 177, 178
    cast of characters, 184
    premiums, 178-179, 202-203, 215
    recordings, 184, 187
    sponsors, 178
rings, 178-179, 186, 203
    Ring of Saturn, 179, 186
    Secret Repeller Ray Ring, 178,
        186, 203, 265, 266
rocket football, 181, 186
rocket pistols, 170, 171-177, 185,
    187, 193
    design of, 172-173

rocket ships, 70, 82, 170, 175, 177, 181, 185, 195
roller skates, 177, 181, 185, 200
rubber-band gun, 183, 187, 216
school supplies, 181, 186
science fiction, 170-171
Scientific Laboratory, 180, 185, 208
set of Britains figures, 179, 186, 203
shoulder patches, 179, 186
sneakers, 180, 185
Solar Scout School Kit, 181, 186
Space Ranger's Halolight Kit, 179, 186, 205
space suits, 175, 177, 185, 198, 199
stationery, 181, 186
Strat-O-Sphere Balloon, 179, 185, 205
strip cards, 182, 187, 212, 234, 236, 250
telescope, 186
timepieces, 127-128, 132, 134, 142, 149, 165, 180, 185, 207-208
    Tootsietoy rocket ships, 82, 183, 185, 218, 219
    Woofian Dictionary, 182-183, 187
Buck Rogers Co., 186
Buck Rogers Story, The, 181, 186
Bugs Bunny, 114
    timepieces, 132, 153
"Bulger Boys, The," 33
Bulletman, 54
Burdick, Jefferson R., 228-229
Burgos, Carl, 52
Burroughs, Edgar Rice, 232
Bush, John A., 120
"Buster Brown" (Outcault), 3, 13
    advertising art, 4
    banks, 4
    buttons, 4
    cameras, 82, 88
    comic books, 48, 57
    comic strip, 4, 13
    dolls, 4
    games, 4
    licensed manufacturers, 4, 120
    merchandise, 4
    original art, 4
    promotions, 120-121
        by midgets, 4
    private museum of memorabilia, 4
    proof pages, 4
    timepieces, 4, 120-121, 133
    toys, 4, 68, 82
Buster Brown Shoe Company, 4
Buster Brown Textile Company, 4
Buttons, 4, 280
    decoders, 261
Buzz Corey's Space Patrol wristwatch, 128

Calkins, Dick, 6, 10, 13, 38, 39, 70, 170, 172, 176, 178, 180, 182, 183, 187, 196, 199, 207, 222
Candy cards, 229, 234, 236
Caniff, Milton, 13
Capp, Al, 79
Captain America, 3, 46, 47, 48, 51, 53, 54
Captain Billy's Whiz Bang, 50
"Captain Easy," 13
Captain Future, 13
Captain Marvel Adventures, 50-51, 54
    Big Red Cheese, 50
    buttons, 280
    decoders, 267
    Lightning Racing Cars, 81, 83, 112
    origin in *Whiz*, 48, 50-51, 59
    timepieces, 129, 133, 152
Captain Marvel, Special Edition, 54, 60
Captain Marvel, Jr., 54
Captain Midnight, 2
    decoders and manuals, 2, 260, 263-266, 273-276
    Ovaltine mugs, 276
    rings, 265, 266, 276, 277
    shoulder patches, 264, 274
Captain Satan, 11, 13
Captain Video, decoders, 277
Card collecting, 228
    art work, 229
    Burdick Collection of Paper Americana, 228-229
    comic-insert cards, 228-259
    price and value, 229
Card inserts, 228-259
    art work, 228, 229, 231
    bubble gum, 228
    Buck Rogers, 182, 187, 212
    collectibles, 228, 235-236
        list of, 236-237
    historical development, 229
    numbered sets, 228, 229
    value and price, 229
Carreras Ltd., 236
Carson, Johnny, 124
Cartoon films. *See* Animated cartoon films
Casting sets, 178
Celluloid paintings, animated films, 11-12
Celluloid toys, 74, 78
Centaur Publications, 54, 56
Century of Progress Exposition, Chicago, 122, 138
Charlie Chaplin
    cards, 235, 237, 252, 253
    comic strip, 9
    timepieces, 134

toys, 76-77, 82, 102
Charlie McCarthy
    buttons, 280
    timepieces, 132, 152
    toys, 80, 83, 110
Cheerios premiums, 266
Chein Company, 73-74, 82-83
Chicago Century of Progress Exposition, 122, 138
Chicago *Tribune*, 8, 236
    comic-strip cards, 255-256
Chicago World's Fair, 119, 182, 187
Cigarette cards, 3, 229
Cinderella, timepieces, 126, 132, 147
Circus cards, 233-234, 237, 252
Circus posters, 4
Clarabelle Cow (studio art), 14
Clark Kent, 49, 128
    See also Superman
Clocks. *See* Timepieces
Cocomalt premiums, 178-179, 182, 187
Collectors and collections, 46-47
    list of collectibles
        Buck Rogers memorabilia, 185-187
        comic books, 54-56
        comic insert cards, 236-237
        decoders and manuals, 266-267
        original art and Sunday pages, 2, 13-14
        studio art, 14
        timepieces, 131-134
        toys, 81-84
    practices of auction houses, 75-76
Columbia Broadcasting Co., 184, 187
Columbia Comics, 54
Columbia Time Co., 132
Comic art, 1-13
    appeal of, 1
    Art Nouveau approach, 5
    artists and illustrators, 1-6, 12-13
    black-and-white inked drawings, 5-6
    collecting, 2, 5-6, 10
    comic books, 10, 13, 48, 50
    commercial preparatory art, 10-11
    cover art, 10, 13
    draftsmanship, 4
    early beginnings, 3-4
    format, 4
    instant recognition of heroes, 50
    price and value, 2
    proof pages, 5
    requested by fans, 10
    studio art, 11-12, 14
    surrealism and realism, 6
    See also Original art

Comic Book Price Guide, The, 4th ed. (Overstreet), 53–54
Comic books, 2, 5, 10, 11, 46–67
 art work, 10, 47, 48, 50, 53
 collecting, 46–47, 53
  complete runs, 48
  condition, 46, 48
  inspecting and evaluating, 47–48, 53–54
  list of collectibles, 13, 46–47, 53–56
  number-one issue and origin issues, 48
  storage in plastic bags, 48
  supply and demand, 47–48
 conventions, 46–47
 cover art, 6, 10, 13
 cultural force, 47
 cut-out-doll books, 67
 distribution of, 48–49
 early history, 48, 51, 57
 horror and science-fiction, 52–53
 price and value, 46–48, 53–54
 "pop-up books," 53
 reprints of newspaper comics, 10, 48–49
 super-hero books, 47, 48, 49
 violence in, 47, 52
 World War II popularity, 48, 51
 See also under name of comic character
Comic-character toys. *See* Toys, comic character
Comic-insert cards, 228–259
 See also Card inserts
Comic strips, 3–10
 art work, 4–5
 artists and illustrators, 4, 6, 183
 balloons to enclose dialogue, 4
 Buck Rogers, 170–171, 172, 177–178, 183
 list of collectibles, 13–14
 merchandise based on, 5
 national syndication, 6
 original art. *See* Original art
 originators, 3–4, 6
 preparation of, 5
 reprinted in comic books, 10, 48–49
 Sunday pages. *See* Sunday pages
 "splash panels," 33
 violence and gangsters, 8
Comics on Parade, 54
Commercial preparatory art, 6, 10
 "Buck Rogers," 39
 "The Shadow," oil painting, 40
Connolly, Joseph V., 80
Correll, Charles, 78
Cover art, 10–11
 collecting, 53
  list of collectibles, 13–14

comic books, 10, 13
 preparatory oil paintings, 40
 pulp magazines, 10–11, 13
Cowboys, timepieces, 128, 131
Crabbe, Larry "Buster," 184
Crack Comics, 54
Crackajack Funnies, 54
Crandall, Reed, 10, 13
Crane, Roy, 13
Cream of Wheat premiums, 177–179, 186, 266
Crime Suspenstories, 54
Crosby, Percy, 13
"Crossover" items, 118, 121
Crowley, Matthew, 179, 184
Crypt of Terror, 54
Cummings, E.E., 9
Cupples and Leon Company, 48
Currier and Ives prints, 229
Cut-out-doll books, 67, 182–183

Dagwood the Driver automotive toy, 80, 83, 109
Daisy Duck, 14
 timepieces, 126, 132, 146
Daisy Mae, 79
Daisy Manufacturing Co., 70, 83
 Buck Rogers rocket pistol, 171–177, 185
Dale Evans, timepieces, 130, 133, 160
Dan Dare, timepieces, 128, 133, 150
Dan Dunn, Big Little Book cards, 236, 248
Dare Devils cards, 237
Daredevil Comics, 54, 60
Daring Mystery Comics, 54
Davis, R. B. Company, 178
Davy Crockett, timepieces, 130, 132, 161, 162
De Beck, Billy, 33
Decoders and manuals, 2, 260–280
 button-type, 261, 268
 Captain Midnight, 260, 263–264, 266, 273, 274, 275, 276
 designs and art work, 260
 Junior Justice Society of America, 278
 Orphan Annie, 260, 261–263, 266, 269, 270, 271
 popularity of, 260
 radio rings, 265
 Tom Mix, 260–261, 266, 268
Defending America cards, 237
Dell Publishing Co., 54–56
 comic books, 48–49
Dennis the Menace, timepieces, 131, 134
Dent Hardware Co., 77
Detective Comics, 48, 49, 53–54
 origin of Batman, 48–50, 59

Detroit *Mirror*, 8
"Dick Tracy," 8–9, 13
 Big Little Book cards, 236
 buttons, 280
 caramels cards, 230–231, 236, 242
 characters, 9
 Color Comics, 54
 commercial preparatory art, 10
 detective comic strip, 8–9, 13, 25
 gum booklets, 232, 236
 Junior Detective Kit, 267, 279
 original art, 6, 10, 25
 Police Station toy, 83, 115
 pop-up book, 53, 66, 67
 popularity of, 8–9
 portrait ring, 265, 267, 277
 Sunday pages, 25
 timepieces, 133, 142, 155
Dictagraph Products Co., 181, 186
Dille, John F., 70, 86, 170–171, 172–175, 176
Dille, John F., Company, 171, 177, 182, 189, 234
Dillinger, John, 231
Dime Mysteries, 13
"Dingbat Family, The," 9
Dirks, Rudolph, 4
Disney, Walt, 5, 73, 230
 manufacturers licensed by, 72
Disney Archives, 121
Disney Productions. *See* Walt Disney Productions
Disneyana, 71–73
 collectors and collecting, 71, 74
 comic-character toys, 71–73
 Donald Duck. *See* Donald Duck
 identifying various periods, 72–73
 Mickey Mouse. *See* Mickey Mouse
 studio art, 12, 14
 ten most wanted collectibles, 73
Disneyland, 125
"Doc Archie and Bean," 9
Doc Savage, 54
Dolls, 5
 Betty Boop, 81, 113
 celluloid, 74, 78
 cut-out-dolls, 67
 Felix the Cat, 81
 Krazy Kat, 100
 Lone Ranger and Tonto, 114
 Mickey Mouse, 81, 94, 95, 96, celluloid, 72, 84, 92
 Popeye, 117
 rubber-band-powered "noddler," 72
 Shirley Temple, 81
 Steiff, 94–95
 The Yellow Kid, 3
Dolly Toy Co., 84
Donald Duck
 buttons, 280

comic books, 54
studio art, 14
timepieces, 126, 132, 145, 146, 165
toys, 84, 91, 99, 116
  Donald Duck and Pluto Lionel handcar, 73, 84, 116
  Donald in the Boat, 99
  in metal, celluloid and cast iron, 73, 91
  Schuco, 73, 91
Don't Let It Happen Here cards, 235, 237
Dora Duck, 14
Double Detective, 13
Dowst Manufacturing Co., 82, 183, 185
"Drago," 7
"Dreams of a Rarebit Fiend," 4–5
Druggist Clock, 119, 131
"Dull Care," 4
Dumbo, 5
Dürer, Albrecht, 229
Dusty Ayres and His Battle Birds, 13

Eagle Comics Co., 128, 130–131
Eastern Color Printing Co., 48, 55
Eastern Publishing Co., 183, 186
E.C. Comics, 13
E.C. Publishers, 52–56
Edison Company, 4–5
Einson-Freeman Co., 181, 187
Eisner, Will, 10, 13
Elgin National Industries, 124–125
  Bradley Division, 124–125
Eppy, Samuel, Company, 236
Evans, Dale, 130, 133, 160
Everbrite Watch Co., 129, 130
Everett, Bill, 52

"Famous Churches of the World," 7
Famous Funnies, 48, 54
Fantasia, 5
Fantastic Adventures, 13
Fawcett Publications, 54–56, 81, 83, 129, 133, 267
  Whiz Comics, 50–51
Feature Book, 54
Feature Comics, 54
Federal Bureau of Investigation, 264
Federal Men, in *Adventure Comics*, 49
Felix the Cat (Sullivan), 14, 31, 74, 81
  studio art, 14
  timepieces, 127, 133
  toys, 73, 83, 111
    advertisement for toys and novelties, 111
    dolls, 81, 111
    on the Scooter, 81, 83, 111
    sparklers, 81, 83, 111
    walking figures, 117

Ferdinand the Bull and Mickey Mouse, 96
Fiction House Magazines, 54–56
Fight Comics, 54
Figures and figurines
  Buck Rogers, 82
  Mickey Mouse, 72
  Popeye, 83, 102
  Seven Dwarfs, 99
Film Funnies cards, 237
Films. *See* Animated cartoon films
Fine, Lou, 10, 13
Finger, Bill, 49
Fireworks, 79
  Buck Rogers, 10, 181, 186, 210
Fisher, Ham, 79–80
Flash, The, 48, 55
"Flash Gordon," 7, 13, 21–22
  Big Little Book cards, 232, 236, 247
  buttons, 280
  collecting, 184
  comic books, 55, 62
  original art, 7, 13, 21, 22
  pop-up books, 53
  space pistols, 93, 115
  syndication, 7
  timepieces, 128, 132
Flea markets as source of collectibles, 75
Fleischer, Max, 11–12
Fleischer Studios, 14, 41, 127
  animation instruction charts, 41–42
Football cards, 228
Foreign Legion cards, 237
Fortune magazine, 69
Foster, Hal, 1, 6–8, 13
  original art, 8
  "Prince Valiant," 8, 24
  "Tarzan," 7–8
Fox, Fontaine, 20, 82
  "Toonerville Trolley" comic strip, 77
Fox Features Syndicate, 54–56
Frank Buck Bring 'Em Back Alive
  gum cards, 228, 233, 236
  portrait ring, 265
Frazetta, Frank, 13
Frontline Combat, 55
Funnies on Parade, 55
  first true comic book, 48

G-8 and His Battle Aces, 10, 11, 13
  cover art, 10
G-Man Big Little Book cards, 236
G-Men and Heroes of the Law cards, 231, 236, 243
Gaines, William, 52–53
"Gasoline Alley," 13
Gene Autry
  portrait ring, 265
  timepieces, 129, 133, 160

General Mills premiums, 266
Generals and Their Flags cards, 237
German character timepieces, 118–119, 164
German toys, 4, 70
  Charlie Chaplin tin and cast-iron wind-up toys, 76–77
  Hi-Way Henry, 76
  Mickey Mouse toys, 72
  "Toonerville Trolley" characters, 77
"Gertie the Dinosaur," 5
Gift Comics, 55, 61
Gilbert Clock Corp., 129, 132, 134
Gimbel, Bernard, 69
Gimbels, Buck Rogers promotion, 171, 174–175
Golden Arrow, origin in *Whiz*, 48
Goodwill Pictures, 184
Goofy studio art, 14
Gordon, Don, 261
Gosden, Freeman, 78
Gottfredson, Fred, 13
Goudey Gum Co., 182, 187, 236–237
Gould, Chester, 8–9, 13, 25
Government Agents vs. Public Enemies cards, 234, 237
Gray, Harold, 13, 77
Great Classic Newspaper Comic Strips, 187
Green Hornet, 55
  ring, 265
Green Lantern, 48, 55
Green Mask, 55
Greeting cards, 228
Gropper Company, 180, 185
"Gulliver Buck Rogers," 10, 39
Gum cards, 229–235, 236
Gum Inc., 236, 237
Gumakers of America, Inc., 236, 237

Haddon Mfg. Co., 130, 132
Hall, Norman, 184
Halloween masks, Buck Rogers, 181
Ham and Sam, the Minstrel Team, 82, 106
Hamilton Chewing Gum, Ltd., 237
Hamlin, V. T., 13
Hammett, Dashiell, 7
Handcars
  Donald Duck and Pluto, 73, 84, 116
  Mickey and Minnie Mouse, 73, 83, 89
  Moon Mullins and Kayo, 80, 82, 105
  Santa Claus and Mickey Mouse, 73, 83, 116
"Happy Holligan," 4
  toys, 82, 85
Harold Lloyd on the Telephone, 83, 109
"Harold Teen" strip cards, 236

Harvey Publications, 55–56
Haunt of Fear, 55
Hearst, William Randolph, 3
Henry and Henrietta, Travelers
  toys, 78, 82, 104
    Henry in the Elephant's Trunk,
     82, 104
    molded Henry rubber doll, 82,
     104
Henry cards, 236, 257
Heroes of the Sea cards, 237
Heroic Comics, 55
Herriman, George, 6, 9, 13
  "Krazy Kat," 27
Hi-Spot, 55
Hi-Time, 133
Hi-Way Henry, 76, 82
Hillman Periodicals, 55–56
Hirschman, Alice, 175
Hit Comics, 55
Hitler, Adolf, 164, 235
Hitt, Oscar, 76, 77, 82
Hogan's Alley, 15
Hogarth Burne, 1, 6, 7, 13
  Tarzan original art, 7–8
Hoge Manufacturing, 83
Hoky Poky Magician wristwatch, 133
Holbein, Hans, 229
Holiday Comics, 55
Hollywood Picture Stars cards, 237
Hoover, Herbert, 78
Hopalong Cassidy
  portrait ring, 265
  timepieces, 130, 133, 161, 162
Horace Horsecollar studio art, 14
Horror comic books, 52–53
Horrors of War cards, 228, 229, 234–
  235, 237, 251
Hough, Cass, 171, 172
  marketing of Buck Rogers, 172–176
Howard Ainslee Company, 48
Howdy Doody
  band toys, 79
  Clock-A-Doodle, 81, 83, 112
  timepieces, 133, 155
Huckleberry Time Co., 133, 134, 180,
  185
Hudson Co., Detroit, 173–174
Hudson-Ross, 83–84
Huey Duck, timepieces, 126, 132
Human Torch, 48, 55
  origin in *Marvel Mystery Comics*,
   48, 51–52, 58
"Hungry Henrietta," 4
Hunted Animals cards, 233, 237

I Am A Spy Smasher button, 280
Ideal and Fleischer, 83
Ideal Novelty and Toy Company, 117

Ignatz Mouse, 73–74
  dolls, 100
  toys, 73, 83, 94
Indian gum cards, 237
Indians, Cowboys, Western Scenes
  cards, 237
Ingersoll, Charles, 119–121
Ingersoll, Robert, 119–121
Ingersoll, Robert H. & Bros., 120–121,
  131–133
Ingersoll Watch Co. Limited, 121,
  123, 130, 132, 133
Ingersoll-Waterbury Co., 121–124,
  129
  Mickey Mouse timepieces, 122–123
  pocket watches, 119–121
Ingraham, E., Co., 119, 127, 128, 130,
  132–133, 180, 185
International Chewing Gum Co., 237
"It's Nice to be Married," 4
"Ivy Hemmanshaw," 7
Iwerks, Ub, 6, 13
  early Mickey Mouse drawn by, 12,
   72

Jack the Giant Killer pop-up book, 53
Jackpot Comics, 55
James Bond 007 wristwatch, 134
Japanese toys, 70, 75
  battery-operated, 75
  "Made in Occupied Japan," 75
  Mickey Mouse toys, 72
Jeff Arnold, timepieces, 130–131, 133,
  162
Jewelry, 5
  Buster Brown, 4
  Orphan Annie celluloid brooch, 103
  See also Timepiece
Joe Carioca, 74
  wind-up toys, 84, 97
"Joe Palooka," 79–80
  Little Max Speshul #1, 79–80, 83,
   109
  strip cards, 236
  timepieces, 133, 158
Joe Penner and His Duck Goo Goo, 80,
  83, 110
Johnson, Walter H., Candy Co., 236
Joker, The (Batman), 45, 50
Jumbo Comics, 55
Junghans, Germany, 118–119, 131
Jungle Comics, 55
Jungle gum cards, 237
"Jungle Jim," 7, 21, 22
Jungle Stories, 11, 13
Junior Justice Society of America,
  decoder, 278

Kagran Corp., 81, 83

Kamen, Kay, 72, 73, 87
  distributor of Disney merchandise,
   69
Kane, Bob, 49
Kastor, Adolph, and Bros. Co., 185
"Katzenjammer Kids, The," 4
Kayo ("Moon Mullins"), 80
Keaton, Russell, 183, 187
Kellogg's premiums, 178, 186
Kickapoo Juice (Li'l Abner), 79
Kid Comics, 55
Kienzle Watch Co., 164
Killer Kane (Buck Rogers), 127, 170
King, Frank, 13
King Comics, 49, 55
King Features Syndicate, 6, 7, 73, 80,
  126
Kirby, Jack, 6, 10, 51
K.K. Publications, 54
Knickerbocker Toy Company, 83, 100
Knobby Walsh ("Joe Palooka"), 80
Koko the Clown, 14
"Krazy Kat," 9, 13, 27
  toys, 83, 100
Krigstein, Bernie, 13
Kurtzman, Harvey, 13

Lacassin, Francis, 7–8
Lady with Fan clock, 118, 131
Lady with Mandolin clock, 118–119,
  131
Leading Comics, 55
Lee-Tex Products, 186
Lev Gleason Publications, 54
Licensing manufacturers, 68
  Buck Rogers merchandise, 171, 173,
   211, 222, 223
  Buster Brown merchandise, 4
  Disney merchandise, 72
  royalty costs, 70
  Yellow Kid merchandise, 3
Lichtenstein, Roy, 12, 48
Life magazine, 43, 71, 124, 234
"Li'l Abner" (Capp), 79
  buttons, 280
  and His Dogpatch Band, 79, 108
  timepieces, 133, 157
  toys, 79, 83, 108
Li'l Beaver, 130
Lionel handcars, 73, 83–84
  Donald Duck, 73, 84, 116
  Mickey Mouse, 73, 83, 89–90, 116
  Moon Mullins, 80, 82, 105
Lithographic printing, 228
"Little Bears and Tigers," 4
Little Lulu, 55
Little Max Speshul #1, 79–80, 83, 109
"Little Nemo in Slumberland," 5, 6,
  13, 18, 19

animated film, 5, 6
original art, 18, 19
Sunday pages, 5
"Little Orphan Annie" (Gray), 3, 13
Big Little Books, 103
celluloid brooch, 103
comic strip, 13
decoders and manuals, 260, 261-263, 266, 267, 269, 270, 271, 272, 273
original art, 6, 10
Ovaltine mugs, 276
pop-up books, 53, 66
portrait ring, 265
Silver Star ring, 263, 267
strip cards, 236
timepieces, 133, 142, 167
toys, 70, 77, 82, 103
Dime Bank, 103
Skipping Rope, 77, 103
Walking Sandy, 103
wind-up platforms in celluloid, 103
"Little Sammy Sneeze," 4
Lone Ranger, 265
buttons, 280
chewing gum cards, 231, 236, 245
Six Shooter Ring, 265, 266, 267
timepieces, 130, 133, 159
toys, 80-81, 110, 114
Lone Ranger Hi-Yo Silver, 80-81, 110
Looney Tunes, 55
Los Angeles *Herald*, 9
Louie Duck, wristwatch, 126
Louis Marx Co. *See* Marx, Louis, Co.
Luks, George, 3-4
Lux animated clocks, 119, 133, 135

McBride, Clifford, 13, 30
McCay, Winsor Zenic, 4-6, 13
influence on other artists, 5
"Little Nemo in Slumberland," 5, 18, 19
McKay, David, Company, 54-55
comic books, 49
McManus, George, 13
"Bringing up Father," 5, 28, 77
MacMurray, Fred, 50
Macy's, 18, 171, 174-175
Buck Rogers promotions, 174-175
Christmas (1934), 181-182, 210
Mad, 55
Magazine Enterprises, 56
Maggie and Jiggs tin wind-up toy, 77, 82
Magic Comics, 55
"Man from Montclair, The," 4

Man on the Trapeze animated clock, 118, 131, 135
Marston, William, 52
Marvel Family, 55
Marvel Mystery Comics, 55
origin of Human Torch and Sub-Mariner, 48, 51-52, 58
price and value, 46, 51, 53
See also Captain Marvel Adventures
Marx, Louis and Company, 69-70, 73-74, 175, 177, 185
Amos n' Andy Fresh Air Taxicab, 78-79
band toys, 79
Big Fight Popeye the Champ, 74
Buck Rogers items, 70, 177
"crazy cars," 80
Joe Penner and His Duck Goo Goo, 80
Little Orphan Annie Skipping Rope, 77
Lone Ranger Hi-Yo Silver toy, 80-81, 110
Merrymakers Mouse Band, 73, 79, 82, 107
Negro toys, 73-74, 78-79
Smitty Scooter, 78
Superman Racing the Airplane, 81
Master Comics, 55
Match folders, 228
Maull, George, 234-235
Max, Peter, 131
"Max und Moritz," 3, 4
Merchandise, character
commercial preparatory art, 10-11
licensing arrangements. *See* Licensing manufacturer
toys. *See* Toys, comic-character
watches. *See* Timepieces, comic-character
Meredith, Burgess, 50
Metropolitan Museum of Art, Burdick Collection of Paper Americana, 228-229
Michener, James, 71
Mickey Mouse, 3, 13, 14
barometers, 97
bread cards, 230, 236, 240, 241
bubble gum cards, 229-230, 236, 238, 239
buttons, 280
Christmas tree lights, 98
collectors, 71-72, 74
Color Comics, 54, 55
commercial preparatory art, 10
cut-out doll books, 67
figures, 95, 96
films, 6
flashlights, 97

Iwerks first artist, 12, 13, 72, 73
jig saw puzzles, 241
merchandise, 71-72, 87
original art, 10, 12
pencil box, 96
pop-up books, 53, 65
radio, 84, 98
school supplies, 96
sculpture by Oldenburg, 12, 44
sketches and cels, 6
Steamboat Willie, 71
studio art, 6, 12, 14
T-shirts, 125
timepieces, 121-132, 138
authenticity, 122-123, 131
Disney franchises, 125
electric clocks, 122-123, 137
English electric clocks, 123, 132
English wind-up clocks, 123, 132, 140
English wristwatch, 123, 132
forties-style Mickey, 124, 143-144
French alarm clock, 125, 132, 144
French wall clock (1933), 143
Japanese reproduction, 122
lapel watch, 123-124, 131
miniature desk clock with Art Deco base, 123, 131, 141
pocket watch, 120-121, 131, 136
pocket watch with fob, 122, 131, 139, 142
postwar production, 124
prices, 122-124
supply and demand, 121-122
thirties-style Mickey, 124, 125, 144
wagging head alarm clock, 123, 125, 131, 140, 142
wind-up clock, 122-123, 131, 137, 140
wristwatch, 122, 124, 131, 139, 140, 142
toothbrush holders, 95
Toreador and Ferdinand the Bull, 96
toys, 68, 71-73, 81, 83, 84
advertisements for, 100
ball trapp game, 84, 93
celluloid, 92
control of designs, 72
Drummer or Saxophone Player, 73, 84, 88
early tooth metal Mickey from Spain, 97
French cast-iron banks, 73, 97
hurdy-gurdy, 73
"knock-offs," 73
Lionel circus toy train, 73

Lionel handcars, 73, 83, 89-90, 116
made in Germany, 72
Marx Merrymakers Mouse Band, 73, 79, 82, 107
Mickey and Minnie Mouse dancing on the piano, 73, 84, 91
molded-rubber figures, 84, 99
1930's Mickeys most desirable, 73
noise-makers, 96
original boxes, 73
price and value, 73
Rosenthal china porcelain figures, 72
Shuco tin and cast-iron wind-up, 73
sparklers, 81
Steiff dolls, 72, 84, 94, 95
tin wind-ups, 72-73
velvet dolls, 72, 84, 94, 95
wooden-jointed doll, 96
Mickey Mouse Book, 55
Mickey Mouse Bubble Gum Co., 236
Mickey Mouse Club, 280
Mickey Mouse Color Comics, 54, 55
Mickey Mouse in King Arthur's Court, 53
Mickey Mouse Magazine, 55
Migra, France, 84
Military Comics, 55
Miller, Frank, 37
Minnie Mouse, 14
   cut-out doll books, 67
   pop-up books, 53, 65
   Pushing a Baby Carriage, 99
   studio art, 14
   wristwatch, 124
"Miracle Jones," 7
Miss Fury Comics, 55
Mr. Peanuts, 83, 114
   wind-up walking figure, 114, 115
MLJ Magazines, 55-56
Montgomery Ward, comic-character merchandise, 127, 130
"Moon Mullins," 35, 36, 80
   and Kayo on a Handcar, 80, 82, 105
   strip cards, 236
Moore, Constance, 184
Moran, Jackie, 184
More Fun Comics, 49, 55
Morrow, Gray, 128
Mortimer Snerd car, 117
Morton's Dime Museum, 4
Morty and Ferdy, 14
Mosley, Zack, 234
Moulton, Charles, 52
"Mouse junkies," 123, 230
Movie Comics, 55

Museum of Modern Art, 5
Museums, interest in comic art, 48
Mystery Men Comics, 55
Mystic Comics, 55

"Napoleon," 13, 30
National Broadcasting Company, 78
National Cartoonists' Society, 8
National Chicle Co., 236, 237
National Comics, 55
National Fireworks Co., 10, 181, 186
National Newspaper Syndicate, 170, 172
National Periodical Publications, 49, 54-55
Negro Banjo Player animated clock, 131
Negro Mammy with Rolling Eyes animated clock, 118-119, 131, 135, 135
Negro toys, 73, 78-79
New Book of Comics, 55
New England Watch Co., 121
New Fun Comics, 49
New Haven Watch and Clock Co., 126-127, 129-130, 132-133
New York *Daily News*, 8-9, 77
New York *Evening Journal*, 9
New York *Evening Telegram*, 4
New York *Herald*, 4, 5, 18, 19
New York *Journal*, 3, 56
New York Public Library, on preservation of paper, 53
New York *World*, 3-4, 9, 15, 16
New York World's Fair Comics, 55, 60, 61
Newspaper comic strips, 3-10, 48
   See also Comic strips
Nickel Comics, 55
Nifty Company (Germany), 77, 81, 82-84
Nita Publications, 56
Nogouchi, Isamu, 184
Novelty Publications, 54
Nowlan, Philip Francis, 170, 172, 183
   Buck Rogers written by, 170

Oldenburg, Claes, 12, 48
   Mickey Mouse, steel sculpture, 12, 44
Olive Oyl, 10, 14, 74, 126
Onward School Supplies, 183, 187
Operator #5, 10, 13
Opper, F. B., 4, 5
Original art, 3-45
   Betty Boop, 14
   black-and-white art, 5-6
   Buck Rogers, 6, 183-184
   collecting, 5-6

comic books, 10, 13
comic strips, 3-10
determining authenticity, 12
list of collectibles, 13-14
oil paintings, 6, 13
Popeye, 14
price and value, 6, 12
pulp magazines, 10-11, 14
reproductions, 12
studio art, 11-12, 14
supply and demand, 5-7
Orphan Annie. *See* Little Orphan Annie
Our Flag, 55
Our Gang Comics, 55
Outcault, Richard Fenton, 3-6, 13, 15-17, 120
   "Buster Brown" created by, 4
   licenses to manufacture toys, 68, 120
   original art destroyed, 6
   "The Yellow Kid" created by, 3-4, 15-16, 48
Ovaltine premiums, 266-267, 276
   Captain Midnight Secret Squadron radio program, 263-264
   Radio Orphan Annie, 261-263
Overstreet, Robert M., 53-54

Packaging design art, 10-11
Pan-American Exposition pocket watch, 120
Paper doll collections, 228
Paper goods, 74
Paper, deterioration of, 53
Parker, Bill, 50
Parker, Fess, 130
Penner, Joe, 80, 83, 110
Pep Comics, 55, 62
Peter, Harry, 52
Peter Pan Peanut Butter
   "Adventures of Sky King" TV program, 265
   premiums, 266-267
Phantom Detective, The, 11, 13
Phantoms Club, button, 280
"Pilgrim's Progress, A," 4
Pinocchio, 84-97
   pop-up books, 53
   timepieces, 126, 132
   wind-up toys, 84, 97
Pirate's Picture Bubble Gum Co., 237
Pirate's pictures cards, 237
Pittsburgh *Post Gazette*, 187
Planet Comics, 55
Planet Outlaws (Buck Rogers film), 225
Planet Stories, 11, 13
Planters Nut and Chocolate Co., 83, 233, 237

Mr. Peanuts, 83, 114, 115
Plastic Man, 55
Playing cards, 228
Playthings Magazine, 121, 138
Pleasure Books, Inc., 53
Pluto studio art, 14
    timepieces, 126, 132
Pocket Comics, 55
Political advertising, 30, 74
"Polly and Her Pals" (Sterrett), 13, 32
"Poor Jake," 4
Pop artists, 12, 48
Popeye, 9–10
    animation instruction chart, 42
    collectors and collecting, 74
    commercial preparatory art, 10, 42
    created by E. C. Segar, 13, 26, 74
    dolls, 83, 117
    original art, 10, 26, 42, 45
    pop-up books, 53, 66
    studio art, 14
    timepieces, 70, 126-127, 132, 147,
      148, 165
    toys, 70, 73–74, 83
      appeal of, 74
      Big Fight Popeye the Champ, 74
      chalk figure of Popeye, 83, 102
      Popeye and Olive Oyl Jiggers, 74,
        83, 101
      Popeye and Olive Oyl on the
        Roof (1936), 74
      Popeye Cowboy, 94
      Popeye Express, 117
      Popeye in the Airplane, 74, 83,
        102
      Popeye in the Barrel, 74, 83, 101
      Popeye on the Delivery Motor-
        cycle, 101
      Popeye the Sailor or Popeye in the
        Rowboat, 74, 83, 101
      Popeye with the Parrot Cages, 74
      Popeye with Punching Bag, 83,
        91, 94
      walking figure, 74
      wood-jointed doll, 117
Popeye by Andy Warhol, 12, 45
Popsicle premiums, 178, 186
Popular Comics, 48-49, 55
Pop-up books, 53, 65-66
    Buck Rogers, 53, 180, 185
    Little Orphan Annie, 53, 66
    Popeye, 53, 66
Porky Pig timepieces, 127, 133, 156
Porter Chemical Co., 180, 185
Post Toasties premiums, 178, 186, 266
Postcards, 228
    comic-characters, 259
    mechanical, 259
Powerful Katrinka toys, 77, 82

Precision Watch Co., 128, 132
Premiums and give-aways
    Buck Rogers, 177-179, 182, 187
    Funnies on Parade, 48
Prentice, John, 7
Pressner, M., and Co., 237
Prince Namor (Sub-Mariner), 52
"Prince Valiant," 8, 13, 24
Prince Valiant Feature Book, 55
Princess Fen of Atlantis, 52
Prize Comics, 55
Prizefighting and wrestling, 74
"Professor Otto and His Auto," 9
Proof pages, 5
Public Enemy, 11
Pulitzer, Joseph, 3
Pulp magazines
    collecting, 11
    cover art, 6, 10-11, 13, 40
    deterioration of paper, 53
    preparatory oil paintings, 13, 40
Puss-N-Boots, 53
    pop-up books, 53
    timepieces, 133, 163

Quality Comics, 54-56
Quaker Oats premiums, 266
Quaker Puffed Wheat and Rice
    premiums, 267

Radios
    Mickey Mouse, 98
    Three Little Pigs and Big Bad Wolf,
      98
Radio programs
    Buck Rogers, 171, 177, 178-179,
      182, 187
    Green Hornet, 265
    Orphan Annie, 261-262
    premiums. *See* Premiums and give-
      aways
    toys based on characters, 78-79
Radio Guide, 11
Ralston premiums, 266-267
    Tom Mix decoder and manuals,
      260-261, 266
Ramos, Mel, 12, 48
    Batmobile and the Joker, oils on
      canvas, 45
Rangers Comics, 55
Rapaport Brothers, Chicago, 178, 185
Rauch, Chauncey, 173
Raymond, Alex, 1, 6-7, 13, 21, 22,
    128, 232
    original art, 6-7
Red Raven, 55
Red Ryder Comics, 55
Red Ryder watch, 130
Reg'lar Fellers, Aggie doll, 114

Reproductions, comic-character toys,
    69
Richardson Co., 182, 187
Richie Prem (clock mfg.), 132
Rings, 265-266, 277
    Buck Rogers, 178-179
    Green Hornet Ring, 265, 277
    portrait, 265-266, 277
    radio, 265
"Rip Kirby," 7
Robin, The Boy Wonder, 50
Robin Hood, 12
    timepieces, 133, 167
Rocket Comics, 55
Rocky Jones Space Ranger, timepieces,
    128, 133, 150
Rogers, Will, 129
Ronson, Adele, 184
Roy Rogers, timepieces, 130, 133, 160,
    162
Rosenthal china porcelain Mickey
    Mouse, 72
Royal Society of Arts, 8
Rozen, G., 10, 40

Sackman Brothers, 175, 177, 185
Sadie Hawkins Day, 79
St. Louis *Post-Dispatch*, 20
St. Louis World's Fair, 4, 120
Sal Metal Products, 80, 83
Schapiro, 134
Schmoo, the (Li'l Abner), 79
Schmoo pendulum clock, 133, 157
School of Visual Arts, New York City, 7
Schuco Company, 84
    tin and cast-iron wind-up toys, 73
Science, 56
Science-fiction comic books, 52-53
    Buck Rogers, 170-171
Sculptural art, comic-character toys,
    68
Sea Raider gum cards, 237
Sears, Roebuck
    Buck Rogers items, 177
    comic-character timepieces, 122,
      125, 128, 142
Second World War cards, The, 237
"Secret Agent X-9," 7, 13
Segar, E.C., 9-10, 13, 70, 126-127
    Popeye created by, 74
    "Thimble Theatre," 26
Seiberling Latex Products, 84
Seiko in Japan, 125
Select, 61
Sendak, Maurice, 5
Sensation Comics, 52, 56
Seth Thomas, 119, 131
Seven Dwarfs, rubber-molded figures,
    99

Shadow, The, magazine, 13, 40, 265
  cover art, 10, 40
Shadow Blue Coal Ring, 265, 266, 277
Shadow Comics, 11, 56
Shaw, C. Montague, 184
Sheena, Queen of the Jungle, 56
Sheffield Watch Corp., 127, 132-133, 134
Shield-Wizard Comics, 56
Shirley Temple
  dolls, 81
  wristwatch, 167
Shock Suspenstories, 56
Shoulder patches, Captain Midnight, 264, 274
Shuster, Joe, 49
Siegel, Jerry, 49
Silver Streak Comics, 56
Simon and Kirby, 13, 51
Single Series, 56
"Skippy" (Crosby), 13
Skippy "Wheaties" cards, 236, 258
Sky King, decoders and manuals, 265, 266, 277
Skybirds cards, 237
Slam Bang, 56
Slam Bradley, 49
Slesinger, Stephen, Inc., 180, 233, 236
Smash Comics, 56
Smilin' Jack cards, 234, 236
Smitty Scooter, 78, 82, 105
Smitty wristwatches, 70, 133
Smokey Stover, timepieces, 133, 167
Snow White and the Seven Dwarfs, 5, 11-12
  animation techniques, 43
  molded-rubber figures, 84, 99
  original art, 11-12, 43
  studio art, 11-22, 13, 14
  timepieces, 126, 132
South African War, Souvenir Watch, 119
Soviet Union, character timepieces, 164
Space heroes
  Buck Rogers, 127-128, 170
  timepieces, 127-129
  toys, 176
Sparkler Comics, 56
Spectre, The, 48
Speed Comics, 56
Spider, 10, 11, 13
  cover art, 11
Spiderman, 56
Spillane, Mickey, 52
Spirit, The, 56
Sports card, 229
Spy and Slam Bradley, 49
Spy Smasher, 48, 56
  buttons, 280

Stalin, Joseph, commemorative clock, 164
Star Spangled Comics, 56
Stars and Stripes Comics, 56
Startling Comics, 56
Steamboat Willie (1928), 71, 72
Stehli, Edgar, 184
Stereoscope cards, 228
Sterrett, Cliff, 13
  "Polly and Her Pals," 32
Stieff, M., and Co., 84
  Mickey Mouse dolls, 72, 94, 95
Strange True Stories cards, 237
Strauss, Ferdinand, Corp., 79
Street and Smith Publications, 54, 56
Studio art
  animated cartoon films, 11-12
  authenticity, 12
  hand-colored cels, 12
  list of collectibles, 13, 14
  pencil sketches, 12
  reproductions, 12
Stuntman Comics, 56
Sub-Mariner, 48, 56
  origin in *Marvel Mystery Comics*, 48, 51-52
Sullivan, Pat, 14, 31, 74, 81
  "Felix the Cat," 31
Sunday pages, 6, 13
  difficulty in finding originals, 6
  list of collectibles, 13
  "Little Nemo in Slumberland," 5
  preparation of, 5
  "Tarzan" by Burne Hogarth, 8
  "Tarzan" by Hal Foster, 8
  Yellow Kid, 3-4
  See also Original art
Super-Mystery Comics, 56
Superboy, 49, 56
Supercat, 49
Super Comics, 56
Superdog, 49
Supergirl, 49
Super-hero books, 47, 48-49, 56
  comic books, 49
  instant recognition, 50
  in World War II, 51
Superior Type Co., 180, 185
Superman, 3, 49, 56, 59
  buttons, 280
  collecting, 46
  comic books, 2, 46, 49, 53, 59
  element of absurdity, 6
  gum cards, 231, 236, 244
  origin in *Action Comics*, 48, 49, 59
  popularity of, 49
  timepieces, 129, 133, 150, 151
  toys, 81, 83
  value of, 53
Superman's X-Mas Adventure, 56

Sweets Company of America, 233-234, 237, 267
Swinnerton, James, 4, 5
Sylvania TV premiums, 179, 186

Tailspin Tommy: gum booklets, 232, 236
  strip cards, 232
Tales of Terror Annual, 56
Tareyton Cigarettes, 236
Target Comics, 56
"Tarzan," 3, 6, 7-8, 21
  buttons, 280
  candy cards, 232-233
  collecting, 184
  drawn by Burne Hogarth (1937-1950), 7-8, 13, 23
  drawn by Hal Foster (1929-1937), 8, 13
  original art, 23
  pop-up book, 53
  strip cards, 233, 236, 249
  Sunday page, 23
  tiger scenes, 23
Tarzan and the Crystal Vault of Isis
  cards, 232-233, 236, 249
Tarzan Ice Cream premiums, 181, 186
Television programs
  Batman, 50
  effect on comic-strip art, 6
Temple, Shirley
  dolls, 81
  wristwatch, 167
"Terry and the Pirates" (Caniff), 13, 56
  pop-up book, 53, 66, 67
  strip cards, 236
"Thimble Theatre," by Segar, 9, 74, 127, 148
  with Popeye, 26
Three Little Pigs and Big Bad Wolf
  acrobats, 99
  radios, 84, 98
  timepieces, 125, 132, 142
Thrilling Comics, 56
Thrilling True Spy Stories cards, 234, 237
Thunda, 56
Tie pins, 3
Tiger Man (Buck Rogers), 128
"Tillie the Toiler," 7, 29
Timely Comics, 54-56
Timely/Marvel, 54
Timely Publications, 54
Timepieces, 118-167
  alarm clocks, 121
  animated-dial clocks, 118-119, 131
  authenticity, 122-123
  Boy Scout watches, 122
  Buck Rogers, 180, 185, 208

commemorative pocket watches, 120
cowboy heroes, 128, 131, 161-162
"crossover" items, 118, 121
Disney licenses for, 122
Ingersoll pocket watches, 119-120
list of collectibles, 131-134
manufacturers, 131-134
Mickey Mouse, 122-124, 131, 137, 139, 140, 141, 142
movements, 118, 119, 131
  alarm clocks, 121
occupational clocks, 119
packages and boxes, 122-123, 125
pocket watches, 119-121, 127
prices and value, 118
space heroes, 127-129
supply and demand, 118-119, 121, 123, 131
tin-can clocks, 118
See also names of comic characters
Timex, 124
Tip Top Comics, 56
Tom Corbett Space Cadet, timepieces, 128, 133, 149
Tom Mix
  blow gun radio premium, 269
  decoders and manuals, 260-261, 266, 268, 271
  gum booklets, 232, 236, 246
  rings, 267
  timepieces, 127, 129, 132
"Toonerville Trolley," 20, 77
  Sunday pages, 20
  tin wind-up toys, 77, 82, 103
Toothbrush holders, Mickey Mouse, 95
Tootsie circus cards, 233-234, 237
Tootsietoys, 82
  Andy Gump in the 348 Car, 116
  Buck Rogers rocket ships, 82, 183, 185, 218, 219
Top-Notch Comics, 13, 56, 64
Torme, Mel, 262
Tortoise and the Hare timepiece, 136
Tough Kid Squad Comics, 56
Toys, comic-character, 68-117
  action toys, 175
  advertising, 70
  art work, 10, 79
  automotive, 80, 81
  band toys, 79
  bank, 4, 114
  based on comic strip characters, 68
  battery-operated, 75
  cast-iron, 68, 74-75, 81
  celluloid dolls, 72
  collectors and collection, 2, 68-69, 74-76
    cast-iron toys, 75
    discovering "new-old" toys, 71

foreign manufactured toys, 70, 75
  list of collectibles, 81-84
  lithographed tin toys, 75
  manipulative practices of auction houses, 75-76
  manufacturers' catalogs, 70
  original boxes, 68-69, 70, 73
  price and value, 69, 75-76
  reproductions, 69
  sample toys, 70
  scarcity and popularity, 74-75, 78
design and packaging, 70, 77
dolls, 74
  See also Dolls
financial risk involved in manufacturing, 69, 70
German-made, 72, 76, 77
  handcard, 73, 80, 82, 83-84, 89-90 105, 116
Japanese-made, 75, 78
licensed manufacturers, 68, 72
lithographed tin wind-ups, 69, 74, 75, 81
Negro, 79
post World War II, 80-81
royalty costs, 70
rubber-band powered "noddler," 72
sparklers, 81
tin, 69, 74, 80-81
  wind-up toys, 69, 74, 75, 77-79, 80, 81
walking figures, 101, 114
wind-up mechanism, 70
See also names of characters
Trade or advertising cards, 228, 229
Trampe, Ray, 184
Trendle, George, 265
Trova, Ernest, 71
Tryon, Edward K., Co., 181
T-shirts, 125

Uncle Sam, 56
Uncle Wiggily, timepieces, 134
Unique Art Manufacturing, 79, 83
United Clock Company, 119
United Features Syndicate, 7, 54, 56
U.S.A. Comics, 56
U.S. Rubber Co., 180, 185
U.S. Time Corp., 124, 126, 128, 130, 132, 133
Universal Pictures, 187, 234
  Buck Rogers films, 184
University of Chicago, 120

Varsity House, Inc., 186
Vault of Horror, 56
Verne, Jules, 7
Victory, 56
Violence, in comic books, 46, 47, 52
Vital Publications, 55

Walt Disney Enterprises, 14, 73, 124
  licenses for timepieces, 122, 130
Walt Disney Productions, 14, 73, 124, 130
Walt Disney's Comics and Stories, 56
War-picture cards, 234-235
Warhol, Andy, 12, 48
  comic art style, 12-13
  Popeye, acrylic on canvas, 12-13, 45
Warren, S. D., Co., 187
Warren Paper Products Co., 181
Watches and clocks, 118-167
  alarm clocks, 121
  authenticity, 122-123
  Boy Scout, 122
  Buck Rogers, 180, 185, 208
  design and packaging, 70
  list of collectibles, 131-134
  manufacturers, 131-134
  Mickey Mouse, 122-123, 137, 140, 141, 142
  pocket watches, 119 121, 127
  supply and demand, 118-119, 121, 123, 131
  See also names of comic-characters
Waterbury Clock Co., 118-121, 131
Weird Fantasy, 56
Weird Science, 56
Weird Tales, 11
Welch, James O., Co., 236
Welch comic-character cards, 236, 256
Welles, Orson, 265
Westover, Russ, 7
  "Tillie the Toiler," 29
Wham Comics, 56
Wheaties, Skippy cards, 236, 258
Whirlwind Comics, 56
White and Wyckoff Co., 181
Whitman Publishing Co., 179-180, 185-187, 236
  Big Little Books, 179, 232
Whiz Comics, 50-51, 53, 56
  origin of Captain Marvel, 48, 50-51, 53
  origin of Spy Smasher and Golden Arrow, 48
Wilane Watch Co., 129, 133
Willard, Frank ("Moon Mullins"), 35, 36, 80
Williamson, Al, 13
Wilma Deering (Buck Rogers girl friend), 127-128, 170, 175, 177
  Cream of Wheat medallion, 178, 186
  space suits, 177
Wimpy (Popeye), 10, 74
  timepieces, 127, 148
  walking figures, 101
Wind-up mechanism in toys, 70
Wings, 56

"Winnie Winkle the Breadwinner," 34
Wise Little Hen, The, (1934), 126
Wolfe, Robert A., 174
Wolverine Gum, Inc., 237
Women's Liberation Movement, 52
Wonder Women, 52, 56, 63
Wonderworld, 56
Wood, Wally, 13
Woodcuts, 229
Woody Woodpecker, timepieces, 132, 154
Woofian Dictionary, 182-183, 187
World's Best Comics, 63
World's Finest, 56
World War II
   cards, 237

comic books, 37, 48, 51
   toys to stimulate bond drives, 80
World Wide Gum Co., 237
Wow Comics, 56
Wristwatches. *See* Timepieces
Wu Fang, 13

Yager, Rick, 38, 183
Yankee, 56
"Yellow Kid, The," 3, 6, 13, 15, 16, 56
   advertising art, 17
   character merchandise, 68
   chewing gum cards, 235-236, 254
   on an Easter Egg, 85
   in the Goat Cart (cast iron), 3, 68, 82, 85

original art, 6, 15, 16, 17
Sunday pages, 3-4
toys, 3, 68, 82, 85
Yellow Kid, The, 48, 57
Yellow Kid Cigars, comic advertising
   art, 17
Yellow Submarine (Beatles film), 12, 131
Young, Chic, 80
Young Allies, 56, 61

Ziegfeld Follies, 129
Zip Comics, 56
Zorro watch, 131